ZAGATSURVEY.

1999

CHICAGO
RESTAURANTS

Edited by Phil Vettel

**Coordinated by Carolyn McGuire
and Jill Van Cleave**

Published and distributed by
ZAGAT SURVEY, LLC
4 Columbus Circle
New York, New York 10019
Tel: 212 977 6000
E-mail: zagat@zagatsurvey.com
Web site: www.zagat.com

Acknowledgments

Thanks to Robert ("Tubby") Bacon, Robert and Jan Batastini, Rebecca Brown, Mel Potash, Fred Rosen, George Schaefer, Brenda and Earl Shapiro and Marian Tripp for their help, encouragement and support; and special thanks to Paula Vettel for her infinite patience.

Contents

Introduction

Here are the results of our *1999 Chicago Restaurant Survey* covering some 860 restaurants in the Chicago area.

By regularly surveying large numbers of local restaurant-goers, we think we have achieved a uniquely current and reliable guide. We hope you agree. Nearly 1,875 people participated. Since the participants dined out an average of 3.4 times per week, this *Survey* is based on about 908 meals per day.

We want to thank each of our participants. They are a widely diverse group in all respects but one – they are food lovers all. This book is really "theirs."

Of the surveyors, 53% are women, 47% are men; the breakdown by age is 13% in their 20s, 22% in their 30s, 22% in their 40s, 27% in their 50s and 16% in their 60s or above.

To help guide our readers to Chicago's best meals and best buys, we have prepared a number of lists. See, for example, Chicago's Favorite Restaurants (page 11), Top Ratings (pages 12–16) and Best Buys (pages 17–18). On the assumption that most people want a quick fix on the places at which they are considering eating, we have tried to be concise and to provide handy indexes.

We are particularly grateful to our editors, Phil Vettel, restaurant critic for the *Chicago Tribune,* Carolyn McGuire, a *Chicago Tribune* travel writer and editor, and Jill Van Cleave, a cookbook author.

We invite you to be a reviewer in our next *Survey*. To do so, simply send a stamped, self-addressed, business-size envelope to ZAGAT SURVEY, 4 Columbus Circle, New York, NY 10019, so that we will be able to contact you. Each participant will receive a free copy of the next *Chicago Restaurant Survey* when it is published.

Your comments, suggestions and even criticisms of this *Survey* are also solicited. There is always room for improvement with your help.

New York, New York   Nina and Tim Zagat
October 26, 1998

Foreword

If it's true that nothing pleases a guidebook publisher more than a changing landscape, you better believe that the *Zagat Survey* loves Chicago, since permutations in our city's restaurant scene are as common as Sammy Sosa's home runs.

While keeping up with all the new developments is a daunting task, one easy way to stay current is to keep your eyes on the west-of-Loop Randolph Street corridor, which had virtually no restaurants five years ago, but is now one of Chicago's hottest dining districts. Vivo and Marché, which established early beachheads, have been joined by a veritable Gold Rush of newcomers: among them, Blackbird, a crowded American hot spot; Bluepoint Oyster Bar, a serious seafooder; Hi Ricky, the newest link in a chain of Pan-Asian noodle shops; and Toque, a hip American with a French twist. On the far eastern end of Randolph, the new Hotel Allegro unveiled the Italian-influenced 312 Chicago, while much farther west, almost at the United Center, we saw the debut of one sixtyblue, a stylish and formal newcomer whose unpublicized silent partner, one Michael Jeffrey Jordan, was the worst-kept secret in town.

Chicago foodies bristle at the largely uninformed suggestion that the city is a meat-and-potatoes mecca. However, there is no denying the popularity of steakhouses here (even if visiting conventioneers are providing much of the business), as proven by the half-dozen that opened in the last year alone. There is the East Coast import Capital Grille, Carmichael's on the Near West Side, EJ's Place on the North Shore, Millennium, a steakhouse named for the times, the New York entry Smith & Wollensky and Tavern on Rush on the Gold Coast. Moreover, at press time, Sullivan's is under construction in River North.

Also new is North Pond Café, a dazzling Regional American that's sited along North Pond in Lincoln Park, and its sister property, Jackson Harbor Grill, a South Side Southern-Creole spot with pretty impressive views of its own. Other notable sequels include a second Bistrot Zinc; Trocadero, a 'European Soul Food' sibling to Hudson Club; and Rudi Fazuli's, a second-generation, urban version of Clara's Pasta di Casa in the western 'burbs.

A couple of high-profile chefs are also generating excitement in new settings. Kevin Schrimmer, formerly of the departed Café Provençal, opened Mimosa. And Eric Aubriot, former chef de cuisine at the acclaimed Carlos', now has himself for a boss at Aubriot on the North Side.

It wasn't all good news in town, though. Churrascos, a Pan-Latin concept that has done famously in Houston and elsewhere in Texas, was short-lived in Chicago. Grappa, an impressive Italian restaurant, was converted into a second Nick & Tony's by their common owners, but within months the space was up for lease. George Kwan closed House of Hunan, his 21-year-old Michigan Avenue stalwart and owner Sophie Madej retired after 33 years of running Busy Bee, the classic Polish restaurant in Wicker Park.

Also of note in '98, Lettuce Entertain You Enterprises, Rich Melman's dining empire, shuttered three spots – Hat Dance, Tucci Milan and Avanzare – and is in the process of replacing them with, respectively: Nacional 27 (a Latin American venue), Vong (a Chicago version of Jean-Georges Vongerichten's popular NYC Thai-French concept) and an as-yet-unnamed venture with the husband-and-wife team of Rick Tramonto and Gale Gand. All three newcomers are expected to debut in early '99.

And while The Pump Room closed in early '98, leaving scores of Chicagoans at a loss for where to go on Valentine's Day, Mother's Day and auspicious anniversaries, fortunately, in July '98, it reopened after a multimillion-dollar redo. Another longtime Chicago establishment, Un Grand Cafe, shut its doors, but a few weeks later emerged as Mon Ami Gabi – the name being a nod to chef and managing partner Gabino Sotelino.

Diners report spending an average of $25.06 per meal in this *Survey*, an 8.2% increase, but only 4.1% annually, over the 1997 figure of $23.16, and if the economy continues to remain strong, there is no reason to suspect that this whirlwind of activity will slow, much less cease. In fact, at press time we're awaiting the opening of a McCormick & Schmick's seafood restaurant on the Gold Coast, John Hogan's Savarin bistro in River North and Tizi Melloul, River North's first Moroccan restaurant. All of which will help make the next *Zagat Survey* as information-packed as we trust you find this one.

Chicago, IL   Phil Vettel
October 26, 1998   Carolyn McGuire
                                                      Jill Van Cleave

Key to Ratings/Symbols

This sample entry identifies the various types of information contained in your Zagat Survey.

(1) Restaurant Name, Address & Phone Number

(2) Hours & Credit Cards

(3) ZAGAT Ratings

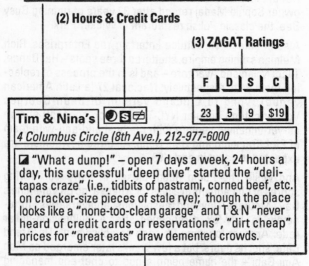

F	D	S	C
23	5	9	$19

Tim & Nina's ◗ 🆂 ⊄

4 Columbus Circle (8th Ave.), 212-977-6000

◪ "What a dump!" – open 7 days a week, 24 hours a day, this successful "deep dive" started the "deli-tapas craze" (i.e., tidbits of pastrami, corned beef, etc. on cracker-size pieces of stale rye); though the place looks like a "none-too-clean garage" and T & N "never heard of credit cards or reservations", "dirt cheap" prices for "great eats" draw demented crowds.

(4) Surveyors' Commentary

The names of restaurants with the highest overall ratings, greatest popularity and importance are printed in **CAPITAL LETTERS**. Address and phone numbers are printed in *italics*.

(2) Hours & Credit Cards

After each restaurant name you will find the following courtesy information:

◗ .... *serving after 11 PM*

🆂 .... *open on Sunday*

⊄ .... *no credit cards accepted*

8

(3) ZAGAT Ratings

Food, **Decor** and **Service** are each rated on a scale of **0** to **30**:

F	D	S	C

F	*Food*
D	*Decor*
S	*Service*
C	*Cost*

23	5	9	$19

0 - 9	*poor to fair*
10 - 15	*fair to good*
16 - 19	*good to very good*
20 - 25	*very good to excellent*
26 - 30	*extraordinary to perfection*

▽ 23	5	9	$19

▽	*Low number of votes/less reliable*

The **Cost (C)** column reflects the estimated price of a dinner with one drink and tip. Lunch usually costs 25% less.

A restaurant listed without ratings is either an important **newcomer** or a popular **write-in**. The estimated cost, with one drink and tip, is indicated by the following symbols.

–	–	–	VE

I	*$15 and below*
M	*$16 to $30*
E	*$31 to $50*
VE	*$51 or more*

(4) Surveyors' Commentary

Surveyors' comments are summarized, with literal comments shown in quotation marks. The following symbols indicate whether responses were mixed or uniform.

◨	*mixed*
◼	*uniform*

Chicago's Favorites

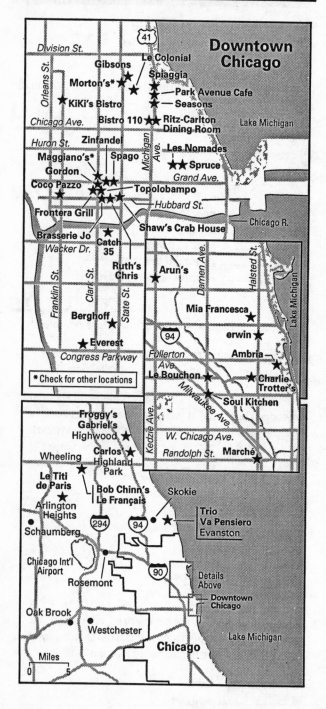

Downtown Chicago

US 41

Division St.

Orleans St.

Gibsons ★
Le Colonial ★

Morton's* ★
Spiaggia ★

KiKi's Bistro ★
Park Avenue Cafe ★
Seasons ★

Chicago Ave.
Bistro 110 ★★
Ritz-Carlton Dining Room

Huron St.
Zinfandel

Michigan Ave.
Les Nomades

Maggiano's* ★
Spago ★
★★ Spruce

Gordon ★★
Grand Ave.

Coco Pazzo ★★
Topolobampo ★

Hubbard St.
Frontera Grill ★★

Lake Michigan

Chicago R.

Brasserie Jo ★
Catch 35 ★

Wacker Dr.

Shaw's Crab House

Ruth's Chris ★

Franklin St.
Clark St.
State St.

Berghoff ★

Everest ★

Congress Parkway

Check for other locations

Arun's ★

Damen Ave.
Halsted St.

Mia Francesca ★

Lake Michigan

94
erwin ★

Fullerton Ave.
Ambria ★

Le Bouchon ★
Charlie Trotter's ★

Soul Kitchen ★

Milwaukee Ave.
Kedzie Ave.

W. Chicago Ave.

Randolph St.
Marché ★

Froggy's ★
Gabriel's ★
Highwood ★

Wheeling
Carlos' ★
Highland Park

Le Titi de Paris ★

Bob Chinn's ★
Le Français ★
Skokie

Arlington Heights
294
94

Trio ★
Va Pensiero
Evanston

Schaumberg ●

Chicago Int'l Airport

90

Rosemont ●

Details Above

Downtown Chicago

Oak Brook ●

Westchester ●

Lake Michigan

Chicago

Miles
0   5

Chicago's Favorite Restaurants

Each of our reviewers has been asked to name his or her five favorite restaurants. The 40 spots most frequently named, in order of their popularity, are:

1. Charlie Trotter's
2. Le Français
3. Ambria
4. Everest
5. Frontera Grill
6. Topolobampo
7. Arun's
8. Brasserie Jo
9. Gibsons
10. KiKi's Bistro
11. Spago
12. Le Titi de Paris
13. Coco Pazzo
14. Trio
15. Carlos'
16. Maggiano's
17. Spruce
18. Le Colonial
19. Berghoff
20. Gordon*
21. Bob Chinn's
22. Les Nomades
23. Seasons
24. Bistro 110
25. Mia Francesca
26. Shaw's Crab Hse.
27. Spiaggia
28. Va Pensiero
29. erwin
30. Ritz-Carlton Din. Rm.
31. Le Bouchon
32. Zinfandel
33. Ruth's Chris
34. Gabriel's
35. Catch 35
36. Park Avenue Cafe*
37. Soul Kitchen*
38. Marché
39. Morton's*
40. Froggy's

It's obvious that many of the restaurants on the above list are among the most expensive, but Chicagoans also love a bargain. Were popularity calibrated to price, we suspect that a number of other restaurants would join the above ranks. Thus, we have listed over 145 Best Buys on pages 17–18.

---

* Tied with the restaurant listed directly above it.

Top Ratings*

Top 40 Food Ranking

29 Le Français	Montparnasse
28 Ambria	Spiaggia
Carlos'	Va Pensiero
Tallgrass	La Sorella di Francesca
27 Le Titi de Paris	Park Avenue Cafe
Topolobampo	Ruth's Chris
Ritz-Carlton Din. Rm.	Entre Nous
Arun's	Les Nomades
Charlie Trotter's	Printer's Row
Everest	24 Le Bouchon
Trio	Cafe 36
Seasons	Gibsons Steakhse.
26 Frontera Grill	Nick's Fishmarket
Morton's	KiKi's Bistro
Méson Sabika	Le Vichyssois
Bistro Banlieue	Oceanique
25 Courtright's	Mia Francesca
Fond de la Tour	Coco Pazzo
Gabriel's	D & J Bistro
Gordon	Cafe Pyrenees

Top Spots by Cuisine

Top American (New)
27 Charlie Trotter's
   Seasons
25 Courtright's
   Gordon
   Park Ave. Cafe

Top American (Regional)
25 Entre Nous
24 Daniel J's
23 Meritage Cafe
   Zinfandel
22 Prairie

Top American (Traditional)
23 Lawry's
21 Genesee Depot
19 Barn of Barrington
   Mrs. Park's Tavern
   Houston's

Top Bar-B-Q
21 Twin Anchors
20 N. N. Smokehouse
19 Carson's Ribs
18 Weber Grill
17 Fireplace Inn

Top Breakfast**
22 Walker Bros.
21 Original Pancake Hse.
   Wishbone
20 Lou Mitchell's
19 John's Place

Top Brunch
27 Ritz-Carlton Din. Rm.
   Seasons
26 Frontera Grill
25 Park Ave. Cafe
23 erwin

---

* Excluding restaurants with low voting.
** Other than hotels.

12

Top Chinese
23 Emperor's Choice
21 Best Hunan
20 Windows of Cuisine
Dee's
Phoenix

Top Coffee Shops/Diners
23 Manny's Coffee Shop
22 Heaven on Seven
15 Sarkis Grill
Nookies
Ed Debevic's

Top Continental
23 Cafe La Cave
22 Zaven's
21 Biggs
20 Lutz Continental
17 Ceiling Zero

Top French
29 Le Français
28 Ambria
Carlos'
Tallgrass
27 Le Titi de Paris

Top French Bistros
26 Bistro Banlieue
24 Le Bouchon
KiKi's Bistro
D & J Bistro
Cafe Pyrenees

Top German
19 Berghoff
18 Schulien's
Golden Ox
Zum Deutschen Eck
– Fritzl's

Top Greek
21 Costa's
Santorini
20 Parthenon
Roditys
Papagus

Top Hamburgers
21 Charlie Beinlich's
20 Pete Miller's Steakhse.
19 Boston Blackie's
16 Hackney's
15 Johnny Rockets

Top Hotel Dining
27 Dining Room
Ritz-Carlton
Seasons
Four Seasons
25 Park Ave. Cafe
Doubletree Guest Suites
Entre Nous
Fairmont Hotel
22 Prairie
Hyatt on Printer's Row

Top Indian
23 Indian Garden
21 Klay Oven
20 Gaylord India
19 Viceroy of India
Moti Mahal

Top Italian
25 Gabriel's
Spiaggia
Va Pensiero
La Sorella di Francesca
24 Mia Francesca

Top Japanese
23 Kuni's
Matsuya
Sai Cafe
22 Akai Hana
21 Itto Sushi
New Japan*

Top Mex/Tex-Mex
27 Topolobampo
26 Frontera Grill
24 Don Juan
22 Salpicón
19 Tecalitlan

---

* Tied with the restaurant listed directly above it.

Top Newcomers/Rated
24 Crofton on Wells
Harvest on Huron
23 Meritage Cafe
Rhapsody
22 Provence

Top Newcomers/Unrated
Aubriot
Mon Ami Gabi
North Pond Café
one sixtyblue
Thyme

Top People-Watching
24 Gibsons Steakhse.
Spago
23 Con Fusion
Soul Kitchen
22 Marché

Top Pizza
22 Pizzeria Uno & Due
21 Lou Malnati's
20 Original Gino's
18 Pizza Capri
Graziano's

Top Power Lunch
27 Seasons
25 Gordon
Spiaggia
Les Nomades
24 KiKi's Bistro

Top Seafood
24 Nick's Fishmarket
Oceanique
23 Shaw's Crab Hse.
22 Cape Cod Room
21 Philander's

Top Spanish/Tapas
26 Mesón Sabika
22 Emilio's Tapas
Emilio's La Perla
21 Cafe Iberico
20 Cafe BaBaReeba!

Top Steakhouses
26 Morton's
25 Ruth's Chris
24 Gibsons Steakhse.
Chicago Chop Hse.
23 Gene & Georgetti

Top Thai
27 Arun's
20 Penny's Noodle Shop
19 Star of Siam
P.S. Bangkok
Thai Star Cafe

Top Worth a Drive
29 Le Français
Wheeling
28 Carlos'
Highland Park
Tallgrass
Lockport
27 Le Titi de Paris
Arlington Heights
Trio
Evanston

Top 40 Decor Ranking

27 Everest
Ambria
Ritz-Carlton Din. Rm.
Le Français
26 Seasons
Entre Nous
Courtright's
Charlie Trotter's
Spiaggia
Cité
25 Le Colonial
Trio
Mesón Sabika
Signature Room
Le Titi de Paris
Gordon
24 Carlos'
Arun's
Biggs
Capital Grille

Topolobampo
Hudson Club
Vivere
Ben Pao
Cafe La Cave
Fond de la Tour
Rhapsody
23 Seasons Cafe
Riva
Les Nomades
Patrick & James
Pasteur Cafe
Tallgrass
Toulouse on the Park
Nick's Fishmarket
Cafe Spiaggia
Spruce
Marché
Primavera
22 Rainforest Cafe

Top Outdoor

Bice Ristorante
Bistro Banlieue
Brasserie Jo
Cafe BaBaReeba!
Carmine's
Charlie's Ale House
Coco Pazzo Cafe

Con Fusion
Dick's Last Resort
Feast
Meritage Cafe
Tavern on Rush
Topo Gigio
Va Pensiero

Top Romantic

Ambria
Biggs
Carlos'
Charlie Trotter's
Coco Pazzo
Cyrano's Bistrot
erwin
Everest

Geja's Cafe
Gordon
KiKi's Bistro
Le Bouchon
Le Français
Pump Room
Ritz-Carlton Din. Rm.
Seasons

Top Rooms

Ambria
Biggs
Carlos'
Charlie Trotter's
Gordon
Le Bouchon
Le Français
Marché

one sixtyblue
Patrick & James
Pump Room
Red Light
Ritz-Carlton Din. Rm.
Seasons
Tallgrass
Vivere

Top Views

Everest
Jackson Harbor Grill
North Pond Café
Oak Terrace

Shark Bar
Signature Room
Smith & Wollensky
Spiaggia

Top 40 Service Ranking

28 Le Français
   Ambria
27 Carlos'
   Charlie Trotter's
   Ritz-Carlton Din. Rm.
   Everest
   Trio
   Seasons
26 Le Titi de Paris
   Tallgrass
25 Arun's
   Entre Nous
   Topolobampo
24 Les Nomades
   Spiaggia
   Gordon
   Gabriel's
   Courtright's
   Nick's Fishmarket
   Seasons Cafe

   Fond de la Tour
23 Cafe La Cave
   Montparnasse
   Va Pensiero
   Primavera
   Spruce
   KiKi's Bistro
   D & J Bistro
   Mesón Sabika
   Printer's Row
   Bistro Banlieue
   Ruth's Chris
   Las Bellas Artes
   Morton's
22 Zaven's
   Biggs
   Cafe Pyrenees
   Ritz-Carlton Cafe
   Park Avenue Cafe
   Coco Pazzo

Top 100 Bangs For The Buck

This list reflects the best dining values in our *Survey*. It is produced by dividing the cost of a meal into the combined ratings for food, decor and service.

1. Fluky's
2. Gold Coast Dogs
3. Ann Sather Cafe
4. Walker Bros.
5. Original Pancake Hse.
6. Sarkis Grill
7. Johnny Rockets
8. Breakfast Club
9. Lou Mitchell's
10. Manny's Coffee Shop
11. Penny's Noodle Shop
12. Aurelio's
13. Russell's Barbecue
14. Charlie Beinlich's
15. Red Apple
16. Ann Sather
17. M Cafe
18. Corner Bakery
19. Athenian Room
20. Bagel
21. My π Pizza
22. Boston Blackie's
23. Lutz Continental Cafe
24. Ed Debevic's
25. Nookies Too
26. Lou Malnati's Pizzeria
27. Cousin's
28. Nookies
29. Cross-Rhodes
30. Bohemian Crystal
31. Tecalitlan
32. Dao
33. LuLu's Dim Sum
34. Oodles of Noodles
35. Duke of Perth
36. Chicago Diner
37. Pizzeria Uno & Due
38. John's Place
39. Addis Abeda
40. Bacino's
41. Dellwood Pickle
42. Blind Faith Cafe
43. Singha
44. Big Bowl
45. Best Hunan
46. Original Gino's East
47. Star of Siam
48. Grecian Taverna
49. Lucky Platter
50. Abril
51. foodlife
52. Dixie Kit. & Bait Shop
53. N. N. Smokehouse
54. Indian Garden
55. Belden Deli
56. Heaven on Seven
57. Hi Ricky
58. Pizza Capri
59. Carmen's
60. Wishbone
61. Thai Star Cafe
62. Edwardo's
63. Red Lion Pub
64. Medici
65. P.S. Bangkok
66. Heartland Cafe
67. Berghoff
68. Las Palmas
69. Bertucci's
70. Graziano's
71. Old Jerusalem
72. Elaine & Ina's
73. Stir Crazy Cafe
74. Giordano's
75. Bar Louie
76. Panda Panda
77. R.J. Grunts
78. Oak Tree
79. Chicago Pizza
80. Dave's Italian Kit.
81. Flat Top Grill
82. Green Door Tavern
83. Mrs. Levy's Deli
84. Father & Son Pizza
85. Club Creole
86. Buca di Beppo
87. Hackney's
88. Bangkok
89. Stanley's Kit. & Tap
90. California Pizza Kit.
91. Leona's
92. Basta Pasta
93. Tommy Nevin's Pub
94. Goose Island
95. Nancy's Original
96. Barry's Ribs
97. Akai Hana
98. Max's Deli
99. Rainforest Cafe
100. Cafe Iberico

Additional Good Values
(A bit more expensive, but worth every penny)

Anna Maria Pasteria
Babaluci
Bacchus Nibbles
Bandera
Bice Grill
Bite Cafe
Blue Mesa
Bones
Bricks
Cafe Borgia
Cafe Luciano
Cheesecake Factory
Clara's Pasta di Casa
Club Lucky
Convito Italiano
Cucina Bella
Daily Bar & Grill
Daruma
Davis St. Fishmarket
Dish
Emperor's Choice
Filippo's
Four Farthings
Frida's

Gale St. Inn
Gaylord India
Genesee Depot
Greek Islands
Gusto Italiano
Hacienda Tecalitlan
Jaipur Palace
Jerome's Red Ginger
Lindo Mexico
Little Bucharest
Mambo Grill
Mandar Inn
Matsuya
Mirabell
Mity Nice Grill
Red Tomato
Reza's
Rose Angelis
Salpicón
Sayat Nova
Tapas Barcelona
Via Veneto
Wild Onion
Zarrosta Grill

Alphabetical
Directory of
Restaurants

Chicago Area

F	D	S	C

Abril ●S
17 | 13 | 17 | $15

2607 N. Milwaukee Ave. (bet. Kedzie Ave. & Logan Blvd.), 773-227-7250

■ "Absolutely consistent" Logan Square Mexican that features "simple but hearty" fare served in an "always friendly" if "nondescript" atmosphere; although "great for kids", singles say it's "best late at night after a few drinks."

Adagio
17 | 20 | 17 | $29

923 W. Weed St. (North Ave.), 312-787-0400

◪ Look for "consciously cool" "beautiful people" at this "noisy", "thirtysomething hangout" in Clybourn Corridor where the Italian cuisine draws comments ranging from "creative" to "nothing special"; the "people-watching" scene gets even hotter from Thursday–Saturday when it turns into a late-night dance club with live entertainment.

Addis Abeda S
19 | 11 | 15 | $14

3512 N. Clark St. (bet. Addison St. & Newport Ave.), 773-929-9383

■ This Wrigleyville Ethiopian combines "complex and unusual taste sensations" with the "novelty of eating with your hands" to produce a "fun ethnic experience"; granted, the "hole-in-the-wall" decor "needs work", but with people proclaiming it "the best Ethiopian in the city", why change?

Akai Hana S
22 | 14 | 18 | $20

3223 W. Lake St. (Skokie Blvd.), Wilmette, 847-251-0384

■ Japanese storefront on the North Shore offering "Downtown quality but better value" on "the freshest sushi around" and "great" tempura; a minority mutters "ugly" decor, but most claim that the "hot towels and terrific food transport you to Japan."

A La Turka S
– | – | – | M

3134 N. Lincoln Ave. (½ block south of Belmont Ave.), 773-935-6447

An "interesting menu" of "more than your typical Turkish offerings" is available at this Far North Sider where "great spreads" are a small part of the many "tasty preparations."

Albert's Café & Patisserie S
– | – | – | M

52 W. Elm St. (Division St.), 312-751-0666

"Charming", "intimate" French cafe on the Near North Side that's a favorite for "outstanding pastries", including "the best croissants this side of Paris", making breakfast the most popular time to visit; however, others prefer to soak up the "European" atmosphere during a "great, light lunch."

Allgauer's §   – – – M
Hilton Lisle/Naperville, 3003 Corporate West Dr. (Naperville Rd.), Lisle, 630-505-0900
Hilton Northbrook, 2855 N. Milwaukee Ave. (1 block north of River Rd.), Northbrook, 847-480-7500
These West and North Suburban Americans are prized for their Sunday brunch, but are "very pleasant" for "leisurely dining" in "elegant" settings whatever the day or hour; the Lisle location is singled out for its view overlooking a "duck-filled pond."

AMBRIA   28 27 28 $62
2300 N. Lincoln Park W. (Belden Ave.), 773-472-5959
■ This Contemporary French "special occasion" jewel garnered the No. 2 spot across-the-board for food, decor and service in this *Survey* and requires both jackets and (far in advance) reservations for entry; surveyors rave about chef Gabino Sotelino's "superb" cuisine, an art nouveau interior that's "classy but unpretentious" and service so attentive, one person testifies "I was afraid to scratch my nose for fear that three waiters would appear with Kleenex"; and romantics, listen up – this is *the* place "for a middle-aged man to propose marriage."

America's Brewpub §   ∇ 17 22 17 $18
205 N. Broadway (New York St.), Aurora, 630-264-2739
☑ A sprawling facility featuring "decent bar food" and handcrafted beers that also boasts a cigar-friendly nook – the Cognac Bar – as well as live music in its summer gazebo; partly owned by Bears Hall of Famer Walter Payton, which explains the Payton's Pilsner on the beverage menu, the "well-designed" space "holds the multitudes without claustrophobia", though some complain that the crowd is "much too young" and the food "could use some spicing up."

Angelina Ristorante §   17 16 18 $23
3561 N. Broadway (Addison St.), 773-935-5933
■ "Charming neighborhood Italian" near Wrigley Field that draws such a hip local crowd that a "black shirt, black jeans and something pierced" are almost mandatory for admission; while the "old-style Italian" food is "yummy" and the cooking "really shines at Sunday brunch", some grouse that seating is "a bit on the crowded side."

Anna Maria Pasteria §   19 13 18 $20
3953 N. Broadway (Irving Park Rd.), 773-929-6363
■ Low decor scores suggest many surveyors haven't visited this Wrigleyville Italian since its recent remodeling; still, most agree that it's "like a visit home to Mom", with "giant portions, lovingly prepared" and an "addictive" calamari.

Ann Sather [S] | 17 | 12 | 17 | $12
929 W. Belmont Ave. (Sheffield Ave.), 773-348-2378
Ann Sather Cafe [S] | 18 | 12 | 17 | $11
5207 N. Clark St. (Foster Ave.), 773-271-6677
Ann Sather Express [S] | ▽ 19 | 11 | 16 | $8
3416 N. Southport Ave. (Roscoe Ave.), 773-404-4475
2665 N. Clark St. (Drummond Pl.), 773-327-9522

■ Kudos abound for these "always great" Swedish-Americans serving "the best breakfast in town for over 25 years" and "decadent" cinnamon rolls that are "reason alone to get out of bed"; though some judge them to be "artery-clogging", "sweet-tooth havens", others contend there's "something to please everybody"; N.B. the Cafe and Express are open for breakfast and lunch only, and the latter doesn't have a liquor license.

Arco de Cuchilleros [S] | ▽ 20 | 16 | 17 | $19
3445 N. Halsted St. (bet. Addison & Belmont Aves.), 773-296-6046

◪ Fans of this Wrigleyville Spanish spot cry "olé!" for its "authentic" fare and "best tapas brunch in town", especially when enjoyed on the "terrific" outdoor patio; valet parking is available at dinner.

Army & Lou's [S] | ▽ 17 | 13 | 17 | $17
422 E. 75th St. (King Dr.), 773-483-3100

◪ "Terrific homestyle cooking" is the draw at this South Side Soul Fooder that has "maintained its reputation" over many years despite several changes in ownership; those not bowled over note that "the place has soul but not the best catfish" and that it "could use a decorator."

ARUN'S [S] | 27 | 24 | 25 | VE
4156 N. Kedzie Ave. (2 blocks north of Irving Park Rd.), 773-539-1909

■ It's an "awesome culinary experience" that awaits those who trek to this North Side Thai where Arun Sampanthavivat offers "impeccable", "top-drawer" cuisine so beautifully presented that "you eat with your eyes first"; while at the time of our *Survey,* many respondents recommended the $75 tasting menu, raving that "there's nothing else like it in North America", it's now the only way to order, which will further disappoint the minority who already gripes about "astronomical prices" and "microscopic portions."

a tavola | 20 | 16 | 18 | $32
2152 W. Chicago Ave. (2 blocks west of Damen Ave.), 773-276-7567

■ "A great find" in Ukrainian Village, this Italian features a "limited menu" of "subtly seasoned", "simple and fresh" food by chef-owner Daniel Bocik, which is served up in a "cozy" setting; N.B. its proximity to the United Center accounts for a sizable pre-event crowd.

Athenian Room 🆂
19 | 10 | 16 | $13 |

807 W. Webster Ave. (Halsted St.), 773-348-5155
■ An "oldie but goodie" in the DePaul area for 25 years, this "cheap" Greek may have "Spartan decor", but students and locals rave about the "finest Greek chicken" that comes with fries for "soaking up the juices."

Aubriot 🆂
– | – | – | E |

1962 N. Halsted St. (Armitage Ave.), 773-281-4211
Simplicity and clean flavors are the hallmarks of this ambitious Contemporary French from ex-Carlos' chef Eric Aubriot; the small dining room is unfussy and very attractive, as are the relatively friendly prices, both of which are finding favor among the Halsted Street restaurant crowd.

August Moon 🆂
▽ 21 | 9 | 16 | $18 |

225 W. 26th St. (Wentworth Ave.), 312-842-2951
■ "Chicago's only restaurant for a rijstaffel feast", this Chinatown BYO has a Chinese and Indonesian menu with "flair"; an "odd location" and "bland decor" are drawbacks, but the "owner has character" and overall most think it's "worth finding" "when in the mood for this type of food."

Aurelio's 🆂
18 | 13 | 16 | $13 |

18162 Harwood Ave. (183rd St.), Homewood, 708-798-8050
601 E. 170th St. (Cottage Grove Ave.), South Holland,
708-333-0310
☑ Supporters of these South Suburban pizzerias, with a "relaxed", "fun, family atmosphere", claim they make a "great thin-crust" pie; others say "there's far better", proving that Chicagoans have no shortage of opinions on the subject; N.B. South Holland does not permit alcohol.

Babaluci Italian Eatery 🆂
16 | 13 | 15 | $21 |

2152 N. Damen Ave. (Webster Ave.), 773-486-5300
☑ A Bucktown Italian that's "a good standby" for "casual, inexpensive" dining in a "funky", "upbeat" atmosphere; the unimpressed call it "decent but nothing special", claiming the kitchen "could use some pizazz."

Bacchanalia 🆂⊅
▽ 23 | 14 | 19 | $21 |

2413 S. Oakley Ave. (bet. 24th Pl. & 24th St.), 773-254-6555
■ "Not trendy, [just] good food" succinctly sums up this "friendly" and "authentic" Heart of Italy veteran; less than spacious seating means you'll "feel like a sardine", but fans say it's "worth dealing with" and "won't let you down."

Bacchus Nibbles ◗🆂
19 | 16 | 19 | $21 |

20817 N. Quentin Rd. (Rand Rd.), Kildeer, 847-438-3212
☑ It's "fun to share" at this Eclectic bistro and wine bar in the Northwest 'burbs that invites "delightful experimenting" with Japanese, Spanish and French munchies ("don't miss the escargot") and lots of "value wines" offered in flights; however, a few complain about "nibble"-sized portions and think it was better under the previous ownership.

Bacino's S   18 | 12 | 15 | $14
75 E. Wacker Dr. (Michigan Ave.), 312-263-0070
2204 N. Lincoln Ave. (Webster Ave.), 773-472-7400
1504 N. Naper Blvd. (Ogden Ave.), Naperville, 630-505-0600
■ This pizzeria minichain makes a strong showing for "best Chicago-style stuffed pizza", with "incomparable spinach" and "super heart-healthy" (i.e. low-fat cheese) versions; the service is generally "pleasant and dependable", but aesthetes think the interiors "could use some ambiance."

Bagel, The S   16 | 11 | 15 | $12
3107 N. Broadway (Barry Ave.), 773-477-0300
Old Orchard Shopping Ctr. (bet. Golf & Old Orchard Rds.), Skokie, 847-677-0100
☑ Admirers recommend these old-fashioned delis that are home to "authentic Jewish soul food" for "excellent corned beef sandwiches", "the best cabbage soup" and other time-tested remedies to "cure all that ails"; some are less impressed ("unreliable", "so-so"), but the fact that they're "crowded" says a lot; N.B. the city location is BYO.

Bandera   19 | 18 | 19 | $21
535 N. Michigan Ave., 2nd fl. (½ block south of Ohio St.), 312-644-3524
☑ "Location, location, location" – specifically, a second-story perch overlooking Michigan Avenue – helps draw a steady stream of expense-account types, moviegoers and shoppers to this New American; it has other appeals as well: a "cozy environment", "great wines by the glass" and chicken turning on the wood-fired rotisserie; but critics come down on a "limited menu" that "lacks creativity."

Bando S   17 | 12 | 14 | $18
2200 W. Lawrence Ave. (Leavitt St.), 773-728-7400
☑ Boosters of this veteran Northwest Sider recommend it for "a good intro" to Seoul food thanks to a "user-friendly" menu and Korean BBQ that's "fun to grill at your table"; others knock the "far too big" space and "Vegas-style dining room" and claim "this is nothing special."

Bangkok S   19 | 15 | 16 | $18
3542 N. Halsted St. (Addison St.), 773-327-2870
■ Surveyors praise this "undervisited" Wrigleyville Thai for being "reliable", with a "good, varied menu", "very reasonable" Sunday buffet and "pleasant service" that make it "worth the parking hassle" on game days.

Bangkok Star S   ▽ 19 | 12 | 14 | $14
1443 W. Fullerton Ave. (bet. Ashland & Southport Aves.), 773-348-8868
☑ Despite "nondescript decor", most patrons have "no complaints" about this Lakeview Thai with "excellent pad Thai" and "the best chicken satay in town"; tougher customers contend "quality is not always consistent."

Bank Lane Bistro   ▽ 17 | 15 | 18 | $21
670 Bank Ln. (Southgate), Lake Forest, 847-234-8802
✓ This French newcomer on the North Shore, a sibling of
South Gate Cafe, has gotten mixed reviews: some gripe that
it's "too expensive" and say the menu "sounds great,
but . . .", while grateful Francophiles call it "a great addition"
and have only one request – "don't tell anyone."

Bar Louie ⬤⬤   16 | 13 | 14 | $15
226 W. Chicago Ave. (bet. Franklin & Wells Sts.), 312-337-3313
1704 N. Damen Ave. (4 blocks north of North Ave.), 773-645-7500
▪ Night owls and hipsters rejoice at this Near North spot,
which keeps extra-late hours and has "dark, edgy music"
and a "cool atmosphere"; despite being "loud and
crowded", it's "fun for drinks and get-togethers" and offers
surprisingly high-"quality" bar food, including "great"
sandwiches and Italian-accented specialties; N.B. the
Bucktown branch is new and unrated.

Barn of Barrington ⬤   19 | 21 | 19 | $27
1415 S. Barrington Rd. (¼ mi. north of Dundee Rd.),
Barrington, 847-381-8585
✓ Seniors say the "unique dining environment" of a restored
red barn distinguishes this Suburban Northwest American,
which is also known for a "stellar Sunday champagne
brunch"; detractors cry 'neigh', dismissing it as "frozen in
the '50s", an "old-school" standby whose food "does not
live up to its reputation"; the even-minded say it "never
changes – that's both a positive and a negative."

Barrington Country Bistro ⬤   22 | 19 | 18 | $31
Foundry Shopping Ctr., 700 W. Northwest Hwy. (bet. Hart Rd.
& Rte. 14), Barrington, 847-842-1300
▪ Aficionados marvel at the "consistently good" cuisine and
"country French feel" of this "cheery" and "comfy" bistro
with monthly wine dinners and a seasonal menu; scattered
service complaints are lost among the general praise.

Barry's Ribs & More ⬤   15 | 12 | 14 | $15
195 W. Dundee Rd. (Buffalo Grove Rd.), Buffalo Grove,
847-537-1000
✓ Supporters claim this simple Northwest Suburban rib
house is "underrated", pointing to its "delicious Southern
pit barbecue" and "great sweet and spicy sauce"; rib snobs
lick their fingers, then sniff "nothing special."

Basta Pasta ⬤   20 | 16 | 18 | $20
6733 Olmsted St. (Northwest Hwy.), 773-763-0667
▪ An Edison Park Italian that draws neighborhood and
North Shore folks who point out that you don't have to
travel "as far as Taylor Street" to encounter homemade
comfort food, a "helpful staff" and portions so generous
you'll cry 'basta' yourself; the few who voice qualms are
uncomfortable with the "barnlike" noise levels.

Belden Deli ◐ [S] — 13 | 9 | 13 | $12

7572 N. Western Ave. (Howard St.), 773-743-4800

◪ Round-the-clock, "cheap" Rogers Park deli that many think "used to be better years ago"; those who keep their expectations in check say "it's not NYC but it's adequate."

Bella Notte [S] — 21 | 14 | 18 | $22

1372 W. Grand Ave. (Noble St.), 312-733-5136

6063 Dempster St. (Austin Blvd.), Morton Grove, 847-470-1405

■ "Italians with flair" sums up the opinion about these city and suburban "neighborhood joints"; they're "noisy" but compensate with "great pastas" in such quantities that "even the half-portions are huge"; P.S. the Dempster street location is now "roomier" thanks to an expansion.

Bella Vista [S] — 19 | 22 | 19 | $26

1001 W. Belmont Ave. (Sheffield Ave.), 773-404-0111

■ This "beautiful" Lakeview Italian occupies a former fiduciary building and is awash in bright colors and "beautiful tile work"; the "very good" food earns nearly as much admiration, and the *Big Night* dinners, which recreate the menu from the movie, are a consistent hit.

Benihana of Tokyo [S] — 19 | 18 | 21 | $27

Summerfield Suites Hotel, 166 E. Superior St. (1 block east of Michigan Ave.), 312-664-9643

747 E. Butterfield Rd. (bet. Highland Ave. & Meyers Rd.), Lombard, 630-571-4440

1200 E. Higgins Rd. (Meacham Rd.), Schaumburg, 847-995-8201

◪ Surveyors' takes on these chain veterans vary with their appreciation for the knife-flashing showmanship of the chefs: pros pronounce a visit an "entertaining" option "for groups", while cons call the concept "passé", "hokey" and "an embarrassment to real Japanese"; your call.

Ben Pao [S] — 18 | 24 | 18 | $26

52 W. Illinois St. (Dearborn St.), 312-222-1888

◪ Sharp reactions abound to this River North Chinese, an upscale creation courtesy of big-time restaurateur Rich Melman: fans feel it's "fresh, fun, inventive" and "rapidly improving", while critics carp about "disappointing" food and "uneven service"; however, as the rating attests, many "love" the "stunning", "slick and chic" decor.

BERGHOFF, THE — 19 | 18 | 18 | $19

17 W. Adams St. (bet. Dearborn & State Sts.), 312-427-3170

■ "A piece of Chicago" that's "a must for tourists", this Loop German-American, which celebrated 100 schnitzel-and-strudel-scarfing years in 1998, is an "institution" that possesses the city's first post-Prohibition beer license; it offers sandwiches in a stand-up bar area ("the place to go") and produces private-label brews, root beer and bourbon; if the service is "brusque" and the atmosphere "hectic", this is what is known as authenticity.

Bertucci's S   15 | 14 | 15 | $15 |

675 N. LaSalle St. (Huron St.), 312-266-3400
140 S. Gary Ave. (Shick Rd.), Bloomingdale, 630-894-1300
1655 N. Milwaukee Ave. (Lake St.), Glenview, 847-296-9660
1311 Ridgeland Ave. (Naperville Rd.), Naperville, 630-505-1200
Westwood Ctr., 2393 63rd Rd. (Belmont St.), Woodridge,
630-434-0070

☑ Offering a "welcome change" – thin-crust pizza – this "kid-friendly" Italian chain also pleases families looking for "large portions" of pasta at a "good value"; while Chicago-style loyalists admit this company "has guts to bring" its version into thick-crust territory, they still find the pies "ordinary."

Best Hunan S   21 | 16 | 18 | $18 |

Hawthorn Fashion Sq., 700 N. Milwaukee Ave. (Rte. 60),
Vernon Hills, 847-680-8855

■ "Best Chinese in the North suburbs" exclaim those who happily skip the trek to Chinatown to indulge in the "great spicy fare" and "yummy" specials here; some say the experience can be "heaven or hell, depending on the night", but it's "always crowded", so they're doing something right.

Betise, A Bistro on the Lake S   19 | 21 | 20 | $28 |

Plaza Del Lago, 1515 Sheridan Rd. (Lake St.), Wilmette,
847-853-1711

■ Surveyors say "ignore the strip mall location" because the interior of this North Shore French bistro is a "charming", "beautiful dining space" and the kitchen turns out "reliable", "creatively prepared" fare served "without pretension."

Bice Grill S   18 | 18 | 16 | $20 |

158 E. Ontario St. (bet. Michigan Ave. & St. Clair St.), 312-266-9168

■ Cut prices and win hearts is the concept behind Bice's casual Italian adjunct, an "unbelievable value at lunch" and "nice" for a "good, quick dinner"; some find this venue "less pretentious", with "better service" than its "naughty sister."

Bice Ristorante S   20 | 20 | 18 | $36 |

158 E. Ontario St. (bet. Michigan Ave. & St. Clair St.), 312-664-1474

☑ It's a battle of extremes over this stylish Streeterville Italian import: while some praise the "excellent pastas" and "exquisite risotto", others find the menu "disappointing" and "a bit pricey" – ditto the service, which gets decent ratings but a barrage of negative comments ("snooty" staff); the consensus, if high-cost chic appeals, dress up and go.

Big Bowl, The S   18 | 17 | 18 | $17 |

159 W. Erie St. (bet. LaSalle & Wells Sts.), 312-787-8297
6 E. Cedar St. (State St.), 312-640-8888

■ These "bargain" Pan-Asian twins provide "oodles of noodles" and a "great variety" of "different and delicious" offerings, making them "a sure thing for vegetarians" and those looking for an "easy, fast" meal; P.S. with flying chopsticks and slurping de rigueur, they're a "tie killer."

BIGGS [S] 21 | 24 | 22 | $42
1150 N. Dearborn St. (Elm St.), 312-787-0900
◪ A Near North mansion transformed by a couple of face-lifts and ownership changes, with generally happy results; "upscale, blue suit" types accompanied by "tall, thin women in black" proclaim that "the old elegance is back" at this "wonderful setting" with "romantic", "classy" interiors; but the jury's still out on the contemporary Continental food, with some declaring it "excellent" and those not expensing the evening saying it "should be better considering the cost."

Biloxi Grill [S] 22 | 17 | 19 | $25
313 E. Liberty St./Rte. 176 (1 mi. east of Rte. 12), Wauconda, 847-526-2420
◪ Former Greenery owners David and Catherine Koelling "have done it again" with this rustic Northwest Suburban charmer on the Bangs Lake shoreline that features "the best chicken-fried steak around" and food that's generally "as good as you get in Louisiana" (though the regional Southern menu takes in a broader field); N.B. the outdoor deck offers pretty lake views.

BISTRO BANLIEUE [S] 26 | 20 | 23 | $31
44 Yorktown Convenience Ctr. (Butterfield Rd. & Highland Ave.), Lombard, 630-629-6560
■ For the third straight year, this "outpost of taste" in DuPage County is the highest-rated bistro in the *Survey*, earning raves for "terrific food" with "well-layered flavors" and such customer-friendly touches as petite portions of some entrees and monthly wine dinners; the "improbable" strip mall location aside, this "real suburban treasure" "could be a star even in the city."

BISTRO 110 [S] 21 | 20 | 20 | $29
110 E. Pearson St. (bet. Michigan Ave. & Rush St.), 312-266-3110
■ This "underrated garlic heaven" is a "high-energy", "authentic French" bistro that's been a "haven for Michigan Avenue shoppers" for more than a decade; surveyors say the menu is filled with such "sensual and decadent" desserts as the "definitive version" of crème brûlée; factor in a "fun", "efficient" staff and a popular Sunday brunch ("jazz and pommes frites") and it's easy to see why it's "worth the wait."

Bistrot Zinc [S] 21 | 20 | 19 | $31
3443 N. Southport Ave. (Roscoe Ave.), 773-281-3443
1131 N. State St. (bet. Cedar & Elm Sts.), 312-337-1131
◪ While there have been a number of chef changes, ratings have held steady for this Lakeview bistro, which some call the "closest thing to Paris in Chicago", as evidenced by the "really cool zinc bar", "out-of-this-world" crêpes and the "biggest mussels in town"; N.B. the Gold Coast branch is new and unrated.

Bistro Ultra 🅂   – | – | – | M |
2239 N. Clybourn Ave. (Webster St.), 773-529-3300
A cozy, 55-seat Clybourn Corridor bistro with affordable
prices (most entrees under $15) and a mostly-French
menu that still leaves room for Juan Hurtado's other
specialties, such as pork piccata; if the food is "very
similar to Rudi's Wine Bar", it's probably because Hurtado
used to cook there.

Bite Cafe 🔵🅂   ∇ 18 | 10 | 13 | $12 |
1039 N. Western Ave. (Cortez St.), 773-226-6403
■ "Quirky, but darn good and cheap" aptly summarizes
the charms of this Eclectic Ukrainian Village BYO, a "hip
place" that draws the same "bohemian" crowd as the jazz
and rock club next door; but as one wag suggests, the low-
rent decor renders it "like the moon – no atmosphere."

Blackbird   ∇ 25 | 20 | 21 | $36 |
619 W. Randolph St. (2 blocks east of Halsted St.), 312-715-0708
■ "Hot, hot" West-of-Loop American that's flying high in its
first year, racking up praise for its "cutting-edge", "creative"
menu, "stark white" decor and "attentive" service; it's easy
to feel at home with the arriviste clientele here "if you are
into black" and like an "energized" atmosphere, but it also
helps to be tolerant, as tables are close together.

Blackhawk Lodge 🅂   21 | 22 | 20 | $29 |
41 E. Superior St. (Wabash Ave.), 312-280-4080
■ Near North veteran sporting a rustic, "faux hunting lodge"
look and a Regional American menu featuring "hearty
Midwestern ribs and pork dishes", "wonderful" corn muffins
and "grits to die for"; all in all, it's probably "the finest
restaurant in Chicago with fried chicken on the menu",
and with service this "gracious" and accommodating,
patrons can "go and celebrate anything."

Blind Faith Cafe 🅂   17 | 13 | 16 | $15 |
3300 N. Lincoln Ave. (School St.), 773-871-3820
525 Dempster St. (Chicago Ave.), Evanston, 847-328-6875
☑ Recommended by the perennially guilt-ridden as the "best
place to pig out and still feel virtuous", these Lakeview and
North Shore vegetarians specialize in "creative, fresh
preparations" that even "nonvegetarians will love";
predictably, the unenlightened grumble over "bland food
for the granola crowd" and warn against it "unless you're
a health nut", but the majority surrenders to the vibes of
"like, laid-back service, man."

Blue Agave 🔵🅂   12 | 13 | 14 | $18 |
1 W. Maple St. (State St.), 312-335-8900
☑ Cons contend this "noisy" Rush Street–area Mexican
dishes up "mediocre", "Americanized" fare; so it's no
surprise some endorse it strictly for the "killer margaritas."

Blue Mesa [S] 18 18 17 $22
1729 N. Halsted St. (Willow St.), 312-944-5990
◩ Chicago's first Southwestern may seem "less exciting" than in days past, but it still has "out of the ordinary" offerings and "hangs in there with solid food"; moreover, it remains "loud and crowded" due to its proximity to Lincoln Park theaters (the Steppenwolf is a short stroll away) and "nice summertime patio" made for sultry evenings.

Bluepoint Oyster Bar [S] 20 19 19 $29
741 W. Randolph St. (Halsted St.), 312-207-1222
◩ West-of-Loop newcomer that offers "awesome fresh oysters" and a menu including "fish you've never heard of"; the "presentation and quality" are notable, and even if the ambiance is "almost too New York", seafood-starved locals generally approve, warning, "watch out, Shaw's."

BOB CHINN'S CRAB HOUSE [S] 22 13 18 $28
393 S. Milwaukee Ave. (bet. Dundee & Palatine Rds.), Wheeling, 847-520-3633
◩ Wheeling's "acoustically challenged", "always crowded" seafooder with a no-reservations policy and a titanic turnover; those used to the wait suggest trying a "world famous" mai tai and checking out the posted bills of lading to see what's arrived fresh; the unimpressed "can't understand the appeal", but a patient plurality counter "it's a circus, but the food is worth the wait."

Bogart's Charhouse [S] ▽ 19 16 18 $24
18225 Dixie Hwy. (183rd St.), Homewood, 708-798-2000
17265 Oak Park Ave. (171st St.), Tinley Park, 708-532-5592
■ Diners prepared for the "insane waits" at these South Suburban steakhouses are treated to "excellent steaks", "big portions" and "little prices"; as the name promises, there's "lots of Bogie atmosphere", with the requisite plethora of gin and smoke.

Bohemian Crystal [S] 19 15 19 $16
639 N. Blackhawk Dr. (¾ mi. west of Rte. 83), Westmont, 630-789-1981
■ A Suburban West Czech that's a "local treasure" to neighbors who love the "helpful service" and "huge portions" of "tasty", "cheap" "Bohemian comfort food", including "great kidney stew" and "breaded pork tenderloin like Grandma's"; you can "forget calorie-watching here."

Bones [S] 17 13 17 $20
7110 N. Lincoln Ave. (Touhy Ave.), Lincolnwood, 847-677-3350
◩ Jewish-style food and barbecue are the unlikely "down-home" combination at this "hectic" North Suburban entry where it helps to "roll up your sleeves to eat" "ample" quantities of "good ribs", burgers and chicken; grouches grumble that the grub's "nothing special" and "not what it once was" and opt for takeout to avoid the "drab" decor.

Boston Blackie's [S] 19 | 12 | 17 | $14

164 E. Grand Ave. (St. Clair St.), 312-938-8700

■ This "cheap", "sporty" hangout off Michigan Avenue is a powerful contender in the "best burger" arena, offers a "yummy salad" and has "swift" service; the "dark", "smoky", "speakeasy-style" room is "noisy", so in case you were in doubt, "avoid proposing marriage here."

Boulevard, The [S] ▽ 23 | 26 | 21 | $43

Hotel Inter-Continental, 505 N. Michigan Ave. (1 block south of Ohio St.), 312-321-8888

■ With new chef Mick Verheyen spicing up the "improving" Mediterranean menu, this "quiet" hotel venue Downtown holds its ground as an undiscovered pleasure, and the "romantic" in spirit give it high marks for "elegant food in an elegant setting", while applauding the "excellent service"; clearly, a room on the rise.

BRASSERIE JO [S] 21 | 21 | 20 | $31

59 W. Hubbard St. (bet. Clark & Dearborn Sts.), 312-595-0800

◪ A "bustling" River North brasserie that "captures the feel of Paris" with such staples as "killer steak with pommes frites" and the "engaging Alsatian concoctions" of proprietor Jean Joho; some find it a tad "hyped" and "noisy", but it remains a "favorite" with the "trendy" crowd; as many already know, the signature "shrimp bag is fabulous" and the "wine list is fantastic."

Brasserie T [S] 20 | 20 | 18 | $29

Northfield Village Sq., 305 S. Happ Rd. (Rte. 94 & Willow Rd.), Northfield, 847-446-0444

◪ Set in a "high-energy room", this American (with French and Italian accents) brings "city dining" to the North Shore 'burbs, winning 'em over with "outstanding salads" and desserts "worth blowing your diet" for; still, cynics find the service "spotty" and food "disappointing, considering the pedigree" of Rick Tramonto and Gale Gand (ex Trio).

Breakfast Club [S] 19 | 12 | 16 | $12

1381 W. Hubbard St. (Noble St.), 312-666-3166

■ "Cute, little" cottage-turned-restaurant in the East Village that serves a breakfast (and lunch) that's "like home cooking, if Mom had been to cooking school" and knew how to whip up "great French toast" and "frittatas that are worth the wait" – which occurs mostly on the weekend.

Brett's [S] 20 | 13 | 17 | $24

2011 W. Roscoe St. (Damen Ave.), 773-248-0999

◪ Owner Brett Knobel "is fussy about everything, and it shows" at this Roscoe Village "neighborhood" Eclectic that's "ideal for lingering"; look for "clever" food that delves into Mexican, Caribbean and Asian idioms, a "solid" brunch and "outstanding desserts"; a few ingrates quibble over "intrusive service" ("staff flirts with you")

Bricks ◗ S
▽ | 22 | 14 | 18 | $15

1909 N. Lincoln Ave. (Wisconsin Ave.), 312-255-0851

■ It's "rathskeller redux" at this subterranean pizza palace in Lincoln Park, where the barbecue pie is the prize; a notably "friendly" place, it makes for a "cozy neighborhood dive" and a "fine family hangout."

Brother Jimmy's BBQ S
15 | 13 | 13 | $17

2909 N. Sheffield Ave. (George Ave.), 773-528-0888

☑ There's "no need to dress up" for this "total frat party" for twentysomethings, a DePaul-area rib shack, replete with U of North Carolina memorabilia and live (no cover) blues and zydeco; while some grumble about only "ok 'cue" and "average Southern" dishes, others insist the "dry rub rocks."

Bruna's Ristorante S
21 | 14 | 19 | $24

2424 S. Oakley Ave. (24th Pl.), 773-254-5550

■ Heart of Italy "charmer" with a "caring" staff "that patiently listens to my dad's lesson on bruschetta"; "terrific", "old-fashioned" food and "affordable wines" woo the wistful who are grateful that this stalwart "still knows how to cook."

Bubba Gump Shrimp Co. S
– | – | – | M

Navy Pier, 600 E. Grand Ave. (Lake Michigan), 312-595-5500

A theatrical seafooder – part of a chain – that's well-placed at the entrance to tourist-magnet Navy Pier; memorabilia and references to the flick *Forrest Gump* abound, including a replica of the bus-stop bench; if that's not enough, there's also an outdoor cafe overlooking a fountain and offering a glimpse of Lake Michigan.

Buca di Beppo S
16 | 20 | 20 | $20

2941 N. Clark St. (bet. Oakdale & Wellington Aves.), 773-348-7673
90 Yorktown Shopping Ctr. (bet. Butterfield Rd. & Highland Ave.), Lombard, 630-932-7673
604 N. Milwaukee Ave. (bet. Dundee Ave. & Lake Cook Rd.), Wheeling, 847-808-9898

☑ "You'll laugh your head off at the wild '50s decor", "old-country" kitsch and photo shrines to Sinatra at these "fun" city and suburban checked-tablecloth chain Italians with family-style "*Flintstone*-esque portions" that are ideal if "you're with a lot of people"; bashers decry "bland", "average" food, but devotees "hope one day to dine at the Pope's table."

Buckingham's S
▽ | 21 | 20 | 19 | $30

Chicago Hilton & Towers, 720 S. Michigan Ave. (bet. Balbo Dr. & 8th St.), 312-922-4000

☑ An "improving" hotel American across from Grant Park that's handy for Downtown theatergoers; pros praise the "good steaks" and "chocolate cake to die for", but a smaller contingent says they "expected much better" and consider the concept "a bit outdated."

Bukhara S
17 | 17 | 16 | $25

2 E. Ontario St. (State St.), 312-943-0188

☑ "Warm decor" and a glass window into the kitchen make it "nice to watch" the chefs work at this "decent" but "nothing extraordinary" River North Indian with a "serviceable buffet at lunch."

Burgundy Bistro S
▽ 19 | 14 | 18 | $28

3462 Vollmer Rd. (Governors Hwy.), Olympia Fields, 708-747-5399

☑ "Much nicer now that it's enlarged" its space, this "hidden neighborhood" French in the South Suburbs is a "pleasant surprise" with "very good food and service"; however, a few holdouts mutter "nothing special."

Butcher Shop Steakhouse S
▽ 22 | 19 | 20 | $33

358 W. Ontario St. (Orleans St.), 312-440-4900

■ Good food ratings for a grill-your-own-steak house point to a clientele with plenty of self-esteem, but the "fabulous" meat does play a part and the appetizers and salads are "quite good too" – it's a "nice concept" that's "great for a family outing"; note that "cigars are welcome", which will mean heaven for some, the opposite for others.

Cafe Absinthe S
22 | 21 | 20 | $37

1954 W. North Ave. (Damen Ave.), 773-278-4488

■ "Funky" and "trendy" are the watchwords at this Bucktown American with an alley entrance and "dark" interior that make it a "challenge" to see "if you can find your way in"; once ensconced, there's "innovative" food and an "edgy", "techno-club" atmosphere with "crowded tables"; while naysayers find it "loud" and "pricey", the "high-quality" food wins 'em over.

Cafe BaBaReeba! S
20 | 19 | 18 | $25

2024 N. Halsted St. (½ block north of Armitage Ave.), 773-935-5000

■ "Sharing can be fun" at this Lincoln Park tapas bar (Chicago's first) with "superb paella", "excellent sangria", a "super outdoor" patio and a "fun and flirty" atmosphere that's "good for groups", especially "adventurous out-of-towners"; despite some moaning that the place "has slipped", most agree it's "still the best" in its genre "if you can stand the long wait."

Cafe Bernard S
20 | 17 | 20 | $28

2100 N. Halsted St. (bet. Armitage & Webster Aves.), 773-871-2100

■ "A Chicago fixture that has weathered well", this "cozy", "low-key" French bistro continues to hold its own against scores of Lincoln Park competitors thanks to "individual attention from Bernard" and his "concerned" staff and "very good" food; still, some are baffled "why it's not busier."

Cafe Borgia [S] 23 | 13 | 19 | $25
17923 Torrence Ave. (I-94), Lansing, 708-474-5515
■ "An oasis of great food in fast-food purgatory" is how admirers see this South Suburban Italian, a former BYO that now boasts a well-chosen wine list; although the seating in this tiny storefront is thisclose and causes some to suggest it "should be smoke-free", it's a "great value" and most are "never disappointed."

Cafe Central [S] 19 | 18 | 19 | $28
455 Central Ave. (Green Bay Rd.), Highland Park, 847-266-7878
◪ Owned by much-acclaimed restaurateurs Carlos and Debbie Nieto (Carlos'), this "charming", "light and airy" North Shore French bistro is recommended as a "good for lunch" choice when you're "just strolling"; while some appreciate the "owners greeting me at the door", others observe that it "does not run as well" when they're gone and think it's an "afterthought" compared to their signature spot.

Cafe Iberico ◐ [S] 21 | 17 | 17 | $20
739 N. LaSalle St. (bet. Chicago Ave. & Superior St.), 312-573-1510
◪ What began as a four-table tapas bar has expanded to more than 400 seats (without much improvement in its decor rating), yet it's "still hard to get a table" at this River North Spaniard, where aficionados claim "the wait is worth it" for food that's "easily the most authentic" in town; some quibble that it was "better when they were smaller" – the restaurant, that is, not the tapas – and that the addition "feels like a Denny's"; still, "for the price, it's great."

Cafe La Cave ◐ [S] 23 | 24 | 23 | $42
2777 Mannheim Rd. (bet. Higgins Rd. & Touhy Ave.), Des Plaines, 847-827-7818
■ "A throwback to the past", this O'Hare-area Continental has "done a wonderful job for years" serving up "old-world" classics (i.e. "steak Diane to die for") in either its grotto-like dining room, for which the place is named, or its banquet facilities; for those who find it "a treat to have an entree prepared tableside", this "swanky", "expense-account" place is "elegance defined."

Cafe Luciano [S] 19 | 19 | 18 | $27
871 N. Rush St. (Chestnut St.), 312-266-1414
2676 Green Bay Rd. (2 blocks north of Central Ave.), Evanston, 847-864-6060
◪ These Evanston and Rush Street trattorias have made converts of those who've sampled the signature dish – a "delicious" country rigatoni – and overall "dependable fare"; others shrug that they're "noisy, garlicky" and merely "decent Italians."

Cafe Matou   ▽ 22 | 23 | 22 | $31
1846 N. Milwaukee Ave. (bet. Armitage & North Aves.),
773-384-8911
■ Surveyors haven't found their way to Charlie Socher's
edge-of-Bucktown bistro in significant numbers, but those
who have dub it "a swell find in the area"; "great French
food" is only enhanced by "clean, quiet" surroundings,
friendly service" and "easy parking."

Cafe Med   ▽ 17 | 14 | 15 | $26
1950 W. North Ave. (½ block east of Damen & Milwaukee Aves.),
773-278-3800
◨ Bucktown newcomer with Mediterranean-Italian cuisine
that shows "promise"; but aside from owners Leonardo
Timatyos and Sandra Burdette, who "make you feel warm
and welcome", a few think "service could be better."

CAFE PYRENEES   24 | 17 | 22 | $34
River Tree Ct. Mall, Rte. 60 & Milwaukee Ave. (Rte. 21),
Vernon Hills, 847-918-8850
◨ This "top-notch" bistro might be "often forgotten, which is
ok by its fans" who gladly make the trek to its Far North
Suburban location in search of "city-caliber food" at a
"reasonable cost"; while some carp about the "so-so"
decor (which has "no waiting area"), to others that's "a
reminder that it's the food that matters."

Cafe Selmarie   – | – | – | M
2327 W. Giddings Ave. (Lincoln Ave.), 773-989-5595
"Hole-in-the-wall" North Sider that's a "terrific place" for
"light" American fare, including "good sandwiches", salads
and "the best desserts around."

Cafe Spiaggia S   23 | 23 | 21 | $35
980 N. Michigan Ave. (Oak St.), 312-280-2750
■ The "little sister to Spiaggia" shares a kitchen with
its more esteemed sibling and though there are "fewer
choices", the prices are more "accessible", making it the
place to go "when you want to impress a date but not too
much"; a recent "stylish" remodeling has made the place
"elegant" and, some point out, more expensive, but most
agree that one should "eat here and dream that you're
eating next door."

CAFE 36 S   24 | 18 | 22 | $33
365 La Grange Rd. (Harris St.), La Grange, 708-354-5722
■ "A real sleeper", this "underrated" ("I don't know of a
restaurant that tries harder") West Suburban French
specializes in wild game and "extraordinary sauces"; it
garners kudos for a menu that "runs with the big dogs in
the city" and might even be "too great for its setting."

California Cafe Bar & Grill S　　− − − M
Woodfield Shopping Ctr., 313-D Woodfield Mall (Rte. 53),
Schaumburg, 847-330-1212
An ambitious Suburban Northwest American that may be
part of a California chain but is a distinct improvement
over mall fare, featuring such upscale amenities as
a wide-ranging menu with multi-ethnic influences,
regular winemaker dinners and a wine list with more
than 150 selections.

California Pizza Kitchen S　　16 13 15 $16
Water Tower Pl., 845 N. Michigan Ave., 7th fl. (bet. Chestnut
& Pearson Sts.), 312-787-7300
414 N. Orleans St. (1½ blocks south of Ohio St.), 312-222-9030
Oak Brook Shopping Ctr., 551 Oak Brook Shopping Ctr.
(bet. Cermak Rd. & Rte. 83), Oak Brook, 630-571-7800
◪ "If you don't mind stepping around strollers", these
"clean", "reliable" city and suburban outposts of this
popular, "solid" chain offer an "interesting variety" of "New
Age" pies that are a "break from tradition" for locals who
mumble about "guilty pleasures" and a barbecue chicken
version "that rules"; but civic priders bemoan the "sterile"
decor, say "the idea is getting stale" and insist "you can
only have great pizza if it comes from Chicago."

Campagnola S　　24 17 21 $29
815 Chicago Ave. (Main St.), Evanston, 847-475-6100
■ This North Shore two-year-old is "a great new Evanston
find" and has "raised the bar" on rustic Italian cooking, even
if some feel that the "amateurish setting" is taking the
rusticity too far; the most common complaint is "not enough
tables" to accommodate everyone who wants to sample
Michael Altenberg's "underrated, innovative" food.

Campeche ◑S　　▽ 14 12 15 $13
3660 N. Clark St. (Addison St.), 773-327-1490
■ "Better when drunk" is the less than complimentary
assessment of this "bare-bones" Wrigleyville Mexican,
whose chief virtues seem to be its proximity to Wrigley
Field (handy for inebriated Cubs fans) and very late
(Sunday–Thursday) and 'round-the-clock hours (Friday–
Saturday); a few belching bleacher bums blurt "decent."

Cape Cod Room ◑S　　22 22 21 $40
Drake Hotel, 140 E. Walton St. (Michigan Ave.), 312-787-2200
◪ You "can feel the history" when you venture into this
Gold Coast hotel seafood "dowager" where, except for
the "steep" tab, the "old-time" staff doesn't "know if it's
1998 or 1958 and neither will you"; partisans say it's a
"classy stalwart" for signature items like the "excellent"
Dover sole and "tasty" bookbinder soup; but crabs carp
that even if it makes "you feel like old money", it's "tired"
and "nowhere near as good as it used to be."

Capital Grille 🅂
22 | 24 | 22 | $46

633 N. St. Clair St. (1 block east of Michigan Ave.), 312-337-9400
▪ "Take your man on his birthday" to this "clubby" DC-transplant steakhouse that strikes most as "a great addition to the competition", serving up "excellent chops" "worthy of a fat cat on an expense account"; the "great wine selection" and "impeccable service" also impress, but beware, cigar "smoke may drift your way."

Capriccio's 🅂
20 | 18 | 21 | $27

300 Happ Rd. (Willow Rd.), Northfield, 847-501-4556
▨ "Old-style" North Shore Italian offering "the best cheese bread in the world" and an "always warm reception" from a staff that "really tries to please"; for diners who originally had different plans for the evening ("for the Brasserie T overflow"), it's a particularly "handy neighborhood place."

CARLOS' 🅂
28 | 24 | 27 | $63

429 Temple Ave. (bet. Green Bay & Half Day Rds.), Highland Park, 847-432-0770
▪ Despite the "ups and downs" of a "chef shuffle", this "small, romantic" North Shore French still remains "a treasure" – "everyone is treated like royalty" by owners Carlos and Debbie Nieto and "every meal is a special occasion"; there are a few scattered quibbles about the high prices, but consistently high marks bear out the sentiment that it's "still one of the best" for "a memorable evening"; N.B. there's no corkage fee on Mondays.

Carmen's 🅂
16 | 11 | 14 | $14

6568 N. Sheridan Rd. (Albion Ave.), 773-465-1700 ◑
1012 Church St. (bet. Maple & Oak Sts.), Evanston, 847-328-0031
▨ While the stuffed-and-deep-dish pies have some hardcore loyalists, the general consensus is that these Northwestern and Loyola U–area pizzerias are "decent but not great", with a few observers indicating they're "slipping."

Carmichael's Chicago Steak House 🅂
– | – | – | E

1052 W. Monroe St. (bet. Morgan & Racine Aves.), 312-433-0025
Handy for the pre-event United Center crowd, pre-theater patrons and Loop-area lunchers, this City West newcomer has an old-fashioned look; in addition to steaks, such signature dishes as shrimp de jonghe and Back-of-the-Yards pork chops are edible evocations of Chicago's culinary past.

Carmine's 🅂
19 | 18 | 19 | $29

1043 N. Rush St. (bet. Cedar & Oak Sts.), 312-988-7676
▪ "A Rosebud cousin with better ambiance", this two-story Rush Street Italian sticks to owner Alex Dana's formula of straightforward cooking and portions so huge "you can eat for a week on what you bring home"; scattered complaints about "inconsistent" service mar the picture somewhat, but constant crowds suggest that he's doing something right.

Carpaccio Ristorante S   ▽ 19 | 15 | 18 | $30
2001 N. Rand Rd. (bet. Dundee & Lake Cook Rds.), Palatine,
847-202-1191
◪ Some appraisers support the "great reviews" that this
Northwest Suburban Italian yearling has garnered, citing
an "imaginative menu" featuring dishes with exceptional
"depth of flavor"; the cautious think it's "still improving",
though they feel it's displaying some difficulty adjusting to
its new-found limelight.

Carson's Ribs S   19 | 13 | 17 | $23
612 N. Wells St. (Ontario St.), 312-280-9200
5970 N. Ridge Ave. (Clark St.), 773-271-4000
5050 N. Harlem Ave. (Foster Ave.), Harwood Heights,
708-867-4200
400 E. Roosevelt Rd. (Highland Ave.), Lombard, 630-627-4300
8617 Niles Ctr. Rd. (2 blocks south of Dempster St.), Skokie,
847-675-6800
◪ These city and suburban rib houses get their share of
nods for the "best gnaw-off in town" if you're into "good,
old-fashioned artery-bangers" and sauce that's rated
"yum, yum, yum"; nonenthusiasts "don't understand the
appeal", complaining of "not much decor" (the remedy
for which is "carryout only") and suggest that true ribs
fans should "go to Kansas City for good BBQ."

CATCH 35 S   23 | 21 | 21 | $35
Leo Burnett Bldg., 35 W. Wacker Dr. (bet. Dearborn &
State Sts.), 312-346-3500
◼ An irresistible lure "for business lunches", this Downtown
seafooder impresses with its "creative", "well-prepared"
Asian-accented fish dishes, its "city buzz" ambiance (lots of
wood and granite) and its handy proximity to Loop theaters;
the only catch seems to be the hefty price point (hope
"someone else is paying").

Ceiling Zero S   17 | 16 | 17 | $28
5000 Anthony Trail (2 blocks west of Pfingsten Rd.),
Northbrook, 847-272-8111
◪ This airplane-themed, retro-hangar hangout on the North
Shore offers "basic" Continental fare ("love the London
broil") to an older crowd; but younger passengers think
the menu doesn't get off the ground ("blah").

Celebrity Cafe S   ▽ 25 | 24 | 24 | $36
Westin River North, 320 N. Dearborn St. (Kinzie St.),
312-836-5499
◪ Despite its name, this "never crowded" River North hotel
dining room enjoys no high-profile among surveyors; the
few that have sampled its Contemporary American fare call
it "Chicago's best-kept secret", with "wonderful food" and
"the best" Sunday brunch; a few naysayers insist "it was
better when Nikko owned it."

Centro Ristorante S
21 | 16 | 18 | $28

710 N. Wells St. (bet. Erie & Superior Sts.), 312-988-7775
■ A member of the Rosebud family, this River North spot, popular with "commodity players" and the buffed East Bank Club crowd, sticks to the tried-and-true formula of "mounds of good Italian" food, including flat noodles that "rule"; some call it "too trendy" and "noisy", and it's so crowded that "long waits" are common even with reservations.

Chaplin's on Church S
– | – | – | M

618 Church St. (Orrington St.), Evanston, 847-864-1445
The name is a play on words (chaplain, church, get it?), but the food is serious at this North Shore American bistro; while the kitchen emphasizes fresh fish, that doesn't prevent diners from recommending the "best brie-crouton salad" or "great pot roast"; overall, a "great place to relax."

Charlie Beinlich's ▱
21 | 14 | 18 | $14

290 Skokie Blvd. (bet. Dundee & Lake Cook Rds.), Northbrook, 847-564-9328
■ This "same as ever" North Suburban "landmark" tavern that will hit the half-century mark in 2000 supplies what supporters insist is "the perfect burger", as well as "great" shrimp cocktail; the only caveat: "I wish it weren't cash only."

Charlie's Ale House S
13 | 15 | 14 | $17

Navy Pier, 700 E. Grand Ave. (Lake Shore Dr.), 312-595-1440
1224 W. Webster St. (Magnolia St.), 773-871-1440
■ DePaul-area and Navy Pier taverns serving up "average bar food", though a few praise the "must-have" chicken pot pie and "wonderful" meat loaf; some advise "go to Webster Street for better atmosphere, no tourists" and the "great patio", but others view that outpost as an "adult frat bar for Golden Domers" (Notre Dame fans).

CHARLIE TROTTER'S
27 | 26 | 27 | $92

816 W. Armitage Ave. (Halsted St.), 773-248-6228
☑ Voted this *Survey*'s most popular restaurant, Charlie Trotter's Lincoln Park temple to New American dining wins raves for his "master of his own domain", never-repeat-a-dish approach and painstakingly presented dishes that are "like going to an art show on plates"; while some find it all "too precious" and "stuffy", many others opine "we will never have a better meal."

Cheesecake Factory ◑ S
18 | 18 | 16 | $19

875 N. Michigan Ave., lower level (bet. Chestnut St. & Delaware Pl.), 312-337-1101
☑ This casual Michigan Avenue American with "circus-like" decor is "teeming with tourists" which makes it a "place to avoid during peak hours"; the "abysmal wait" allows time to peruse a menu "as big as a dictionary" that yields "large portions" and "rich desserts"; however, purists argue that it suffers from a "jack-of-all-trades syndrome."

Chicago Chop House [S] 24 | 18 | 20 | $37

60 W. Ontario St. (bet. Clark & Dearborn Sts.), 312-787-7100

■ Given its River North location, this steakhouse may have "too many tourists", but locals like it too, particularly the "men's club atmosphere" and "decidedly Chicago decor", including historic city photographs; overall, a "contender for the best steaks" and "the best value" in its class.

Chicago Diner [S] 16 | 12 | 17 | $14

3411 N. Halsted St. (Roscoe St.), 773-935-6696

581 Elm Pl. (bet. 1st & 2nd Sts.), Highland Park, 847-433-1228

◪ This veteran North Sider and its year-old Highland Park sequel get a mixed review; acolytes find them "admirable in their struggle for purity" and ask "why aren't there more places like this?"; however, the disenchanted decree "vegetarian doesn't need to be this mediocre."

Chicago Flat Sammies [S]⊄ – | – | – | I

811 N. Michigan Ave. (bet. Chicago Ave. & Pearson St.), 312-664-2733

Located in the historic Pumping Station (a survivor of the Chicago Fire), this casual cafe/sandwich shop serves three meals a day to Michigan Avenue workers, tourists and shoppers; its outdoor cafe, which seats 60, is pooch-friendly, providing complimentary water and dog biscuits.

Chicago Pizza & Oven Grinder Co. [S]⊄ 18 | 14 | 15 | $17

2121 N. Clark St. (bet. Dickens & Webster Sts.), 773-248-2570

◪ Lincoln Park mainstay where the "must-try" house specialty is an "upside-down pizza pot pie" that respondents agree is a "different way to experience Chicago pizza"; the "excellent grinders" (Italian sausage sandwiches) are also touted by regulars who don't seem to mind the "dungeonlike" interior and "long waits."

Chinoiserie [S]⊄ – | – | – | M

509 Fourth St. (Linden Ave.), Wilmette, 847-256-0306

An "innovative" BYO North Shore French-accented Chinese that has only seven tables, not nearly enough for the scores who want to try the "quite good" offerings; insiders advise "go for the show", referring to the banter between the chef and his wife; though service can be "sketchy", this "chic" nook is apparently worth a little inconvenience.

Ciao Tutti [S] ▽ 20 | 17 | 21 | $23

50 S. La Grange Rd. (2 blocks south of Ogden Ave.), La Grange, 708-352-6466

◪ The name can mean 'hello, everybody' or 'goodbye, everybody' and surveyors seem similarly conflicted over this West Suburban Italian, with some viewing it as "a gem" that's "getting better" and others finding it "disappointing"; there's some positive consensus on the live music on Thursdays and asking "for Dominic for the royal treatment."

Cielo [S] ▽ 18 | 22 | 20 | $36

Omni Chicago Hotel, 676 N. Michigan Ave. (Huron St.), 312-944-7676

■ Despite "glittery views of Michigan Avenue", a "lovely setting" that includes a trompe l'oeil ceiling mural of the sky, live piano music nightly and "better-than-average" Italian-accented American food, this handsome hotel dining room is "never crowded"; appreciative patrons say it "deserves more accolades", so have a look.

CITÉ [S] 20 | 26 | 21 | $46

Lake Point Tower, 505 N. Lake Shore Dr., 70th fl. (bet. Grand Ave. & Illinois St.), 312-644-4050

■ This American spot on the 70th floor of Lake Point Tower recently amended its Continental ways to focus on steaks, seafood and pasta, but the food seems incidental here – "go on a clear day", "don't go when it's windy"; it's also the place to "take someone to impress them because everyone falls in love with the view", even though "you pay for it."

Claim Company [S] 14 | 14 | 15 | $16

Northbrook Ct., 2124 Northbrook Ct. (bet. Lake Cook & Waukegan Rds.), Northbrook, 847-291-0770

◪ A miner-motif burger joint down to its last productive vein, having tapped out of its Oak Brook and Chicago locations; fans must now trek to a northern suburb for the "great" Motherlode hamburger and "good" salad bar; still, some claim "standards aren't as high as they used to be."

Clara's Pasta di Casa [S] ▽ 20 | 12 | 18 | $18

6740 S. Rte. 53 (Hobson Rd.), Woodridge, 630-968-8899

◪ Clara Melchiorre, daughter of the famed Mama Celeste, is the guiding light behind this West Suburban pasta parlor where the food "is better than most on Taylor Street at half the price"; while some complain about the "out-of-the-way" location, "long waits" and "tiny" space, others believe the "good homemade pastas" are worth a little inconvenience.

Clark Street Bistro [S] 18 | 14 | 17 | $24

2600 N. Clark St. (Wrightwood Ave.), 773-525-9992

■ "You don't know what you're missing" if you overlook this "reliable" Lakeview Italian-French "neighborhood place" where "flavorful food" is available at "reasonable" prices, albeit in "bland surroundings"; it also serves "one of the better" Sunday brunches in the area.

Club Creole 19 | 13 | 16 | $17

226 W. Kinzie St. (1 block west of Wells St.), 312-222-0300

■ Some wags dub this "cramped" Cajun-Creole tucked behind the Merchandise Mart "the Small Easy" – a "good Dixie find" that's "great for lunch" for area businessmen; nitpickers scoff that it's a "poor man's Heaven On Seven", with "no atmosphere", but the majority seems to like this "cute theme place" and its "decent prices" just fine.

Clubhouse, The 🅂   18 | 21 | 17 | $24
298 Oak Brook Shopping Ctr. (bet. Cermak Rd. & Rte. 83),
Oak Brook, 630-472-0600
☑ Owned by celebrities (Kevin Costner, Robert Wagner and
Jack Nicklaus, among others), this "stylishly decorated",
country club–themed Traditional American in Oak Brook
opened in late '97; while its decor and golf pro shop win
points and the "average" food's not an issue, some are
teed off by the "noisy" atmosphere and "disorganized"
service; clearly, it "still has growing pains."

Club Lucky 🅂   18 | 16 | 17 | $23
1824 W. Wabansia St. (bet. Ashland & Damen Aves.),
773-227-2300
■ "Wicked martinis" garnished with blue cheese–stuffed
olives are one of the lures at this Bucktown Italian that's a
pre-game fave of Bulls and Blackhawks boosters and a
"good neighborhood drop-in place", even if dropping in
means "fighting through the crowded bar" to sample the
"amazing calamari"; assessments of its retro decor –
variously attributed to the '30s, '40s and '50s – suggest
patrons don't study many decorating magazines.

Club Macanudo ◐   – | – | – | E
60 E. Walton St. (bet. Michigan Ave. & Rush St.),
312-642-4200
This four-level Rush Street–area cigar bar, which is owned
by the company that manufactures Macanudos, features an
American menu with Latin influences ranging from prime
steaks to a Cuban sandwich; the clubby space includes
overstuffed chairs, cigar-store Indian figures, a top-of-the-
line ventilation system and, of course, a logo-filled gift shop.

COCO PAZZO 🅂   24 | 22 | 22 | $38
300 W. Hubbard St. (Franklin St.), 312-836-0900
■ "A sure winner" say fans of this NYC import where
"amazing", "sophisticated" Tuscan cuisine and a "classy
but homey" atmosphere add up to a "topflight" dining
experience Downtown; the food is "about as good as Italian
gets in this town" and the "attentive", "well-informed"
service makes it a "fine celebratory choice", though some
wish it would "lose the New York prices."

Coco Pazzo Cafe 🅂   23 | 21 | 21 | $30
Motel 6, 636 N. St. Clair St. (Ontario St.), 312-664-2777
■ Not much has changed at the former Il Toscanaccio
aside from the moniker shift, which better reflects its
status as a moderately priced sibling of Coco Pazzo; it's
still an "intimate" trattoria with "tasty", "hearty Tuscan
food" and an outdoor patio that remains one of the city's
prettiest sidewalk cafes.

Cocoro [S] ▽ 18 | 15 | 18 | $26

668 N. Wells St. (Erie St.), 312-943-2220

■ The nondescript exterior may explain why few voters have sampled this River North Japanese, but those who have laud the "authentic" sushi and sashimi, "great soups and grilled items" and "friendly, eager" staffers; considering the recent closings of nearby competitors, some sigh "thank God for affordable, decent Japanese" in the area.

Cohiba Restaurant & Cigar Bar ◐ [S] – | – | – | M

2642 N. Lincoln Ave. (bet. Sheffield & Wrightwood Aves.), 773-871-2180

This Lincoln Park Cuban restaurant and cigar bar is a sister property to next-door Lindo Mexico, which speaks well of its chances of success, as does the relative dearth of Cuban establishments in town.

Como Inn [S] 18 | 20 | 19 | $27

546 N. Milwaukee Ave. (bet. Grand Ave. & Halsted St.), 312-421-5222

◪ "Throw a dart at the menu" and you'll hit a winner say fans of this Near West Side Italian, a "Chicago landmark" (since 1924) with a "charming old-world atmosphere" that can be "romantic if you get a booth" in one of its myriad small rooms; foes say it's "living on its reputation" and catering to the "Greyhound bus crowd", but free parking and shuttle service to sports and cultural events are appealing.

Con Fusion [S] 23 | 20 | 20 | $37

1616 N. Damen Ave. (½ block north of North Ave.), 773-772-7100

■ A "happening place" populated by a "cool and trendy city crowd", this Bucktown Eclectic's name alludes to chef Kevin Shikami's "inventive", ever-changing, fusion menu; the "artistic dishes" and "minimalist" decor are "cutting edge", but "take a cushion" to combat the uncomfortable seating and "ear plugs" for the "excessive noise."

Convito Italiano [S] 18 | 14 | 16 | $21

Plaza del Lago, 1515 Sheridan Rd. (Westerfield Rd.), Wilmette, 847-251-3654

◪ With its "excellent" carry-out counter and wine shop, this North Shore country Italian is a "great choice for catered events" and at-home meals; while some find the dining room less impressive, it's popular with "ladies who lunch" and has a "nice patio in the summer"; however, a critical contingent claims the place "lacks its former enthusiasm."

Cornelia's Roosterant [S] ▽ 21 | 21 | 21 | $25

750 W. Cornelia St. (bet. Broadway & Halsted St.), 773-248-8333

◪ Being in "a beautiful summer garden" "amongst the birds" is something to crow about at this "comfy and romantic" Lakeview Italian-American; it's a "good, all-purpose place to go" for "unbelievable chicken", and those in a rush should know that there's "rarely a wait" for a table.

Corner Bakery S
18 | 15 | 14 | $13 |

1121 N. State St. (Cedar St.), 312-787-1969
676 N. St. Clair St. (Erie St.), 312-266-2570
516 N. Clark St. (Grand Ave.), 312-644-8100
638 Central Ave. (1 block east of Green Bay Rd.),
Highland Park, 847-433-4638
Oak Brook Shopping Ctr., 240 Oak Brook Shopping Ctr.
(bet. Rte. 83 & 22nd St.), Oak Brook, 630-368-0505
1901 E. Woodfield Rd. (Rte. 53), Schaumburg,
847-240-1111
Old Orchard Shopping Ctr., 175 Old Orchard Ctr. (bet. Golf Rd.
& Skokie Blvd.), Skokie, 847-933-1555
■ For "the staff of life at its best", check out any location
of this "soon to be on every corner" chain, which "smells
wonderful" and features an "amazing selection of baked
goods", including "imaginative sandwiches" and "crusty"
take-home breads; although it "fills the gap between fast
food and fine dining", many decry the "haughty" service
and "the most poorly organized cashier lines ever."

Costa's ●S
21 | 21 | 20 | $25 |

340 S. Halsted St. (Jackson Blvd.), 312-263-9700
1 S. 130 Summit Ave. (½ block south of Roosevelt Rd.), Oak
Brook Terrace, 630-620-1100
■ This "stunning", "exceptionally well-appointed" Greek,
with the "best" grilled lamb chops and "fisherman's risotto
to die for", ranks in "the upper end of Greektown" spots;
the complimentary valet parking at lunch and dinner is a
customer-friendly bonus; N.B. the Oak Brook Terrace
branch is new and unrated.

COURTRIGHT'S S
25 | 26 | 24 | $41 |

8989 S. Archer Ave. (2 blocks west of Willow Springs Rd.),
Willow Springs, 708-839-8000
■ "A perfect 10" "headed for four stars" enthuse supporters
of this South Suburban American that's a "high aspiration"
operation with "wonderful food", a "top-notch" (600-label)
wine list and a "unique" setting featuring double-height
windows that showcase forest preserve vistas; "what
one expects and doesn't always get Downtown" says one
convert to this "gem in the 'burbs."

Cousin's S
17 | 16 | 17 | $15 |

2833 N. Broadway (Diversey Pkwy.), 773-880-0063
5203 N. Clark St. (Foster Ave.), 773-334-4553
■ These North Side Middle Easterns are "good" local spots
offering "reasonably priced", "above-average" choices in
"artifact-filled" dining rooms; admirers appreciate the
variety of vegetarian selections and recommend the "great
hummus", Turkish coffee and "succulent" baklava.

Crawdaddy Bayou S   17 20 18 $24
412 N. Milwaukee Ave. (bet. Dundee & Lake Cook Rds.),
Wheeling, 847-520-4800
☑ Opinion is divided over this theatrical Northwest Suburban
Cajun whose "faux bayou atmosphere" comes complete
with an indoor "swamp", animatronic alligators and live
music: for some, its "authentic" menu means it's "Mardi
Gras all year long", while others brand it a "cutesy"
"insult to Louisiana"; beyond dispute are the crowds
nearly every night ("go early"), the "incredible noise" and
the "fun-fun-fun" party atmosphere.

Crofton on Wells   24 19 20 $40
535 N. Wells St. (bet. Grand Ave. & Ohio St.), 312-755-1790
■ This River North American marked chef Suzy Crofton's
"dazzling debut" in mid-'97 and praise for her "world-class",
"nuanced cooking" continues to build, even though her
"very tasteful" dining room – which seats fewer than 75 –
makes reservations mandatory and difficult to obtain;
some suggest that the place "needs polish", particularly
on the service end, but overall, this "jewel among
newcomers" is a "keeper."

Cross-Rhodes S ⊄   18 8 16 $13
913 Chicago Ave. (Main St.), Evanston, 847-475-4475
■ A North Shore storefront serving "unforgettable"
Greek fries seasoned with garlic, herbs and lemon;
while easy on the wallets of nearby students, the "not
much to look at" decor causes collegians to quip "get
the chicken, rent a movie."

Cucina Bella S   19 18 19 $23
543 W. Diversey Pkwy. (2 blocks east of Clark St.),
773-868-1119
☑ "Nice little neighborhood" Italian on the North Side
offering a "warm and comfortable" atmosphere for
sampling "wonderful bruschetta" and "fantastic calamari";
others wax less enthusiastic, dubbing it "nothing special",
"worth a walk, not a ride"; N.B. ask about the chef's table.

Cucina Paradiso S   ▽ 22 20 21 $23
814 North Blvd. (bet. Lake St. & Oak Park Ave.), Oak Park,
708-848-3434
■ "Consistently good", "Downtown-style" West Suburban
trattoria featuring "to-die-for" pastas and "creative"
fish dishes; although its "backstreet" location makes it
tricky to find, apparently plenty do, as it's "crowded,
especially on weekends."

Cucina Roma 🅢   20 20 19 $23
Village Green Ctr., 185 N. Milwaukee Ave. (Old Half Day Rd.),
Lincolnshire, 847-478-9600
Iroquois Ctr., 1163 E. Ogden Ave. (Naperville Rd.),
Naperville, 630-355-4444
James Crossing Shopping Ctr., 800 E. Ogden Ave. (83rd St.),
Westmont, 630-654-9600
■ These popular West and North Suburban trattorias
provide "old-world" ambiance for locals who rejoice at
finding "thumbs-up" Italian cuisine within a quick drive;
the "huge portions" at "reasonable prices" also win favor,
but quibblers complain that they're "always too busy."

Cuisines 🅢   ▽ 21 19 20 $35
Renaissance Hotel, 1 W. Wacker Dr. (State St.), 312-372-7200
■ A "restful" place for North-of-Loop business types and
shoppers, this hotel dining room may be quieter than the
owners would like since it remains largely ignored by voters;
those who've visited point to "excellent" Mediterranean
food and steps-away proximity to the Chicago Theater.

Cyrano's Bistrot & Wine Bar   21 18 19 $32
546 N. Wells St. (bet. Grand Ave. & Ohio St.), 312-467-0546
■ Didier and Jamie Durand's "bustling, friendly" River North
bistro features a menu from the Bergerac region (hence
the name) and contiguous parts of Southwest France;
there's an "unusual and reasonably priced wine list" and
"very good" "rustic" cooking, with patrons singling out
the four-course express lunch as a "great bargain."

Cy's Crab House 🅢   15 13 15 $21
3819 N. Ashland Ave. (2 blocks north of Addison St.),
773-883-8900
◪ "Don't expect fine dining" at this Northwest Side Persian
seafooder where lowered expectations help overcome its
"not-too-good" atmosphere; still, adherents appreciate the
"good variety" of fish, "reasonable prices" and free parking.

Cy's Steak & Chop House 🅢   – – – M
4138 N. Lincoln Ave. (1 block north of Irving Park Rd.),
773-404-5800
Northwest Side counterpart to Cy's Crab House that serves
"excellent" steaks, chops and bargain-priced sandwiches in
a unintimidating atmosphere "that doesn't mind my toddler
dining with me"; P.S. try the "wonderful pies and cakes."

Czech Plaza 🅢⊄   ▽ 20 13 18 $13
7016 W. Cermak Rd. (bet. Harlem Ave. & 22nd St.),
Berwyn, 708-795-6555
■ Bargain-hunters savor this West Suburban Bohemian's
"good ethnic food at ethnic prices", including "flavorful"
duck and roast pork with bread dumplings; "you can't
cook as cheaply" as they can, but when it's time to say
'Czech, please', remember this place takes no plastic.

D'Agostino's Conversational Cafe [S] ▽ 17 | 15 | 16 | $18
1967 N. Halsted St. (Armitage Ave.), 312-951-9059
■ "Almost the definition of a neighborhood restaurant", this Italian on hotly competitive Halsted Street survives thanks to live music on weekends and a series of theme parties throughout the year; while definitely a "fun" place with a "cool atmosphere", no one seems excited about the "decent" food.

Daily Bar & Grill [S] 16 | 17 | 16 | $19
4560 N. Lincoln Ave. (Wilson Ave.), 773-561-6198
■ "You'd think Dick Tracy would be a regular" at this Northwest Side American, a "kitschy", '50s retro "hangout" with "good, basic comfort food", a few updated specials and, most noteworthy, "great martinis"; as one barfly observes: "meat loaf and vodka – what's not to love?"

D & J BISTRO [S] 24 | 19 | 23 | $32
466 S. Rand Rd. (Rte. 22), Lake Zurich, 847-438-8001
■ "Dollar for dollar the best restaurant in Chicagoland" and "getting better all the time" enthuse supporters of this Far Northwest Suburban French bistro tucked into a strip mall; expect "excellent", "authentic" fare ("great steak frites"), "dependable" daily specials, "value" wines and a "knowledgeable staff"; in addition to being a "local favorite", city folk find it's "great for a ride in the country."

Da Nicola 18 | 13 | 18 | $24
3114 N. Lincoln Ave. (bet. Ashland & Belmont Aves.), 773-935-8000
■ A recent remodeling isn't reflected in the decor scores for this "cute" North Side Italian that despite unspectacular numbers receives lots of positive comments ("overlooked gem", "quality" kitchen); the good news is its "depressed neighborhood" is now rebounding; the bad news, at least for regulars, is this place has now "caught on with yuppies."

Daniel J's [S] 24 | 13 | 21 | $29
3811 N. Ashland Ave. (Grace St.), 773-404-7772
■ Epitomizing the adage of not judging a book by its cover, this "unassuming", "off-the-beaten-path" North Side storefront may have "drab" decor and "cramped" seating, but it whips up "sophisticated", "always interesting", "kick ass" American bistro cooking at "small town prices"; P.S. don't leave without trying the "to-die-for" bread pudding.

Daniello's [S] 17 | 16 | 18 | $23
913 N. Milwaukee Ave. (Lake Cook Rd.), Wheeling, 847-459-7200
■ Marks are up for the second straight *Survey* for this "cozy" Northwest Suburban Italian that's recommended "for lunch"; while some still find it an "average" place, for "homemade food" without a lot of fuss, it'll do.

Dao S   17 | 12 | 15 | $14 |
230 E. Ohio St. (bet. Columbus Dr. & St. Clair St.), 312-337-0000
☒ Respondents are sharply divided on this Thai off Michigan Avenue; while some shower it with praise as an "excellent", "Chicago mainstay", detractors decry its "cookie-cutter" cooking; the truth may be closer to those office workers who find it "quick", "serviceable" and "inexpensive."

Daruma S   19 | 17 | 17 | $20 |
2901 Central St. (Lincolnwood Ave.), Evanston, 847-864-6633
Poplar Creek Shopping Ctr., 1823 W. Golf Rd. (Walnut St.), Schaumburg, 847-882-9700
☒ These Evanston and Schaumburg sushi shacks are "institutions" where "you always know what you're getting" – namely, "very good", "fresh" sushi at a "bargain"; on weekends, "the wait can be a killer."

Dave & Buster's S   11 | 15 | 13 | $17 |
1030 N. Clark St. (bet. Maple & Oak Sts.), 312-943-5151
1155 N. Swift Rd. (bet. Army Trail Rd. & Lake St.), Addison, 630-543-5151 ☻
■ "Chuck E. Cheese for the over-30 crowd", these city and suburban "adult playgrounds" offer video and skill games to a "frat party with tourists" crowd – "an ugly combination"; sustenance comes in the form of "basic", "unimpressive" bar fare, though there's an "extensive beer selection."

Dave's Italian Kitchen S   17 | 11 | 15 | $15 |
906 Church St. (3 blocks east of Ridge Rd.), Evanston, 847-864-6000
■ You'll either "feel like you're back in college" or really old at this North Shore Italian where bargain-hunting Northwesterners line up for "industrial-strength" portions of pasta; some sniff students love it "because they're used to dorm food", but most find it "cozy" and "a great value."

Davis Street Fishmarket S   20 | 15 | 18 | $24 |
501 Davis St. (Hinman Ave.), Evanston, 847-869-3474
■ A "boisterous" North Shore seafooder that brings in fish from all directions, making it alternately an "East Coaster's fish heaven", a "slice of New Orleans" thanks to "great gumbo", and for displaced San Franciscans, there's even cioppino – plus, of course, a fantastic assortment of oysters; some call it "overrated", but the tide's against them.

Dee's S   20 | 16 | 18 | $22 |
1144 W. Armitage Ave. (bet. Halsted St. & Racine Ave.), 773-477-1500
☒ Despite rumblings that this Lincoln Park Chinese "has declined", ratings remain essentially the same for the "well-seasoned", "wonderful food", including the "best sizzling rice soup and egg rolls"; veterans say "ask for a seat in the back", which is the prettiest; prices are higher here, befitting the neighborhood, but fans say it's "worth it."

Deleece [S] 19 | 16 | 19 | $23
4004 N. Southport Ave. (Irving Park Rd.), 773-325-1710
◪ An "out-of-the-way location" near Wrigley Field means this Eclectic-Californian is a "very pleasant surprise" offering "budget gourmet food and sincere service"; while it "occasionally misses", is "sometimes too ambitious" and "too crowded for its own good", it's a "fine place for a date" or for partaking in the "creative" Sunday brunch.

Dellwood Pickle [S] 18 | 13 | 18 | $15
1475 W. Balmoral Ave. (Clark St.), 773-271-7728
■ "Funky, hippie-ish" Far North Sider that's great for "comfort foods with a modern twist", such as New Orleans shepherd's pie and a "sublime" bananas Foster; since prices are fairly "cheap" and it's still BYO at press time (though it's working on a liquor license), "you can go regularly."

Del Rio 18 | 15 | 19 | $25
228 Green Bay Rd. (Rte. 22), Highwood, 847-432-4608
◪ While still "the essential Highwood restaurant", some find that this Italian dating back to 1916 "has lost some of its old-world charm" and that its recipes are out of step with the '90s; nonetheless, the "best linguini in the world" continues to pack them in, as does the "divine wine list" ("best on the North Shore") that a few think "overwhelms the food."

Dick's Last Resort [S] 11 | 13 | 13 | $18
River East Plaza, 435 E. Illinois St. (Lake Shore Dr.), 312-836-7870
◪ Where "sassy servers sell so-so burgers" is what alliterative surveyors say about this North Pier BBQ and seafood shack that's part of a chain that prides itself on its wisecracking waiters and down 'n' dirty atmosphere; it's "tourist and conventioneer heaven" and "an experience not for the timid" – though amid complaints like "I'd rather eat in hell", there is admiration for the "knockout" Sunday gospel brunch.

Dionne's Cafe ▽ 26 | 21 | 25 | $37
606 N. Dixie Hwy. (6th St.), Momence, 815-472-6081
■ As in *Surveys* past, the few who visit this "unpretentious" Far South Suburban country French rave about "excellent food", "artwork decor" and "friendly owners who enjoy speaking to customers" ("like being in someone's home"); N.B. dinner is served only on Friday and Saturday.

Dish [S] 19 | 14 | 17 | $22
3651 N. Southport Ave. (Addison St.), 773-549-8614
■ "Creative flavors" and "funky diner decor" ("old-time radios everywhere") are the hallmarks of this "unique" Southwestern that delights North Siders with its "excellent" blackened catfish and Bloody Marys; critics would like to see more reliability in the "inconsistent" service, as well as "an expansion – this isn't a comfy place."

Dixie Kitchen & Bait Shop S   19 | 19 | 18 | $19
Harper Ct., 5201 S. Harper St. (53rd St.), 773-363-4943
825 Church St. (Benson Ave.), Evanston, 847-733-9030
■ Hyde Parkers are happy to call this lively Southerner their own since it offers "terrific food and fun in a neighborhood that badly needs both"; look for "great catfish, corncakes and peach cobbler", plus Creole-Cajun offerings that prime patrons for the restaurant's annual Mardi Gras celebration; N.B. the Evanston outpost is new and unrated.

Don Juan S   24 | 13 | 18 | $26
6730 N. Northwest Hwy. (bet. Devon & Touhy Aves.), 773-775-6438
■ Cognoscenti call this Edison Park "gourmet" Mexican "a diamond in the rough" because Patrick Concannon's "astoundingly creative" cuisine (especially his "exciting specials") seems out of place in the "modest", no-frills dining room; however, a recently opened, more upscale room named Patricio's eases the dissonance considerably.

Don Roth's S   19 | 16 | 19 | $27
61 N. Milwaukee Ave. (Dundee Rd.), Wheeling, 847-537-5800
■ Veteran restaurateur Don Roth's city restaurants are long gone, but this 30-year-old Northwest Suburban survives on the strength of its "great prime rib" and signature, vintage touches like the "spinning salad bowl ritual"; the menu may seem limited to "beef and more beef" and the crowds are often "conventioneers galore", but in between the calls of "tired", there is still respect for "classic dining."

Don's Fishmarket S   20 | 17 | 19 | $29
9335 Skokie Blvd. (Golf Rd.), Skokie, 847-677-3424
☑ Surveyors indicate this "convenient" North Suburban seafooder across the street from the Old Orchard shopping center is "much improved over two, three years ago"; some think it's "better for lunch" because prices are lower.

Dover Straits S   21 | 18 | 20 | $28
1149 W. Golf Rd. (Gannon Rd.), Hoffman Estates, 847-884-3900
890 E. Rte. 45 (Rte. 83), Mundelein, 847-949-1550 ◑
■ Savvy surveyors take advantage of the early-bird menus ("a steal") at these nautically decorated Northwest Suburban seafood twins; if you must pay full price, be aware that the "consistently" "excellent" (if "conventional") fish and winning salads are still "worth it" and that staffers "know how to treat you well."

Duke of Perth S   16 | 16 | 16 | $15
2913 N. Clark St. (Oakdale Ave.), 773-477-1741
■ An "authentic Scottish pub serving terrific fish 'n' chips" and other "hearty" standards; this Lakeview local also elicits ayes for its "excellent beer selection" and "tremendous collection" of more than 100 single-malt whiskeys, which naturally make the atmosphere "warm" and "fun."

Earl of Loch Ness S   – | – | – | M |
2350 N. Clark St. (Fullerton Pkwy.), 773-529-9879
"Homey", "pub-type" newcomer that brings a touch of
Scotland to Lincoln Park, though with tongue firmly in
cheek (fried calamari is billed as 'Loch Ness Monster
Tentacles'); but the selection of single-malt scotches is
quite serious, as is the list of Scottish and English drafts.

Earth   21 | 17 | 18 | $24 |
738 N. Wells St. (bet. Chicago Ave. & Superior St.),
312-335-5475
■ "A pleasant surprise" awaits at this "minimalist" River
North American where "natural" is the watchword and
organic, additive-free ingredients are whipped into "fresh,
innovative" offerings; it's a "great concept and the results
are mostly "very tasty."

Ed Debevic's Short Orders Deluxe S   15 | 18 | 17 | $15 |
640 N. Wells St. (Ontario St.), 312-664-1707
660 W. Lake Cook Rd. (bet. Pfingsten & Waukegan Rds.),
Deerfield, 847-945-3242
◪ Appreciation for these city and suburban "kitsch king"
burger palaces, with their "rollback to the '50s" motif, is
proportional to your tolerance for "smart aleck" (phobes
say "rude") service; it's either "a fun trip back in time" or "a
total gimmick" that's suitable only "if you're five years old."

Edelweiss Bistro S   ▽ 19 | 19 | 19 | $22 |
7650 W. Irving Park Rd. (Cumberland Ave.), Norridge,
708-452-6040
■ Loyalists claim there's "never a letdown" at this North
Suburban German-Austrian whose "hearty fare", Alpine
trappings and live "oompah band on weekends" are
just *wunderbar*; to the exacting eye it may seem "a poor
imitation" that's "too Americanized", but aren't you saving
yourself the trip to Munich?

Edwardo's S   17 | 10 | 13 | $14 |
2662 N. Halsted St. (1 block south of Diversey Pkwy.),
773-871-3400
1212 N. Dearborn St. (Division St.), 312-337-4490
521 S. Dearborn St. (bet. Congress Pkwy. & Harrison St.),
312-939-3366
1937 W. Howard St. (Damen Ave.), 773-761-7040
1321 E. 57th St. (bet. Kenwood & Kimbark Aves.),
773-241-7960
240 Skokie Blvd. (bet. Dundee & Lake Cook Rds.), Northbrook,
847-272-5222
◪ The various outposts of this pizza chain win kudos for
their "excellent wheat crust" and the "definitive" spinach
and pesto combo, but a scattered minority says "decent
not great" and adds that the "dismal" decor means "get it
to go"; N.B. the East 57th Street location is BYO.

EJ's Place [S] — | – | – | – | E |

10027 Skokie Blvd. (Old Orchard Rd.), Skokie, 847-933-9800
North Suburban Italian-accented steakhouse where white tablecloths coexist with a rustic, North Woods atmosphere; owner E.J. Lenzi is a descendant of the Gene & Georgetti clan, which is a pretty good pedigree.

Elaine & Ina's [S] — | 19 | 16 | 17 | $18 |

448 E. Ontario St. (bet. Lake Shore Dr. & McClurg Ct.), 312-337-6700
■ While some still "miss the Lincoln Park" site, this Contemporary American, now relocated near the lake in Streeterville, still receives hosannas for its "wonderful breakfasts", brunches and "sublime sweets" from the "very good" in-house bakery.

Eli's the Place for Steaks [S] — | 21 | 18 | 20 | $35 |

215 E. Chicago Ave. (2 blocks east of Michigan Ave.), 312-642-1393
◪ This venerable Streeterville haunt may be named for its steak, but it's also notable for the "best calf's liver on the planet" and, of course, for the famous cheesecake; otherwise mixed emotions abound, and what some call "first-class beef" will seem "ordinary" to others; ditto the decor, which is either "classic" or "passé."

El Jardin ◐ [S] — | 14 | 13 | 14 | $17 |

3335 N. Clark St. (bet. Addison St. & Belmont Ave.), 773-528-6775
◪ "Don't plan on driving home" after consuming one of the "lethal margaritas" at this "hole-in-the-wall" Wrigleyville Mexican that gets "crowded after Cubs games"; while the "great garden" also appeals, the chow is "standard" at best.

El Nandu [S] — | – | – | – | M |

2731 W. Fullerton Pkwy. (California Ave.), 773-278-0900
"If you live close by and have the late-night munchies", night owls recommend this lively, "friendly" Northwest Side Argentinean for "great empanadas"; those not into deep-fried pastries can order some of the "excellent" grilled meats or take in the "funky" artwork.

El Presidente ◐ [S] — ▽ | 14 | 8 | 16 | $11 |

2558 N. Ashland Ave. (Wrightwood Ave.), 773-525-7938
■ "A dive", but "it's open 24-hours", is the long and short of this North Side Mexican with "ok" grub; a few who see more at work say the sopa is "good" and the salsa is "spicy."

El Tipico ◐ [S] — ▽ | 16 | 14 | 16 | $16 |

1836 W. Foster Ave. (Wolcott Ave.), 773-878-0839
3341 W. Dempster Ave. (McCormick Blvd.), Skokie, 847-676-4070
■ "Dark, cozy" North Side and North Suburban Mexicans whose "tons of cheap food" and "very heavy" cooking make them a guilty pleasure ("I can't believe I ate the whole thing"); those less interested in quantity find the "typical", "very beany, cheesy" menu just "decent."

Emilio's La Perla S　　22 | 19 | 20 | $28
2135 S. Wolf Rd. (Cermak Rd.), Hillside, 708-449-1070
◪ With its spacious dining rooms and a "nice outdoor garden cafe", this Suburban West spot qualifies as Emilio Gervilla's "prettiest" effort; it's generally agreed to be an "interesting experience", particularly now that the menu is focused exclusively on tapas.

Emilio's Tapas Bar & Restaurant S　22 | 19 | 20 | $26
444 W. Fullerton Ave. (Clark St.), 773-327-5100
4100 W. Roosevelt Rd. (Mannheim Rd.), Hillside, 708-547-7177
◼ These Lakeview and West Suburban flagships of Emilio Gervilla's empire inspire fierce loyalty among fans who laud the "superb", "always interesting menu choices" and swear that "no other tapas compare"; scattered complaints that "to get enough, it gets pretty expensive" are countered with "it's cheaper than a plane ticket to Spain."

Emperor's Choice ◖ S　　23 | 14 | 19 | $22
2238 S. Wentworth Ave. (Cermak Rd.), 312-225-8800
◼ "Chicago's best Chinese by a long shot" is the verdict on this tiny, "upscale" Chinatown facility whose "great seafood entrees" include "yummy Peking lobster" and "huge oysters"; though the "minimalist", "dark" decor draws low marks, the kitchen has "great hours for hungry night people" who recommend the 'acquired taste' menu.

ENTRE NOUS　　25 | 26 | 25 | $51
Fairmont Hotel, 200 N. Columbus Dr. (Wacker Dr.), 312-565-7997
◼ For "lovely hotel dining", it's hard to outdo this "elegant" Regional American room east of Michigan Avenue, whose lavish appointments and soft piano music make it "a place for a special dinner"; although "it looks like it needs people", the atmosphere is "so romantic, you can recharge your love here" (or slip over to the gift shop for new batteries).

Erie Cafe S　　20 | 18 | 20 | $38
536 W. Erie St. (Kingsbury St.), 312-266-2300
◪ This "undiscovered" Italian steakhouse in River North is a "masculine", "older crowd" type of place where servings are so sizable that respondents wonder "who do they think can eat this much food?"; admirers tout the "excellent" beef and "great" grilled calamari, but nonenthusiasts dismiss it as a "wanna-be."

ERWIN, AN AMERICAN CAFE S　23 | 20 | 21 | $32
2925 N. Halsted St. (Oakdale Ave.), 773-528-7200
◼ Erwin Drechsler's "creative American dishes" are a hit with Lakeview locals and pre-theater passersby seeking "superb regional cuisine" and a "hospitable staff"; if the "innovative" menu is "limited, it's limited to only great items" and the overall consensus is that this "warm, comfy room with warm, comfy food" "deserves a visit."

Ethiopian Village 🅂   ▽ 17 | 10 | 13 | $16 |
3462 N. Clark St. (bet. Cornelia Ave. & Newport St.), 773-929-8300
▣ Picky eaters "should not be afraid" of this Wrigleyville
Ethiopian prized for its "interesting" selections, "good"
vegetarian buffet, low prices and live music on weekends.

EVEREST   27 | 27 | 27 | $73 |
*One Financial Plaza, 440 S. LaSalle St., 40th fl. (Congress Pkwy.),
312-663-8920*
■ A Top 10 scorer in food and service and No. 1 in decor, this
Downtown Contemporary French showcases "the most
beautiful view in Chicago" from its 40th-floor aerie; chef
Jean Joho's "attention to subtle detail shines through" a
"wonderfully creative" menu that's tempered with a "touch
of Alsace"; factor in "impeccable service", "superb wines"
and it's "clearly at the top of the mountain"; the only question
that remains: "how do you get a window table?"

Fadó Irish Pub ◑🅂   ▽ 16 | 23 | 17 | $21 |
100 W. Grand Ave. (Clark St.), 312-836-0066
▣ This "authentic", "well-done pub", which is part of a
chain, offers River North patrons a piece of Ireland – several
pieces, in fact, since the interior was built on the Emerald
Isle and shipped here for assembly; the unenchanted call
it "Planet Dublin" and say the food "leaves something to
be desired", proving that atmosphere isn't everything.

Famous Dave's 🅂   – | – | – | M |
*1126 E. Ogden Ave. (bet. Naperville Rd. & Washington St.),
Naperville, 630-428-3500*
Suburban West link of a Minneapolis-based chain that
incorporates several regional barbecue styles, from Texas
brisket to Carolina pulled pork, but it's the St. Louis–cut ribs
that are the specialty; the kitschy decor includes references
to Chicago's West Side and there's plenty of blues music.

Father and Son Pizza ◑🅂   14 | 12 | 14 | $14 |
2475 N. Milwaukee Ave. (Sacramento Blvd.), 773-252-2620
Marcello's, a Father and Son Restaurant 🅂
645 W. North Ave. (bet. Halsted & Larrabee Sts.), 312-654-2560
▣ Though these North Side Italian "old standbys" are best
known for "good thin-crust pizza", they're getting more
ambitious, what with a bakery being added onto the North
Avenue location; while some characterize the food as just
"acceptable", they remain "a good place for kids" or takeout.

Feast 🅂   19 | 16 | 17 | $26 |
1835 W. North Ave. (bet. Ashland & Damen Aves.), 773-235-6361
■ Much of the praise for this Wicker Park Eclectic is
inspired by the "great summer courtyard", "one of the
best in the city", where a young, casually-dressed crowd
passes sultry evenings; foodwise, surveyors applaud the
"creative" menu "from around the world", though as far
as portions go, some find this feast "more like a nibble."

Fernando's 🅂   ▽ 18 | 12 | 18 | $18
3450 N. Lincoln Ave. (1½ blocks south of Addison St.),
773-477-6930

■ "Don't be put off by the decor or lack thereof" at this "basic" North Side Mexican that's a "better-than-average" hangout offering "friendly, good service", "wonderful *chilaquiles*" and "the best chips and salsa in the city"; occasional gripes ("how can so many dishes look and taste the same?") suggest that this is a haven for locals rather than a destination.

Fifth Avenue Bistro   ▽ 21 | 19 | 19 | $32
200 E. Fifth Ave. (Ogden Ave.), Naperville, 630-961-8203
■ Occupying the loft space above the formal Montparnasse, this "lively" West Suburban French features a "delicious" bistro menu ("as good as downstairs"); locals dub it "a great value", possibly offering "the best lunch in Naperville."

56 West ◐   ▽ 19 | 24 | 16 | $31
56 W. Illinois St. (Dearborn Ave.), 312-527-5600
■ Dazzling decor in a below-street-level Eclectic proves what a designer can accomplish even without windows at Chicago's "best-looking basement"; that this "trendy boîte", a River North yearling, pulls in a "great-looking", yup-oriented clientele is another plus, unless you have an aversion to cigars; most find the food "good but pricey", and there's a late-night "light" menu to fortify the party crowd.

Filippo's 🅂   ▽ 18 | 14 | 17 | $24
2211 N. Clybourn Ave. (Webster Ave.), 773-528-2211
☑ An "always crowded" Clybourn Corridor Italian known for "great risotto" and a kitchen that's "glad to add or delete ingredients" to your liking; former fans say it's "not as good as it once was" and the "tables are too close together."

Fireplace Inn ◐🅂   17 | 15 | 17 | $22
1448 N. Wells St. (1½ blocks south of North Ave.),
312-664-5264
☑ "The aroma from the street brings you in" to this "cozy" Old Town barbecue shack with a "dark", throwback ski lodge atmosphere; while the "you-got-to-have" ribs are "some of the best around", surveyors are silent on the rest of the menu; P.S. make sure to "sit outside in summer."

Fireside Beverly 🅂   ▽ 15 | 15 | 14 | $22
10730 S. Western Ave. (107th St.), 773-779-3606
☑ "Uneven but promising" is a common take on this South Side American whose "well-rounded" menu displays its Southern influence, from Cajun pastas to pecan-coated trout; locals appreciate its presence in an area not teeming with dining options and find the outdoor patio "pleasant", but while it "tries hard", it apparently also "needs work."

Flatlander's 🅂   – | – | – | M |
200 Village Green (bet. Milwaukee Ave. & Rte. 45),
Lincolnshire, 847-821-1234
The name refers to one of the more polite appellations
people have for Illinoisans, and this Northwest Suburban
microbrewery abounds with Prairie State spirit, from the
Midwestern menu to the sprawling Frank Lloyd Wright
inspired setting that's frequently filled to capacity.

Flat Top Grill 🅂   17 | 13 | 15 | $16 |
319 W. North Ave. (Orleans St.), 312-787-7676
1000 W. Washington Ave. (Carpenter St.), 312-829-4800
707 Church St. (bet. Orrington & Sherman Aves.),
Evanston, 847-570-0100
■ It's "interactive dining" at these city and suburban
Americans where customers choose from a buffet of raw
ingredients and sauces that are then cooked by stir-fry
chefs; enthusiasts say it's "great for us yuppie, health food–
eating, cheap North Siders", and popular for carnivores'
"all-you-can-eat" binges.

Fluky's 🅂⇱   16 | 11 | 13 | $7 |
6821 N. Western Ave. (Pratt Ave.), 773-274-3652
■ Chicagoans are as passionate about frankfurters as they
are about pizza and this Far North Sider, "a favorite for 30
years", still gets hosannas for "hot dogs at their finest"
(that's Chicago-style, with salad on top) and "the best Polish
sausage" in town; all told, it's this *Survey's* No. 1 Bang for
the Buck, even if some argue that the quality "has fallen."

Fly Me to the Moon   – | – | – | M |
3400 N. Clark St. (Roscoe Ave.), 773-528-4033
Wrigleyville newcomer offering "good" Italian fare in an
environment that includes live music and a cigar lounge;
although surveyors concede it's "interesting", some think
it hasn't quite reached the stratosphere.

Fog City Diner 🅂   – | – | – | M |
Hampton Inn & Suites, 33 W. Illinois St. (Dearborn St.),
312-828-0404
This River North clone of the San Francisco original offers a
diverse menu of American comfort food and West Coast
contemporary creations; it's all dished up in a re-created
diner with mahogany booths and black-and-chrome tables.

FOND DE LA TOUR   25 | 24 | 24 | $42 |
40 N. Tower Rd. (bet. Butterfield & Meyers Rds.), Oak Brook,
630-620-1500
■ West Suburbanites in the mood to play dress-up head to
this jacket-required Classic French, an "elegant, special"
place where the food "is rich and fattening but oh, so good";
though some observe that the "menu is in a time warp" and
the "decor is lagging behind 20 years", where else can
you count on "an experience" like this?

Fondue Stube S
17 ｜ 14 ｜ 17 ｜ $27

*2717 W. Peterson Ave. (1½ blocks east of California Ave.),
773-784-2200*

☑ Despite sneers that it's nothing more than "Geja's' homely
sister" and a "'70s throwback", this Northwest Side fondue
hangout remains "fun for a group" or for couples looking
for a "romantic, quiet" do-it-yourself dinner.

foodlife S
16 ｜ 15 ｜ 13 ｜ $14

*Water Tower Pl., 835 N. Michigan Ave., mezzanine level
(bet. Chestnut & Pearson Sts.), 312-335-3663*

■ This "cafeteria for the trendy" is an upscale, "creative"
food court where individual stations offer "anything your
little heart desires", with an emphasis on veggie and organic
selections; even if it's "more expensive than you think", the
"amazingly decent food" makes this "a welcome option
for shoppers and tourists" who, after all, are the people
Water Tower Place was built for.

Founders Hill Brewing Co. S
16 ｜ 19 ｜ 16 ｜ $19

5200 Main St. (Grove St.), Downers Grove, 630-963-2739

☑ A West Suburban microbrewery in a restored vintage
building that gets a few plaudits for its "above-average"
crafted brews and a bar food menu that's "better than
most"; a minority finds the pub grub "typical", but still
advises going "for the beer and music" (live bands are
on hand Thursday–Saturday).

Four Farthings S
16 ｜ 16 ｜ 16 ｜ $20

2060 N. Cleveland Ave. (Lincoln Ave.), 773-935-2060

■ Lincoln Park tavern catering to a young, neighborhood
crowd but, as some surveyors cheerfully note, "it's too
expensive for the frat boys"; the menu of "stock pub food
plus some extras" has its fans, especially those who manage
to snag a table on the "great outside patio."

Francesca's North S
23 ｜ 17 ｜ 18 ｜ $26

1145 Church St. (Shermer Rd.), Northbrook, 847-559-0260

Francesca's on Taylor S
23 ｜ 19 ｜ 20 ｜ $27

1400 W. Taylor St. (Loomis Ave.), 312-829-2828

Francesca's by the River
– ｜ – ｜ – ｜ M

200 S. Second St. (Illinois St.), St. Charles, 630-587-8221

☑ "Go very early or late to avoid crowds" at these city and
suburban spinoffs of Mia Francesca, which stick with the
winning formula of "exquisite" Italian fare dished up at
"reasonable prices"; the North Suburban incarnation, "a
mecca for suburban yuppies", takes hits for having "close
quarters" and being "too noisy", while the Taylor Street
location wins hearts with its "movie set atmosphere" and –
"hooray!" – reservations-yes policy; N.B. Francesca's by
the River is new and unrated.

Francesco's Hole in the Wall 🅂⊘ 23 14 20 $24
254 Skokie Blvd. (bet. Dundee & Lake Cook Rds.),
Northbrook, 847-272-0155
■ "Substantial menu choices" and "exceptional Italian
food" await patient North Suburban diners who make it to
the front of the line at this "small", "mobbed" hangout;
dishes like "real chicken Vesuvio", "exceptional" pastas
and "too large" salads are generally "worth the wait."

Franconello's 🅂 ▽ 23 17 17 $23
10222 S. Western Ave. (103rd St.), 773-881-4100
◩ "Promising" homestyle Italian offering "huge portions"
of "very good food" in an environment that "reminds me
of places grandparents go"; but while fans feel it's a
"wonderful addition to the South Side", the unconvinced
think it needs work, citing an "inconsistent" experience
that "doesn't quite match up to expectations."

Fresh Starts Restaurant & Bakery ▽ 22 16 19 $26
1040 Sterling Ave. (north of Flossmoor Rd.), Flossmoor,
708-957-7900
■ Staunch supporters of this New American featuring
"outstanding fish, pasta" and "innovative" light dishes
say it's "consistently the best restaurant on the South
Side"; comments about a "very fresh alternative" refer to
the "ambitious menu", not the "good service."

Frida's 🅂 17 17 16 $21
2143 N. Damen Ave. (Webster Ave.), 312-337-4327
◩ Once again it's a split decision for this "interesting"
Bucktown Mexican, which takes its name from artist
Frida Kahlo and consequently is decorated with colorful
artwork that "provides excellent ambiance"; though the
menu is "very inventive" and "they make a good mole",
some think the kitchen "tries too hard" and that some
items "just don't work."

Fritzl's 🅂 – – – M
Rte. 30 (Old Rand Rd.), Lake Zurich, 847-540-8844
"The best German restaurant in the area", this Suburban
West spot offers a "great variety" of Teutonic and American
dishes, "quality service" and a cozy, burgundy-and-green
dining room that's romantic enough to be "our special place."

Froggy's French Cafe 23 17 22 $33
306 Green Bay Rd. (Highwood Ave.), Highwood, 847-433-7080
■ "Perhaps the best buy for sophisticated French" fare is
the take on this unassuming North Shore bistro, which
receives lots of kudos for "always polite" service and for
providing "a gourmet meal at a great value"; the only
brickbats are aimed at the less-than-thrilling decor, but
even detractors concede it's gotten "a little brighter."

FRONTERA GRILL
26 | 21 | 22 | $29

445 N. Clark St. (bet. Hubbard & Illinois Sts.), 312-661-1434

■ "There aren't enough superlatives" to describe Rick Bayless' seminal, nationally renowned River North establishment, but that doesn't stop surveyors from trying; the praise rolls in for "the best Mexican restaurant in the US (take that, LA)" whose "imaginative", "scrumptious" food is "damn near perfect"; Bayless may indeed be "a sorceror", but even he can't conjure up enough seating to meet the demand – "you could qualify for Social Security waiting for a table."

Furama S
▽ 18 | 9 | 13 | $16

2828 S. Wentworth Ave. (31st St.), 312-225-6888
4936 N. Broadway (Argyle St.), 773-271-1161

■ These Cantonese-Mandarin "dives" in Chinatown and Uptown aren't much to look at, but there is consistent praise for their "excellent" dim sum; waits can be lengthy, but for diners who can adjust to the "real Hong Kong–like ambiance", it's "worth it."

GABRIEL'S
25 | 21 | 24 | $47

310 Green Bay Rd. (Highwood Ave.), Highwood, 847-433-0031

■ "As good as it gets" on the North Shore, this French-Italian hybrid marries a "first-class atmosphere" with "creative" food by "meticulous" chef-owner Gabriel Viti that "meets all expectations"; aesthetes add that the "open kitchen concept works well here."

Gale Street Inn S
19 | 16 | 18 | $21

4914 N. Milwaukee Ave. (Lawrence Ave.), 773-725-1300
906 Diamond Lake Rd. (bet. Rtes. 45 & 60/83), Mundelein, 847-566-1090

■ Two Americans that share a name and similar menus but have different owners; nonetheless, they get equal treatment from assessors who dub them "old standbys" and give the edge to the Northwest 'burb locale because of its "pretty Diamond Lake setting"; both are considered "laid-back, casual" hangouts featuring "melt-in-your-mouth" barbecued ribs and a particularly "nice lunch menu."

Gary Barnett's S
▽ 14 | 15 | 14 | $16

Orrington Hotel, 1710 N. Orrington Ave. (bet. Church & Davis Sts.), Evanston, 847-473-4279

■ After leading his team to consecutive bowl bids, NU football coach Gary Barnett received the ultimate sporting accolade – his own memorabilia-laden restaurant; while alums find "some charm" in the place and praise the "decent food", most agree that the American fare is "generally disappointing" and that the "coach should stick to football."

Gaylord India [S] 20 14 17 $22

678 N. Clark St. (Huron St.), 312-664-1700

■ An "upscale" River North veteran that's a "favorite" among area workers who enjoy "the best Indian buffet in town" at lunch and à la carte dinner creations that are "richer, subtler and more varied" than the competition.

Geja's Cafe [S] 21 22 19 $34

340 W. Armitage Ave. (bet. Clark St. & Lincoln Ave.), 773-281-9101

■ Lincoln Park fondue specialist that gets lots of votes for "most romantic restaurant in Chicago", thanks to dark interiors, live flamenco guitar music and a sophisticated wine list; while the gestalt of communal cooking makes fondue "a foreplay to foreplay", some wisecrack that "nothing says I love you like skewered meat in boiling oil"; regulars advise arriving late "just for the chocolate fondue dessert", but note that there are no reservations Friday–Saturday after 6 PM.

Gene & Georgetti ◐ 23 14 19 $38

500 N. Franklin St. (Illinois St.), 312-527-3718

◪ This River North "Sinatra of restaurants" where Ol' Blue Eyes used to dine is the "quintessential Chicago steakhouse", which regulars think serves the "best" beef in town, along with "good garbage salad and cottage fries"; lots of nonregulars grouse "you're in trouble if the maitre d' doesn't know you" at this "old man's club", but a recent remodeling that expanded seating by 100 and added a fireplace should make newcomers feel (at least physically) more comfortable.

Genesee Depot [S] 21 15 21 $22

3736 N. Broadway (bet. Grace & Waveland Sts.), 773-528-6990

■ A neighborhood fixture for 25 years, this North Side German-accented American BYO is a "reliable" place for "quality home cooking" and "good service"; the "poor parking" situation keeps the crowd mostly local, though "your out-of-town auntie would love it."

Giannotti Steak House [S] 22 17 19 $30

8422 W. Lawrence Ave. (Cumberland Ave.), Norridge, 708-453-1616

17 W. 400 22nd St. (Midwest Hwy.), Oak Brook Terrace, 630-833-2700

■ Veteran airport-area Italian that recently added a West Suburban outpost; both branches serve up "big portions" of "fabulous" pastas, seafood and steaks, including the "best lobster diavolo" and the "greatest chicken Vesuvio"; while a few say they're "not crazy about the decor" ("tacky"), most applaud the "old-time feel and service."

GIBSONS STEAKHOUSE ◐ S   24 | 19 | 21 | $44

1028 N. Rush St. (bet. Bellevue Pl. & Oak St.), 312-266-8999
■ "Big steaks, tall martinis, long cigars and short skirts"
make up the "good show" at this "loud", "glamorous" Rush
Street steakhouse that draws a "colorful" mix of "who's
who in Chicago" and conventioneers; those taking a break
from the "top-notch people-watching" add that the food's
"wonderful", especially dessert, which consists of the
"largest pieces of cake in the city."

Gilardi's S   20 | 20 | 20 | $29

23397 N. Rte. 45 (Rte. 21), Vernon Hills, 847-634-1811
■ A "warm, family-run place", this North Suburban Italian
features "excellently flavored pastas" served in an
"intimate" space where one "always feels at home"; a
few label it "very suburban", but the general feeling is
"nice and friendly."

Gilles   – | – | – | E

(nka Cuisine Française)
1791 St. Johns Ave. (bet. Central & Laurel Aves.),
Highland Park, 847-926-0855
This Highland Park Mediterranean has made fast friends
with the North Shore foodie crowd, though the loss of chef
Gilles Epie could take its toll and the high-priced wine list
may take some warming up to.

Gino's Steak House S   ▽ 21 | 17 | 18 | $33

16299 S. Wallace Ave. (3 blocks east of Halsted St.),
Harvey, 708-331-4393
☑ "Beef and lots of it" is the attraction at this South
Suburban steakhouse, an "old-time place" that features
such bygone touches as a complimentary relish tray;
supporters note "for Harvey, it's a neat place", while the
nostalgic say "used to be better."

Giordano's S   17 | 11 | 13 | $14

5159 S. Pulaski Rd. (51st St.), 773-582-7676 ◐
5927 W. Irving Park Rd. (Austin Ave.), 773-736-5553 ◗
310 W. Randolph St. (Franklin St.), 312-201-1441
747 N. Rush St. (Chicago Ave.), 312-951-0747
5311 S. Blackstone Ave. (Lake Park Ave.), 773-947-0200 ◗
1840 N. Clark St. (bet. Lincoln Ave. & Wells St.), 312-944-6100 ◐
500 Davis St. (Hinman Ave.), Evanston, 847-475-5000
Crest Creek Sq., 796 Royal St. (Ogden Ave.), Naperville,
630-717-6446
17 W. 048 W. 22nd St. (bet. Meyers & Midwest Sts.), Oak
Brook Terrace, 630-620-7979 ◐
☑ Depending on who's talking and which location you visit,
this stuffed-pie chain is either a strong pizza contender
("second best in town") or just "very average"; respondents
are of one opinion, however, on the decor – "needs a
lift" – and nearly unanimous on their favorite pie: the
"excellent spinach deep dish."

Gladys Luncheonette 🅂🚭   ▽ | 23 | 6 | 14 | $12 |
4527 S. Indiana Ave. (Michigan Ave.), 773-548-4566
■ Its high food score and dismal decor rating suggest that this South Side "neighborhood institution" still kicks out "great Soul Food" and the "best peach cobbler", but in generally bleak surroundings; a secured parking lot eases qualms about the dicey neighborhood.

Gold Coast Dogs 🚭 | 17 | 8 | 13 | $7 |
*159 N. Wabash Ave. (bet. Lake & Randolph Sts.),
312-917-1677* 🅂
2 N. Riverside Dr. (bet. Canal St. & Madison Ave.), 312-879-0447
Union Station, 225 S. Canal St. (Jackson Blvd.), 312-258-8585 🅂
418 N. State St. (Hubbard St.), 312-527-1222 🅂
■ These popular, fast-food lunch counters provide "no-frills, cheap thrills" sustenance, including "classic" Chicago-style dogs, char dogs (not the same thing), "mmm good" burgers and for the health-conscious, veggie burgers and grilled fish sandwiches; since "service is not for the fainthearted", this is "no place to take a date", but you still might "rub elbows with celebrities and cab drivers."

Golden Ox 🅂 | 18 | 18 | 18 | $26 |
1578 N. Clybourn Ave. (North Ave.), 312-664-0780
■ You'll think you're in the Black Forest at this long-running North Side "schnitzelfest", though new owners have added non-Germanic dishes like osso buco to an otherwise traditional menu that includes sauerbraten that "equals one month's protein"; portions are big enough that "you won't have to eat for a week" and "heavy" enough that you may not want to.

Goose Island Brewing Co. 🅂 | 14 | 16 | 15 | $16 |
1800 N. Clybourn Ave. (Sheffield Ave.), 312-915-0071
☑ "The beer needs no improvement" at this Clybourn Corridor brewpub, the city's oldest, though many find the food "less than memorable", with the exception of the "can't stop eating them" homemade potato chips, a longtime fave; stalwarts counter that the "young, fun atmosphere" more than makes up for any culinary lapses.

GORDON 🅂 | 25 | 25 | 24 | $48 |
500 N. Clark St. (Illinois St.), 312-467-9780
■ Gordon Sinclair's "cutting edge" River North New American continues to wow 'em after 23 years with an "elegant, contemporary atmosphere" where an "oh so cool" crowd dons (required) jackets for dinner and the entrees are available in full and half-portions to encourage multi-course nibbling; it "gets better with age no matter who the chef is" (and there've been many over the years) and Gordon himself "still has the magic touch."

Granada S
▽ 25 | 21 | 21 | $28

(fka Emilio's Granada)
14 S. Third St. (Rte. 38), Geneva, 630-262-1000
■ Emilio Gervilla is no longer affiliated with this "charming" West Suburban Spaniard, but tapas fans feel that "grazing through the menu is still fun" and a visit continues to be a "nice alternative", especially if you're in the mood for fiery flamenco dancing.

Grapes S
20 | 17 | 19 | $32

733 N. Wells St. (bet. Chicago Ave. & Superior St.), 312-943-4500
☑ This River North storefront represents a foray into the Mediterranean arena by chef Steven Chiappetti (Mango, Rhapsody); while many assessors label it "another winner" and "hope the prices and portions last", most everyone agrees that the "very tight seating" means "please space out the tables."

Graziano's Brick Oven Pizza S
18 | 17 | 19 | $19

5960 W. Touhy Ave. (bet. Caldwell & Lehigh Rds.), Niles, 847-647-4096
■ A "very kid-friendly" atmosphere draws families to this North Suburban Italian whose menu includes, of all things, a peanut butter and jelly pizza; it's "booming on the weekends" (and "a little too noisy") as fans dig into "excellent" calamari and "great, bottomless" salads.

Grecian Taverna ◗S
20 | 17 | 20 | $19

4535 N. Lincoln Ave. (bet. Sunnyside & Wilson Aves.), 773-728-1600
☑ Visiting this Lincoln Square "cozy neighborhood retreat" is like a "cheap trip to Greece" for "authentic" fare, including "good fish and lamb dishes"; though some scoff at "inconsistency", others find that the "not trendy" atmosphere translates into "no waiting."

Greek Islands S
19 | 17 | 18 | $22

200 S. Halsted St. (Adams St.), 312-782-9855
300 E. 22nd St. (Highland Ave.), Lombard, 630-932-4545
☑ These "fun" Greektown and West Suburban spots have "lots of hustle and bustle" and a "kitschy" ambiance; well-wishers say a visit is a "safe bet" and "love their lamb anything", but critics think they're "rushed", "noisy barns."

Green Dolphin Street S
21 | 20 | 18 | $38

2200 N. Ashland Ave. (Webster Ave.), 773-395-0066
■ "Sleek and showy", this DePaul-area complex houses a "huge" French-American dining room, an "up-and-coming" jazz club (with no cover charge for diners), a cigar-friendly bar and a Bentley-filled parking lot; the scene might not have much to do with the "above-average" but "overpriced" food, yet everyone agrees it's "great for people-watching."

Green Door Tavern   16 | 17 | 16 | $17
678 N. Orleans St. (Huron St.), 312-664-5496
■ The 1921 building housing this River North "landmark" has "great charm" if you like "sloping floors" and out-of-plumb doorways; the pub grub inspires some ("hamburger heaven") and confounds others ("don't expect great things"), but this "old standby" "feels like home" to most.

Gusto Italiano S   17 | 13 | 17 | $22
Carillon Shopping Ctr., 1470 Waukegan Rd. (Lake Ave.), Glenview, 847-729-5444
☑ In a convenient shopping center location, this "pleasant" North Suburban Italian is assured a certain amount of "drop-in" clientele for its "exceptional" eggplant rotolo and "wonderful garlic rolls"; while some label it only "fair to middling", its 14-year history speaks for itself.

Hacienda Tecalitlan S   18 | 20 | 17 | $23
820 N. Ashland Ave. (Chicago Ave.), 312-243-1166
☑ Fans love the "beautiful" interior of this Near West Side Mexican; while the strolling "serenade" on weekends helps explain why it's "worth a trip for the atmosphere", reviewers are less enamored with the "average" food, even though it's a "solid, pig-out" spot.

Hackney's S   16 | 13 | 16 | $16
1241 Harms St. (Lake St.), Glenview, 847-724-5577
1514 Lake Ave. (Waukegan Rd.), Glenview, 847-724-7171
880 N. Old Rand Rd. (Rte. 12), Lake Zurich, 847-438-2103
La Grange Rd. (123rd St.), Palos Park, 708-448-8300
241 S. Milwaukee Ave. (bet. Dundee & Hintz Rds.), Wheeling, 847-537-2100
■ These "suburban quintets" with a "must-try" French fried onion loaf, "great", "reliable" burgers and "patio dining in summer" (except La Grange) are "like an old friend" to many; others say "loved it in high school", but the "greasy reminiscence" now seems less appealing; of course, that doesn't prevent reviewers from introducing a new generation – it's "fun to take children" there.

Half Shell ●S⋻   18 | 10 | 15 | $21
676 W. Diversey Pkwy. (Orchard St.), 773-549-1773
■ A basement Lakeview seafooder that's "like eating in a submarine"; however, locals still squeeze in for "affordable" oysters and "the best" crab legs in a climate "conducive to flying crab shells and enthusiastic finger licking."

Happi Sushi S   18 | 15 | 17 | $24
561 Roger Williams Ave. (Green Bay Rd.), Highland Park, 847-432-1516
■ "Low-key" Highland Park sushi bar that can be counted on for "reliable, basic Japanese food" at "good prices"; while few gush about the variety ("standard"), the majority finds the quality "very good."

Hard Rock Cafe S   12 | 20 | 13 | $18
63 W. Ontario St. (bet. Clark & Dearborn Sts.), 312-943-2252
◪ The Chicago outpost of this worldwide rock 'n' roll chain caters to out-of-towners and "teeny boppers" who seem impervious to the "extreme noise level", but quite focused on the "cool guitar" memorabilia and "great T-shirt" souvenirs; sure, "it's all about atmosphere" and "fun" decor, but "good hamburgers" help; those rolling their eyes mutter "juvenile", "hokey" "rip-off."

Harry Caray's S   20 | 19 | 19 | $28
33 W. Kinzie St. (Dearborn St.), 312-828-0966
■ Cubs announcer Harry Caray passed away in early '98, but his spirit lives on at this Italian-American in River North where, in his honor, staffers sing 'Take Me Out to the Ball Game' every day at 7:30 PM; while "overpriced" and a bit "touristy", it's reliable for "celebrity visits", a "fun bar" (especially during "important games"), "outstanding chicken Vesuvio" and "terrific steaks."

Harvest on Huron ◐S   24 | 21 | 20 | $40
217 W. Huron St. (bet. Franklin & Wells Sts.), 312-587-9600
◪ Chef Alan Sternweiler's "delicious", "interesting" Contemporary American fare and an interior that's "pure elegance" are why many dub this River North spot a "best newcomer", "along with Crofton on Wells"; however, the Harvest also yields more than a few complaints of "inattentive" service and "unacceptably loud" noise.

Hashalom ⏢   ▽ 19 | 8 | 16 | $14
2905 W. Devon Ave. (Francesco Ave.), 773-465-5675
■ "A feast from the Middle East" awaits diners at this "super casual" Far North Sider where "delicious Cornish hen", "wonderful soup" and "excellent Friday night couscous" compensate for the "dive" atmosphere; it's a "great bargain" that's "good for its purpose."

Hatsuhana   20 | 15 | 17 | $32
160 E. Ontario St. (bet. Michigan Ave. & St. Clair St.), 312-280-8808
◪ Some still insist that this Japanese just off the Mag Mile "continues to offer high-quality", "tasty" sushi delivered by an "eager" staff; however, critics counter that it "used to be the best" in Chicago, but is now "living on its reputation" and has become an "overpriced tourist trap."

Havana Café Cubano S   19 | 22 | 18 | $29
230 W. Kinzie St. (Franklin St.), 312-595-0101
■ An "intimate", "faux tropical room" complete with plantation shutters and "slow turning" ceiling fans is just part of the "wonderful" atmosphere at this "lively", "noisy" River North Cuban-Caribbean "hot spot"; while "the food needs a little more attention", all is forgiven when you enter the downstairs cigar bar and "feel like Castro."

Heartland Cafe S   15   13   14 $14
7000 N. Glenwood Ave. (Lunt Ave.), 773-465-8005
■ It's the "'60s, here we come" at this Rogers Park "hangout" that's an "aging hippie's delight", with poetry readings, folk bands and "mostly vegetarian" food, though there is a "good buffalo burger" for carnivores; bashers would like to tune out the "chain-smoking staff" and think the "place could use a good scrubbing."

Heaven on Seven ⊅   22   15   18 $18
Garland Bldg., 111 N. Wabash Ave., 7th fl. (Washington St.),
312-263-6443

Heaven on Seven on Rush S   20   18   17 $21
600 N. Michigan Ave., 2nd fl. (bet. Ohio & Rush Sts.),
312-280-7774
■ Though they share a name (and chef-owner Jimmy Bannos) these Cajun-Creole establishments are vastly different: the "cramped" Loop location ("go early" or "consider carryout") is a 7th-floor luncheonette that serves dinner only on the first and third Fridays of the month; the Michigan Avenue spot is a bigger, "slicker" operation serving lunch and dinner daily; while the nostalgic say "stick with the original" Loop locale, both feature "fab crab cakes" and "awesome gumbo."

Hickory Pit, The S   15   9   15 $21
(fka Glass Dome Hickory Pit)
2801 S. Halsted St. (bet. Archer Ave. & 31st St.), 312-842-7600
☑ The name's been shortened, but this seasoned (since 1933) South Side ribbery remains "a must on the way to Comiskey Park" and "worth the drive for serious rib lovers", even without ball game tickets; wise guys commenting on the decor declare "they used up the world's supply of Formica to decorate the place."

Hi Howe S   14   7   11 $16
6015 N. Cicero Ave. (Peterson Ave.), 773-725-2257
☑ While some surveyors continue to tout the "best egg rolls" and "huge portions" at this Northwest Side Cantonese, more warn that this "once great" local is now "a relic of the past"; since there's "absolutely no atmosphere" or liquor license, consider takeout.

Hi Ricky S   16   13   15 $15
941 W. Randolph St. (2 blocks west of Halsted St.), 312-491-9100
1852 W. North Ave. (Wolcott Ave.), 773-276-8300
3730 N. Southport Ave. (Irving Park Rd.), 773-388-0000
☑ With locations in Bucktown, the Near West Side and the Wrigley Field–area, these "trendy", "twentysomething" noodle shops are making friends all over the city thanks to "fresh, tasty", "quick" Pan-Asian fare, like "interesting" satays and curry dishes that are a "bargain"; but not all agree: "Penny's Noodle Shop is better" – "bye, Ricky."

Hong Min ◗⬛   22 | 5 | 13 | $16
221 W. Cermak Rd. (Wentworth Ave.), 312-842-5026
■ Someone had to get the lowest decor rating in the
Survey, and this "dumpy" and "chaotic" Chinatown BYO
storefront is the lucky winner; while "surly service" doesn't
help matters, its stellar food score supports claims that it
has "the best dim sum in Chicago", and that's just a small
part of the "incredibly extensive, exotic" menu.

Hopcats Brewing Co. ◗⬛   – | – | – | M
2354 N. Clybourn Ave. (Fullerton Ave.), 773-868-4461
Clybourn Corridor microbrewery featuring "food with a
latitude", meaning the menu embraces just about anything
found between the Tropics of Cancer and Capricorn (and,
truth be told, more than a few regions further north); there
are at least a half-dozen fresh beers daily, along with "guest
brews" from other makers.

House of Blues ⬛   16 | 22 | 16 | $22
329 N. Dearborn St. (Kinzie St.), 312-527-2583
■ The New Orleans–style food served at this nightclub
chain's River North link is "unexpectedly good" say
surveyors who came for the music and the "dark",
"dramatic" decor with a "style of its own", but left thinking
"the mashed potatoes are amazing"; P.S. the "Sunday
gospel brunch is a hoot."

Houston's ⬛   19 | 16 | 17 | $21
Lenox Hotel, 612 N. Rush St. (Ohio St.), 312-649-1121
■ "Dark", "clubby" booths create a "warm, comfortable"
atmosphere at this Traditional American just off Michigan
Avenue that's "always crowded" with business lunchers
and after-fivers; while a few snobs sniff "mass-produced
and middlebrow", the majority "gotta have the spinach-
artichoke dip" and "love the grilled chicken salad"; a "staff
that excels in hospitality" further underlines why it's "one
of the better chains."

Hubbard Street Grill   20 | 18 | 19 | $26
351 W. Hubbard St. (Orleans St.), 312-222-0770
■ David Schy's River North American across from the East
Bank Club is "always good" for comfort food "with a few
wrinkles"; highlights include "the best skirt steak in the
city", a "wonderful tuna burger", "delicious" pot roast
and "great" fries with jalapeño-laced ketchup; it may be
"off the beaten path", but many regularly make the trip.

Hudson Club ⬛   19 | 24 | 19 | $33
504 N. Wells St. (bet. Grand Ave. & Illinois St.), 312-467-1947
◪ "Eating is secondary" at this stylishly laid out, "trendy
with a capital T", River North American in an "enormous
airplane hangar setting"; the "hopping bar" offers 100 wines
in "flights" (fittingly) or by the glass to a "smart-looking"
crowd angling to mingle.

Indian Garden [S] 23 | 16 | 17 | $19

2548 W. Devon Ave. (Rockwell Ave.), 773-338-2929
247 E. Ontario St., 2nd fl. (bet. Fairbanks Ct. & Michigan Ave.), 312-280-4910
855 E. Schaumburg Rd. (Plum Grove Ave.), Schaumburg, 847-524-3007

■ Fans praise these Indian "standouts", with Streeterville residents particularly delighted to have a "much-needed ethnic" nearby; the "brilliant" lunch buffet is a "better buy than dinner", but for any meal expect "beautifully spiced" food and "friendly" waiters.

Irish Oak Restaurant & Pub ◐ [S] – | – | – | M

3511 N. Clark St. (Addison St.), 773-935-6669

Guinness and Murphy's are on tap at this Wrigleyville pub whose interiors were manufactured in Ireland and shipped to Chicago for assembly; the menu includes traditional favorites, such as Irish stew, and enough offbeat items (smoked haddock lasagna?) to avoid total predictability.

Iron Mike's Grille [S] 18 | 21 | 19 | $33

Tremont Hotel, 100 E. Chestnut St. (½ block west of Michigan Ave.), 312-587-8989

◩ Your take on this chophouse may depend on your opinion of its namesake, ex Bears coach Mike Ditka; fans praise "da pork chops" and the tasteful memorabilia, but boo-birds hiss at the "jock food, jock ambiance, jock crowd" and note the menu has "a lot of cholesterol for a guy with a bad heart."

Itto Sushi ◐ 21 | 14 | 19 | $25

2616 N. Halsted St. (Wrightwood Ave.), 773-871-1800

◩ Regulars at this "bare-bones" Lakeview sushi spot with "very fresh" and "dependable" fare think of it more as a "Japanese sports bar" because the TV is often tuned to the big game (usually the Bulls); the "social club" atmosphere extends to the "happy to see you" staff.

Jack Gibbons Garden [S] ▽ 19 | 14 | 18 | $28

14700 S. Oak Park Ave. (147th St.), Oak Forest, 708-687-2331

■ Locals claim this "old-school" Southwest Suburban steakhouse serves beef "as good as Morton's at half the price"; more reserved fans say "best steaks on the South Side"; modernists who object to the "stuck in a time warp" ambiance cry "change the decor, for Pete's sake."

Jack's American Blend [S] 21 | 17 | 21 | $22

(nka Jack's on Holstead)

3201 N. Halsted St. (Belmont Ave.), 773-244-9191

■ This Lakeview newcomer, a sibling of Daniel J's, features clever decor by Nancy Warren and an eclectic American bistro menu offering "high-end food at reasonable prices"; the clientele, which can be as unconventional as the fare, extols the "lovely wine selection" and "great service", concluding that this is "the best addition to Halsted in years."

Jackson Harbor Grill S   – | – | – | M
6401 S. Lake Shore Dr. (64th St.), 773-288-4442
A South Side Southern-Creole that occupies a Park District
boathouse on Jackson Harbor offering diners, especially
those who eat alfresco in summer, spectacular lake and
skyline views; few know of this gem (though thousands
cruise past it on Lake Shore Drive daily), but those who do
call it a "superb setting" for "romantic waterfront dining."

Jaipur Palace S   ▽ 17 | 18 | 16 | $22
Marriott Suites, 22 E. Hubbard St. (State St.),
312-595-0911
☑ River North Indian set in a "pretty room" that's a favorite
with its nooner business clients who praise the "excellent
buffet" bargain; otherwise, comments are split between
"a cut above" and "nothing special."

Jane's S   22 | 18 | 19 | $23
1655 W. Cortland Ave. (bet. Ashland & Damen Aves.),
773-862-JANE
■ "Please, please stop telling people about this" "homey"
Bucktown American with an "exposed brick" interior and
"consistently excellent", "healthful" food with a strong
vegetarian component; don't be surprised by "long waits"
on weekends as "artsy folks and MBAs" converge over
the "great brunch"; overall, a "solid first date" choice.

Jerome's Red Ginger S   14 | 16 | 15 | $20
2450 N. Clark St. (bet. Arlington Pl. & Fullerton Pkwy.),
773-327-2207
☑ When the weather's warm, brunch on the patio of this
Lakeview Eclectic is "super", but surveyors differ over
whether visits are otherwise justified: optimists say "it's
finding its way" with new Asian-accented dishes, but
others think the nonbrunch experience is just "ordinary."

Jia's S   16 | 12 | 15 | $17
2 E. Delaware Pl. (State St.), 312-642-0626
2545 N. Halsted St. (bet. Fullerton Pkwy. & Wrightwood Ave.),
773-477-6256
☑ Delivery that's "almost instant" and an accommodating
kitchen that'll "make it the way you like it" are two features
of these Gold Coast and DePaul-area Chinese; while the
majority says "solid", contrarians counter: "nothing special."

Jilly's Cafe S   21 | 17 | 21 | $30
2614 Green Bay Rd. (Central St.), Evanston, 847-869-7636
■ "Cute" North Shore Contemporary American "small
jewel" offering a "wonderful blend of flavors and textures"
at an "excellent value"; while many think the "tables are
too close", "cooking with flair" and "attentive service"
more than compensate.

Jimmy's Charhouse [S] 16 | 14 | 17 | $21
1111 N. Milwaukee Ave. (Deerfield Rd.), Riverwoods, 847-465-9300
◪ While some sniff that this "crowded" North Suburban neighborhood steakhouse is "nothing to write home about", a loyal contingent finds it a "favorite for lamb chops"; overall, it earns respect for providing "a decent meal at a decent price."

Jimmy's Steakhouse [S] ▽ 16 | 12 | 16 | $31
440 Green Bay Rd. (½ mi. north of Half Day Rd.), Highwood, 847-266-1700
◪ The younger sibling of Jimmy's Charhouse, this budget-friendly North Shore spot offers "quantity" beef with a cost incentive that includes a "good early-bird deal"; but critics say the food is "indifferent" and "the decor is tired."

Joe's Be-Bop Cafe & Jazz Emporium [S] 17 | 18 | 15 | $20
Navy Pier, 600 E. Grand Ave. (Lake Shore Dr.), 312-595-5299
■ This Navy Pier rib joint may be a "tourist mecca" (and what operation on the pier is not?), but the combination of "good barbecue" and live jazz nightly has surveyors tapping their toes, particularly if they snare an outdoor table that adds a lake view to the package.

Joe's Crab Shack [S] 15 | 16 | 15 | $22
745 N. Wells St. (bet. Chicago Ave. & Superior St.), 312-664-2722
1461 Butterfield Rd. (Finley Ave.), Downers Grove, 630-960-2033
2000 E. Golf Rd. (Hwy. 53), Schaumburg, 847-517-1212
◪ "Red Lobster with an attitude" is how wits describe these nautical shacks in the city and 'burbs featuring various "crab entrees at low prices" and theatrical servers who are prone to "jumping on tables to sing and dance"; the family-friendly menu contributes to a prime-time atmosphere that's so "noisy" you should "go with someone you don't like."

Johnny Rockets [S] 15 | 15 | 16 | $11
901 N. Rush St. (Delaware Pl.), 312-337-3900
■ With its "good and greasy" chow, "great egg salad" sandwiches and no-liquor policy, this Rush Street retro diner "brings you back to *Happy Days*"; the "clean, stainless steel" setting attracts the nostalgic, but the core of its appeal is simplicity itself: "nothing beats a great burger and fries done right."

John's Place [S] 19 | 15 | 18 | $16
1202 W. Webster St. (Racine Ave.), 773-525-6670
■ Geographically Eclectic "comfort" dishes translate into "solid" "Mom food with a kick" at this "cute" and "friendly" Lincoln Parker; the "great crowd" of locals and Gen Xers make it "Chicago's answer to a SoHo restaurant", but if you want to take in the scene be prepared for "waits", especially for the "hearty" weekend brunches.

J.P.'s Eating Place　　18　14　17　$25
1800 N. Halsted St. (Willow St.), 312-664-1801
☑ Lincoln Park seafooder with a core of devotees who note that it's "convenient to the Steppenwolf Theater" and "makes an effort" with a "varied and fun" ("almost tapas-like") selection of offerings from the sea; however, the unimpressed find it only "so-so."

Julie Mai's Le Bistro 𝕊　▽ 18　15　14　$22
5025 N. Clark St. (Winnemac Ave.), 773-784-6000
☑ "Adventurous cuisine" is the objective at this Edgewater hybrid where French bistro and Vietnamese dishes leave some saying "wow", but others muttering "disappointing"; service too comes in for criticism, but is easily overlooked by couples who snare one of the "cozy booths."

Julio's Latin Cafe ◑𝕊⊅　　−　−　−　M
3801 N. Kedzie Ave. (Grace St.), 773-866-2800
South American, Caribbean and Mexican dishes coexist on the lively menu of this 24-hour Northwest Side "gourmet Latin", a favorite with locals for its "excellent" food, "lovely dining room" and live entertainment on weekends that "excites the soul."

Kamehachi 𝕊　　23　17　18　$26
1400 N. Wells St. (Schiller St.), 312-664-3663
■ "Hot spot" serving "the best sushi east of Tokyo" in "hip" surroundings that include "the young, beautiful" and "every yuppie on the North Side"; since there's "almost always a wait" at this Old Town Japanese, many diners "ask to sit upstairs" where there's "more atmosphere" or out on the "beautiful summer patio."

Kerouac Jack's 𝕊　　17　16　17　$20
3407 N. Paulina St. (bet. Lincoln Ave. & Roscoe St.), 773-348-4321
■ The food "continues to improve" at this North Side Eclectic whose "*Pulp Fiction* atmosphere" (with some Beat Generation influence) pleases the "funky, local" crowd; highlights include "perfect risotto", "trendy pastas" and "delicious" brunchtime banana pancakes; though some remark it's "trying too hard to be hip", the majority labels it "a good place to share interesting stuff."

KIKI'S BISTRO　　24　22　23　$35
900 N. Franklin St. (bet. Chicago Ave. & Oak St.), 312-335-5454
■ There's beaucoup praise for this "très, très bien" bistro, just north of River North, with cooking "so wonderful you can't wait to go back" and "superb service"; a "real charmer", its "cozy" ambiance makes some feel they're in Provence and it's so "ideal for a romantic date" that many devotees wish "it stayed open later."

King Crab S
19 | 14 | 17 | $23

1616 N. Halsted St. (bet. Armitage & North Aves.), 312-280-8990
■ This "relaxed" Lincoln Park seafooder is handy for residents and Steppenwolf theatergoers who come for the "great crab legs" and other fishy fare at "reasonable" prices; while some caution that it's "ok for the price but not the best", they concede that it's "convenient."

Kinzie Chophouse S
19 | 17 | 18 | $29

400 N. Wells St. (Kinzie St.), 312-822-0191
■ A favorite "before the opera", this steakhouse also draws a business lunch crowd because of its proximity to the Merchandise Mart; though some deride it as a "lower-echelon" entry in the beef wars, stalwarts speak up for "good steaks, fish and pasta", as well as "great meatless options" presented in "comfortable", albeit "noisy", digs.

Klay Oven S
21 | 19 | 18 | $28

414 N. Orleans St. (Hubbard St.), 312-527-3999
■ One of "Chicago's best and its only haute Indian restaurant", this elegant River North spot might be "higher priced" than competitors but is "well worth the splurge" say respondents; it's a big "step up from Devon Avenue", with "polished service" and "outstanding food", including an "awesome" lunch buffet.

Kuni's S
23 | 16 | 18 | $25

511 Main St. (bet. Chicago & Hinman Aves.), Evanston, 847-328-2004
■ An "unpretentious" North Shore "gem" that ranks as the No. 1 Japanese and wins the title of "best sushi in Evanston", thanks to "fair prices" and the "freshest raw fish in Chicagoland"; insiders say that the "well-crafted" maki rolls are best "if made by Kuni himself" and stress that with plenty of cooked offerings, it's "more than a sushi bar."

Kyoto Japanese Restaurant S ▽
23 | 13 | 20 | $23

2534 N. Lincoln Ave. (Fullerton Pkwy.), 773-477-2788
■ Long on quality but short on looks, this "favorite sushi dive" among DePaul-area locals succeeds with an "excellent", "bargain" menu; diners note that a friendly atmosphere and attentive chefs mean that "after you go a few times, you won't have to order."

La Bocca della Verità S
22 | 16 | 21 | $27

4618 N. Lincoln Ave. (bet. Eastwood & Wilson Aves.), 773-784-6222
■ "The friendly owner will cook to please" at this "very good" Lincoln Square Italian with an "unpretentious" "neighborhood feel"; while "parking is a problem", the food is worth the hassle", especially for those who order the "great bruschetta" or the chef's signature *ravioli all'anatra*.

La Borsa

▽ 17 | 17 | 17 | $24

375 N. Morgan St. (Kinzie St.), 312-563-1414

☑ "You need a compass to find" this Near West Side "value" Italian located in a "large", "funky" "renovated railroad station" that has "fine views" of the city; "great ravioli" and "good sauces" contribute to the "solid" food, and since this place is "undiscovered, you can park."

La Canasta S

14 | 14 | 16 | $17

1119 W. Webster Ave. (bet. Racine & Sheffield Aves.), 773-975-9667

☑ DePaul-area cantina that's derided by some as a "warehouse of Mexican mediocrity", but "after a Cubs game" more than a few surveyors head here for "basic", "serviceable" dishes and "vicious margaritas."

La Cantina S

▽ 21 | 20 | 21 | $26

71 W. Monroe St. (bet. Clark & Dearborn Sts.), 312-332-7005

■ This basement restaurant in the Loop, which is part of the Italian Village trio, labors literally in the shadows of its better-known brothers (Village and Vivere); however, it's a handy lunch and pre-theater destination that offers a "great wine list."

La Crêperie S

19 | 14 | 16 | $19

2845 N. Clark St. (bet. Diversey Pkwy. & Surf St.), 773-528-9050

■ It "hasn't changed since the '70s", but that's ok with nostalgic surveyors and "first daters" who choose this Lakeview French for "inexpensive, filling" crêpes, including "crêpes suzette to die for" at dessert; the decor may be "cheesy", but there's always the "wonderful garden in back."

La Donna S

21 | 15 | 19 | $23

5146 N. Clark St. (Foster Ave.), 773-561-9400

■ Edgewater sibling to Via Veneto with "wonderful Italian" specialties, such as "first-rate raviolis" and "excellent risotto"; service is "friendly", even though the staff must work its way around "tables so close you can eat off your neighbor's plate" (not a bad idea).

La Gondola S

19 | 14 | 19 | $25

2425 N. Ashland Ave. (1 block north of Fullerton Pkwy.), 773-248-4433

☑ For "authentic Northern Italian" that's "not some trendy rip-off", this "neighborhood Tuscan" on the fringe of Lakeview "is it"; "terrific veal" and "exceptional eggplant" earn raves, but a few think the "old-fashioned" decor has "no atmosphere" – therefore, it's "great for carryout."

Lan's Bistro Pacific

– | – | – | M

680 N. Lake Shore Dr. (Erie St.), 312-397-1800

Chinese, Thai, Japanese and Vietnamese dishes mingle happily at this Streeterville Pan-Asian bistro; its 11-seat sushi bar and 150-seat dining room draw an eclectic mix of area residents and Michigan Avenue shoppers.

La Rosetta
18 | 17 | 16 | $24

3 First National Plaza, 70 W. Madison St. (bet. Clark & Dearborn Sts.), 312-332-9500

☑ Part of the Rosebud group, this Italian's principal drawing cards are "large portions" and a convenient Loop location near the theaters, United Center and office buildings; it's "always crowded" at lunch, leading critics to carp that the service can be "haphazard", with "tables too close."

La Sardine
– | – | – | M

111 N. Carpenter St. (bet. Randolph & Washington Sts.), 312-421-2800

Jean-Claude Poilevey of très-popular Le Bouchon has expanded by opening this Near West French bistro; while it's a bit more upscale than his first venture, he'll probably pack 'em in like sardines since the price is right.

Las Bellas Artes S
23 | 19 | 23 | $32

112 W. Park Ave. (York Rd.), Elmhurst, 630-530-7725

■ An "upscale", "gourmet Mexican" in the western suburbs, set in a "wonderfully romantic", antiques-laden room; the "outstanding" kitchen "sometimes reaches very high levels" and the "attentive" service is "excellent"; overall, "the 'burbs need more places like this."

Las Fuentes S
▽ 15 | 12 | 15 | $17

2558 N. Halsted St. (Wrightwood Ave.), 773-935-2004

☑ A DePaul-area Mexican that gets a nod or two for "great margaritas", but is primarily valued for its handy location and low prices; the menu covers "all the standards" and the food is "competent" but "not worth a special trip."

LA SORELLA DI FRANCESCA S
25 | 19 | 19 | $26

18 W. Jefferson St. (bet. Main & Washington Sts.), Naperville, 630-961-2706

■ "Hidden in Naperville", this "trendy" sibling of the Mia Francesca family may be the "best Italian in the 'burbs", offering "consistently flavorful" rustic dishes at moderate prices; while some complain that it's "very noisy", and more note that "they need to take reservations", everyone agrees the food's "excellent."

Las Palmas S
18 | 15 | 17 | $17

86 E. Dundee Rd. (Buffalo Rd.), Buffalo Grove, 847-520-8222
1642 Maple St. (Church St.), Evanston, 847-328-2555
1150 Ogden Ave. (Naperville Rd.), Naperville, 630-717-9030
3111 W. Ogden Ave. (Washington St.), Westmont, 630-963-9999

☑ Amigos of this Mexican chain say it offers "well-prepared" dishes, including the "best snapper Veracruzana in Chicago" and "excellent chile rellenos", but dissenters declare that it serves "pedestrian" "food for gringos"; a truce is called over the friendly staffers who help make it "a great family place."

La Strada Ristorante 19 | 18 | 19 | $32

155 N. Michigan Ave. (Randolph St.), 312-565-2200

◪ Some surveyors give this Continental near Grant Park points just for surviving the North Michigan Avenue reconstruction, which made it all but inaccessible for much of '97; now that the streets are clear, the tuxedoed waiters can resume serving the "good" food, even if dissenters find the place merely "acceptable."

Lawry's The Prime Rib [S] 23 | 22 | 22 | $35

100 E. Ontario St. (Michigan Ave.), 312-787-5000

■ "For prime rib there's nowhere else" besides this 25-year-old Chicago institution, which also serves lobster tail, a daily fish special and nothing else (discounting the "creamed spinach to die for" and chef Jackie Shen's famed chocolate bag dessert); but that's plenty for the business types and tourists who crowd into the "'60s setting" just off Michigan Avenue and concur that it's still "a terrific place to celebrate special occasions."

LE BOUCHON 24 | 18 | 21 | $33

1958 N. Damen Ave. (Armitage Ave.), 773-862-6600

■ "Pinch me, I'm in Paris" marvel those who secure a table in this "tiny", "cozy" Bucktown bistro, which the smitten promote as home to "the best French food in the city", citing the "great" onion tart and "amazing" roast duck for two; though the noise level makes the "cramped" dining room "no place for conversation", fans shrug "who cares – I love this place."

LE COLONIAL [S] 23 | 25 | 20 | $38

937 N. Rush St. (bet. Oak & Walton Sts.), 312-255-0088

■ You'll feel "transported to another world" – specifically, French-occupied Saigon – at this Rush Street Vietnamese with a "bamboo everywhere" interior that gets nominations for the "best decor in town"; the "tony" crowd adds that the "excellent", if "small portioned", food ("try the spicy beef salad"), is a close second, so "bring a group and try everything"; P.S. don't miss the "very sexy bar upstairs."

LE FRANÇAIS 29 | 27 | 28 | $77

269 S. Milwaukee Ave. (bet. Dundee & Willow Rds.), Wheeling, 847-541-7470

■ Once again, surveyors rate this Wheeling wonder the "epitome of good taste and tastes" and Chicago's No. 1 in food and service; while a No. 4 decor score prevented an across-the-board sweep, it's still "what the Bulls are to basketball", thanks to Roland Liccioni's "incomparable" French cooking and his wife and pastry chef Mary Beth's supervision of an "excellent" dining room staff that sees everything ("they even have reading glasses for people who forget"); while "perfection" doesn't come cheap ("very expensive"), lunch and the early bird are relative bargains.

Le Loup Cafe 🖢 — ▽ | 19 | 14 | 18 | $22 |
*3348 N. Sheffield Ave. (2 blocks north of Belmont Ave.),
773-248-1830*

■ A "fun and cozy" "poor man's bistro", this Wrigleyville
BYO spot has a year-round outdoor patio; its simple French-
Mediterranean specialties, such as "excellent Merguez
sausages" and "spiced couscous", are a "great value."

Leona's 🖢 — | 16 | 14 | 16 | $16 |
*6935 N. Sheridan Rd. (Morse Ave.), 773-764-5757
848 W. Madison St. (1½ blocks west of Oak Park Ave.),
Oak Park, 708-445-0101*

Leona's Neighborhood Place 🖢 ▽ | 17 | 15 | 16 | $17 |
1936 W. Augusta Blvd. (Damen Ave.), 773-292-4300

Leona's on Taylor 🖢 — ▽ | 14 | 13 | 16 | $19 |
1419 W. Taylor St. (Ashland Ave.), 312-850-2222

Leona's Sons ◑🖢 — | – | – | – | M |
3215 N. Sheffield Ave. (Belmont Ave.), 773-327-8861

☑ Chain of city and suburban pizzerias whose defenders
appreciate their "large, varied menu", "big portions" and
"basic" pies; however, foes feel they're "nothing special."

Leo's Lunchroom 🖢⌿ — ▽ | 18 | 8 | 13 | $14 |
1809 W. Division St. (bet. Ashland & Damen Aves.), 773-276-6509

■ For "funky" BYO dining on the Wicker Park border, head
to this "divey treasure" where "the best breakfast burritos"
are served to early risers and those who "look as if they've
been out all night"; later on, the likes of mac 'n' cheese and
other blue plate specials are also proffered by "hip slackers"
but remember, you "go for the prices, not the decor."

LES NOMADES — | 25 | 23 | 24 | $58 |
*222 E. Ontario St. (1½ blocks east of Michigan Ave.),
312-649-9010*

☑ Owned by the Liccionis of Le Français, this city sibling
just off the Mag Mile earns stellar, if not as spectacular,
marks from surveyors who call the Classic French cooking
"luscious" and the cheese course "the best in town"; "the
sophisticated ambiance" lends a "secluded feeling" – not
unlike the private club it used to be – so while a few find it
"snooty" and "stuffy" (jacket required and "hushed tones
necessary here"), that's just the way regulars like it.

LE TITI DE PARIS — | 27 | 25 | 26 | $55 |
*1015 W. Dundee Rd. (Kennicott St.), Arlington Heights,
847-506-0222*

■ "How does Pierre Pollin do it?" ask awestruck surveyors
who find this more than 25-years-old Northwest Suburban
French "still alive with new ideas" – well, let's give chef
de cuisine Michael Maddox some credit; in addition, a
"wonderful welcome at the door", a "warm", "attentive"
staff and prices that are, relatively speaking, an "amazing
bargain" contribute to the "fond memories."

LE VICHYSSOIS 🆂　　　24　22　22　$47
220 W. Rte. 120 (2 mi. west of Rte. 12), Lakemoor,
815-385-8221
■ Bernard Cretier's pioneering Far Northwest Suburban is
"a long trip from anywhere", but acolytes happily fill up their
gas tanks for "superb" Contemporary French in a charming
country setting – a freestanding building that makes some
proclaim "now *this* is a roadhouse!"; the atmosphere is
"romantic" and it's "the best value in the area."

Lindo Mexico 🆂　　　16　15　15　$18
2638 N. Lincoln Ave. (bet. Sheffield & Wrighwood Aves.),
773-871-4832 ◗
1934 Maple Ave. (bet. Emerson & Foster), Evanston, 847-475-3435
☑ Opinion is divided on these city and suburban Mexicans:
the nays call them "mediocre" and "hit and miss", while
the olés cheer for "great fajitas", "healthy options" and
overall "reliable" cuisine; P.S. the outdoor garden on North
Lincoln is perfect for those "strong margaritas."

Lino's Ristorante　　　22　18　21　$29
222 W. Ontario St. (bet. Franklin & Wells Sts.),
312-266-0616
■ "One of the last of the old-time, family-style" Italians, this
River North sibling to Stefani's and Riva has "checkered
tablecloths" and a "simple" menu that "never disappoints";
the "warm staff" makes patrons feel welcome – maybe
that's why President Clinton ate here in '98.

Little Bucharest ◗🆂　　　17　14　18　$21
3001 N. Ashland Ave. (bet. Belmont Ave. & Diversey Pkwy.),
773-929-8640
☑ When dining at this "charming" Romanian on the fringe of
Lakeview, surveyors say, "be prepared for overload" in the
form of "humongous" portions and the owner's over-the-top
host act; while a few gripe about the "limited" menu and
"boring" food, the proprietor's efforts and "value" prices
blunt any disappointment.

Lloyd's　　　12　12　14　$22
200 W. Madison St. (Wells St.), 312-407-6900
☑ This American's Loop locale ensures a steady stream
of business lunchers and pre-opera and pre-theatergoers,
though one critic wonders if "anyone orders anything other
than the Cobb salad?"; for some who consider the food
"tired" and "uninspired", convenience is its principal virtue.

L'Olive　　　19　13　18　$20
3915 N. Sheridan Rd. (Irving Park Rd.), 773-472-2400
■ North Side BYO ethnic that's "one of Chicago's few
Moroccan options" and offers "fabulous b'steeya" and
"superb tagines", though portions can be "small"; still,
it's a "special place" with a "warm, inviting atmosphere."

Lone Star Steakhouse S   16 | 16 | 17 | $19
6250 S. Main St. (63rd St.), Downers Grove, 630-852-7037
High Point Plaza, 569 E. Roosevelt Rd. (bet. Highland &
Meyer Aves.), Lombard, 630-953-9442
▨ A "fun", "noisy" suburban steakhouse chain that's known
for having "peanuts on the table", a "dancing staff" ("needs
lessons"), "long waits", "excellent" sweet potatoes "as
big as Texas" and "good steaks"; however, that doesn't
stop critics from judging them "not as good as Outback."

Louisiana Kitchen S   – | – | – | M
2666 N. Halsted St. (Diversey Pkwy.), 773-529-1666
Lincoln Park Cajun-Creole that isn't shy on spice, but enough
locals like it that way to keep it packed on weekends;
the menu includes alligator, jambalaya and "blackened
everything", and the kitchen sells packets of its secret
seasoning mix to do-it-yourselfers.

Lou Malnati's Pizzeria S   21 | 13 | 16 | $15
439 N. Wells St. (Hubbard St.), 312-828-9800
1050 E. Higgins Rd. (Arlington Hts. Rd.), Elk Grove,
847-439-2000
6649 N. Lincoln Ave. (2 blocks south of Touhy Ave.),
Lincolnwood, 847-673-0800
■ While ratings-wise Pizzeria Uno & Due edged out this
family-run chain of city and suburban pizzerias, they still
receive lots of votes for the "best deep-dish pies" in town;
"excellent antipasto salad" and cheddar cubes that many
"could eat all night" further explain why they're a "must
try" for visitors to Chicago.

Lou Mitchell's S⊭   20 | 11 | 18 | $12
565 W. Jackson Blvd. (Jefferson St.), 312-939-3111
Lou Mitchell's Express ◐S⊭   – | – | – | I
O'Hare Airport, International Terminal 5, 773-601-8989
■ Big eaters head for this "high-grade diner" near Union
Station (or its airport kiosk) for "awesome breakfasts" (the
"best omelet in the city" and "dependable French toast")
that are served by waitresses that some say are "ebullient
bordering on obnoxious"; the Loop location is equally
popular for lunch, even though "the American Heart
Association should put a warning label on this place."

Lucca's S   21 | 22 | 21 | $30
2834 N. Southport Ave. (1 block north of Diversey Pkwy.),
773-477-2565
■ This "gem on the Southport strip" in Lakeview is a French-
American hybrid (with a bit of Greek thown in too) that's
"a neighborhood find" featuring such unusual dishes as
shiitake mushroom pancakes; staffers "go out of their way to
please" and the "comfortable", "handsome" room with
"great appointments" adds to an "intimate atmosphere."

Lucky Platter 🟦 | 17 | 13 | 16 | $15 |
1400 N. Lake Shore Dr. (Schiller Ave.), 312-337-8130
514 Main St. (bet. Chicago & Hinman Aves.), Evanston,
847-869-4064
■ These Gold Coast and Evanston Eclectics are "campy classics" where "'50s" "comfort food" gets a modern spin; regulars rave about the "yummy" sweet potato fries, cornbread, turkey meatballs and breakfast omelets and find the decor as "funky" as the prices are low.

LuLu's Dim Sum & Then Sum 🟦 | 19 | 11 | 16 | $14 |
1333 E. 57th St. (Kenwood Ave.), 773-288-2988
626 Davis St. (bet. Chicago & Sherman Aves.), Evanston,
847-869-4343
◪ "Hip" Pan-Asians in Hyde Park (near U of Chicago) and Evanston (Northwestern) with prices that lure hungry collegians for "different dim sum" on weekends and "interesting" Thai, Japanese, Korean and Vietnamese interpretations all the time; certain combos may be "Americanized", but "oh, those noodles!"

Lupita's 🟦 | ▽ | 19 | 14 | 17 | $18 |
700 Main St. (bet. Chicago & Ridge Aves.), Evanston,
847-328-2255
◪ "Innovative", "very good" North Shore Mexican that offers "possibilities other than the standards", particularly when it comes to its "truly special" daily specials, which may include a recipe culled from *Like Water for Chocolate.*

Lutnia 🟦 | ▽ | 21 | 22 | 19 | $29 |
5532 W. Belmont Ave. (Central Ave.), 778-282-5335
■ "The most elegant Polish restaurant" around is actually "more Continental than Polish", though this Northwest Sider's menu has plenty of "excellent" specialties to take you back to Warsaw; "white-glove service" and classic piano music add to the "European atmosphere", though a few find it all a bit "pretentious."

Lutz Continental Cafe | 20 | 18 | 17 | $16 |
& Pastry Shop 🟦
2458 W. Montrose Ave. (Western Ave.), 773-478-7785
■ "Fabulous pastries" are the highlight of this venerable Northwest Sider, and though some "would die without the napoleons", there's more than just desserts here; there are "tasty" European noshes perfect for "ladies who lunch", especially in the "beautiful" outdoor garden.

Machu Picchu 🟦 | ▽ | 19 | 12 | 22 | $24 |
5427 N. Clark St. (bet. Bryn Mawr & Foster Aves.), 773-769-0455
■ This Far North Side Peruvian has "uneven but sometimes outstanding food" and "lots of character" – specifically the owner/chef/waiter who runs the place; there's a five-course prix-fixe dinner that's "a treasure", but it's only served from Thursday–Saturday.

Madam B 🅂　　　21 | 21 | 20 | $34
3441 N. Halsted St. (bet. Cornelia & Newport Aves.),
773-248-4040
■ "Au courant", "sleek and classy" dining rooms and a
"quiet and romantic" atmosphere are part of the appeal of
this Lakeview Asian-American; while a new chef arrived
post-*Survey*, if he's as good as his predecessor, this place
will continue to be an "outstanding new addition."

Madison's 🅂　　　▽ 21 | 19 | 20 | $29
1330 W. Madison St. (2 blocks east of Ashland Ave.),
312-455-0099
■ Located near the United Center, this Italian steakhouse,
with "generous and tasty portions", definitely "adds class
to a rejuvenated neighborhood"; while it's a "great place
before and after games", some prefer it "when the Bulls
are out of town" and the crowds are more manageable.

MAGGIANO'S LITTLE ITALY 🅂　20 | 18 | 19 | $24
516 N. Clark St. (Grand Ave.), 312-644-7700
240 Oakbrook Ctr. (bet. Butterfield & Spring Rds.), Oak Brook,
630-368-0300
1901 E. Woodfield Rd. (Rte. 53), Schaumburg,
847-240-5600
175 Old Orchard Shopping Ctr. (bet. Golf & Old Orchard Rds.),
Skokie, 847-933-9555
☑ "Doggie bags are mandatory" at these theatrical Italian-
Americans whose "very good", family-style entrees come
in "hilariously" large portions; their incredible popularity
means "go by 5 PM" or "give your name and go to the
movies", but some surveyors don't get the big deal, dubbing
them "as authentic as silicone."

Magnum's Steak & Lobster 🅂　22 | 18 | 20 | $38
225 W. Ontario St. (Franklin St.), 312-337-8080 ◗
777 E. Butterfield Rd. (bet. Highland Ave. & Myers Rd.),
Lombard, 630-573-1010
☑ "Bring your ear plugs" and a big appetite to these
River North and West Suburban beef emporiums; they're
considered "suitable for politicians" and win votes in their
own right for "awesome steak" and lobsters "so big, they're
frightening", though at prices that scare some surveyors
as well; scattered opponents grouse about the "bar noise"
in the background, but that didn't keep the food rating
from going up.

Mama Desta's Red Sea 🅂　　▽ 16 | 9 | 16 | $15
3216 N. Clark St. (Belmont Ave.), 773-935-7561
■ "The food makes up for the lack of atmosphere" at this
"dive" of a Wrigleyville Ethiopian where the prospect of
eating sans utensils is not too intimidating given the "tasty",
"wonderfully spiced" food and "very friendly" servers;
regulars say it's "great fun for a large group."

Mambo Grill S   17 | 15 | 16 | $21
412 N. Clark St. (bet. Hubbard & Kinzie Sts.), 312-467-9797
■ This "underappreciated" River North Pan-Hispanic
touches on everything from Tex-Mex to South American,
resulting in a "good variety" of "creative drinks and peppy
food", particularly the Cuban sandwich and Chicago's "best
(maybe only) poblano-mushroom sandwich"; business
lunchers appreciate "a good alternative to traditional
choices" and couples dub it "a great night out."

Mandar Inn S   ▽ 18 | 14 | 17 | $16
2249 S. Wentworth Ave. (Cermak Rd.), 312-842-4014
☑ Fans of this "plain" Chinatown mainstay say it's got
"good food"; less enthused diners opine that the cooking
is "unexciting" but "ok."

Mango S   22 | 18 | 20 | $33
712 N. Clark St. (Superior St.), 312-337-5440
■ An "intimate" and "inventive" American-Eclectic that's
one of the most popular spots in River North owing to
Steven Chiappetti's "robust and flavorful" menu and
"spectacular presentations"; only a few gripes ("what's all
the fuss about?") surface amid raves for an "absolute must"
that may be "cramped" and "noisy, but worth it."

Manhattan's   – | – | – | M
415 S. Dearborn St. (bet. Congress Pkwy. & Van Buren St.),
312-957-0460
Steven Schnur (no, not the NU quarterback) is chef at this
self-styled 'bold American' concept in the Loop – a handy
location for the Financial District lunch crowd and a short
walk from the Auditorium Theater.

Manny's Coffee Shop ⊄   23 | 10 | 16 | $12
1141 S. Jefferson St. (Roosevelt Rd.), 312-939-2855
■ "The closest thing Chicago has to a New York deli" is this
Near South Side cafeteria where the mighty and the humble
stand elbow to elbow for "Jewish comfort food" that
includes "humongous corned beef sandwiches", "wonderful
kugel" and "chicken soup that'll cure what ails you"; addicts
call it a "treasure" and "the most interesting lunchroom in
town" (they serve breakfast too, but no dinner).

Mantuano Mediterranean Table S 23 | 20 | 20 | $33
NBC Tower, 455 Cityfront Plaza Dr. (Columbus Dr.), 312-832-2600
■ Those who come expecting "great food at reasonable
prices" from this lively Mediterranean in the NBC Tower
find that it "delivers on its promise" due to Tony Mantuano,
"one of the great chefs of Chicago"; the "convenient
downtown location" is a boon to Michigan Avenue goers,
and nearby residents appreciate the gourmet take-out
option; the "dynamic menu" showcases "exotic dishes"
that find favor with every taste.

Maple Tree Inn　　　　20 | 15 | 18 | $25
13301 S. Western Ave. (under the bridge at 133rd St.),
Blue Island, 708-388-3461
■ Venerable South Suburban Cajun-Creole that "saves you
a trip to New Orleans" for "comforting" catfish, oysters, and
cornbread that's "worth every crumb"; an "outstanding beer
selection" offsets the somewhat "shabby" decor.

MARCHÉ S　　　　22 | 23 | 19 | $37
833 W. Randolph St. (1 block west of Halsted St.), 312-226-8399
■ One of the pioneers in the now sizzling West Randolph
corridor, this "very trendy" French-American bistro is a
"see-and-be-seen" place with "good, interesting" fare and a
"funky" design that leads some to dub it "the Cirque du
Soleil of restaurants"; there's the predictable amount of
"noise", but the "beautiful crowd" doesn't seem to mind.

Mashed Potato Club S　　　　15 | 17 | 15 | $21
316 W. Erie St. (bet. Franklin & Orleans Sts.), 312-255-8579
☑ "Twentysomethings" who want to "eat in a disco" head to
this River North American-Eclectic with a "huge selection"
of potatoes-as-entrees and a "hundred interesting
toppings"; however, those who feel cold about the concept
criticize the "bad techno music and Day-Glo decor" and
conclude: "yuppies and mashed potatoes, oh my!"

Matsuya ●S　　　　23 | 13 | 17 | $21
3469 N. Clark St. (Sheffield Ave.), 773-248-2677
■ Surveyors figure the "predominantly Asian clientele" at
this "crowded" Wrigleyville Japanese is "a good indicator"
of high-quality fare, including "the most innovative maki
selection in town" and fish "so fresh it glistens"; the "cheap
prices" make up for what some feel are "cramped" quarters.

Max's Deli S　　　　14 | 10 | 13 | $14
2301 N. Clark St. (Belden Ave.), 773-281-9100
Crossroads Shopping Ctr., 191 Skokie Valley Rd. (Lake
Cook Rd.), Highland Park, 847-831-0600
☑ "It's not the Lower East Side" say patrons of this Lincoln
Park/Highland Park duo, "but it's the closest we have"; fans
praise the "large portions", "tremendous matzo balls" and
"yummy potato pancakes", but a fair number kvetch that
they're "second-rate", with service that can be "rude."

M Cafe S　　　　18 | 18 | 14 | $13
Museum of Contemporary Art, 220 E. Chicago Ave. (1 block
east of Michigan Ave.), 312-397-4035
■ The "best museum food in Chicago" (ok, not the toughest
category) may well be the "inventive sandwiches" and
other "good" light fare offered at this lunch-only Eclectic
inside the Museum of Contemporary Art; patrons praise the
"stark, modern decor", the eye-catching views of the
outdoor sculpture garden and Lake Michigan; it's "good for
first dates" and a "quiet Sunday lunch outside."

Medici [S] 16 | 14 | 15 | $15

2850 N. Sheridan Rd. (Surf St.), 773-929-7300

Medici on 57th ◐ [S]

1327 E. 57th St. (Kimbark Ave.), 773-667-7394

◪ "Stick to the hamburgers" at these "inexpensive" Americans since most maintain the food is only "average"; still, some say the Hyde Park original is the "only normal college hangout on the U of C campus" and "isn't bad if you don't mind grunge."

Meritage Cafe & Wine Bar [S] 23 | 19 | 20 | $35

2118 N. Damen Ave. (2 blocks north of Armitage Ave.), 773-235-6434

■ "One of the best new finds in Bucktown" is this Pacific Northwest specialist that's a sibling to Starfish and "a rising star" in its own right; big pluses in the estimation of many are the "fantastic food" from "a creative menu", a "great wine selection" and a "delightful" and "romantic" outdoor garden (much of it weather-protected).

Merlot Joe [S] 16 | 15 | 18 | $24

2119 N. Damen Ave. (2 blocks north of Armitage Ave.), 773-252-5141

■ This French-accented Eclectic bistro offers "terrific value" say bargain-conscious Bucktowners who laud the "hearty, well-cooked" fare; a few gripe about the "idiosyncratic setting" and cramped seating, but romantics feel that just makes it "unpretentious" and a "perfect first-date place"; in the summer, most opt to sit in the "wonderful garden" anyway.

MESÓN SABIKA [S] 26 | 25 | 23 | $28

(fka Emilio's Meson Sabika)

1025 Aurora Ave. (bet. Rte. 59 & Washington St.), Naperville, 630-983-3000

Northfield Village Ctr., 310 Happ Rd. (Willow Rd.), Northfield, 847-784-9300

■ Though Emilio Gervilla has moved on from this Naperville Spaniard (he sold out to former partners), "the dining is still great", winning raves for "splendid tapas" and "wonderful sangria"; those with a taste for "elegant surroundings" particularly appreciate the setting – a "romantic", "old white mansion" with a "gorgeous patio in summer"; N.B. the Northfield branch is new and unrated.

Mia Cucina [S] 20 | 20 | 18 | $31

56 W. Wilson Ave. (2 blocks north of Palatine Rd.), Palatine, 847-358-4900

◪ "Noisy sista to Spasso" is one take on this Northwest Suburban Italian and indeed a number comment on the acoustics ("fun but not the place for intimate conversation") in the "loft-style" dining room; the kitchen is well regarded, winning high marks for "excellent" pizzas and pastas; the outdoor patio may provide relief from the noise level inside.

MIA FRANCESCA 🟥 |24| |16| |19| |$26|
3311 N. Clark St. (School St.), 773-281-3310

🔳 The restaurant that launched three sequels is a proven Wrigleyville phenomenon – a no-reservations Italian where patrons "gladly line up or dine at 5 PM" to secure a precious table; skeptics wonder what "makes it the Microsoft" of the Chicago scene, while pros praise "always delicious" and "affordable" food, especially the "superb pastas", and, of course, the "great people-watching."

Mi Casa Su Casa 🟥 |16| |15| |16| |$20|
2524 N. Southport Ave. (1 block north of Fullerton Pkwy.), 773-525-6323

🔲 "Good" Lakeview Mexican that lives up to its name with a "cozy setting" designed to make you feel "as if you're in someone's living room"; this "standard Mexican" isn't setting any new standards, but it's an "old favorite" that still makes for "great late nights" on weekends.

Michael Jordan's 🟥 |13| |18| |14| |$23|
500 N. La Salle St. (Illinois St.), 312-644-DUNK

🔲 "I saw MJ here!" pretty much sums up the appeal of this River North American, which might be deserted if it "were named for anyone else", but is a hit with die-hard fans and "out-of-town guests" hoping to catch a glimpse of His Airness; while the memorabilia may be "a must-see for the kids", that doesn't make the chow a must-eat, though the "excellent crab cakes" and "yummy" macaroni and cheese have their advocates.

Millennium Steaks & Chops 🟤   ▽ |19| |19| |19| |$37|
832 W. Randolph St. (1 block west of Halsted St.), 312-455-1400

🔲 Boosters of the only steakhouse on the West Randolph Street corridor praise the "terrific food and service", calling the porterhouse "the tastiest in town"; however, some foes gripe about the prices and ambiance, saying "they have managed to make a simple" concept "feel complicated."

Miller's Pub 🟤🟥 |17| |14| |17| |$20|
134 S. Wabash Ave. (Adams St.), 312-263-4988

🔲 An "old Chicago haunt" and "after-work favorite" that's also popular for its late-night hours, this Loop "meat-and-potatoes" American is "a blue-collar joint with white-collar customers" who cheer for the "great ribs" and lamb chops; but critics counter that its "location is better than its food."

Mill Race Inn 🟥 |18| |22| |19| |$26|
4 E. State St. (bet. Rtes. 38 & 25), Geneva, 630-232-2030

🔲 People drive to Geneva for the view and they dine at this venerable riverside American for the same reason, i.e. the "lovely setting" – especially the outdoor patio ("be sure to feed the ducks"); it's hard to argue with a "great lunch outside along the Fox", but a few find fault with the "average" food and say they "would not race" to get here.

Millrose Brewing Co. S   19 | 21 | 19 | $27
45 S. Barrington Rd. (Central Rd.), Barrington, 847-382-7673
☑ Opinion varies on this "always crowded" Northwest
Suburban brewpub: while enthusiasts urge "order anything
from the [American] menu – it's great", the less enthused
say that's "it's easy to be above-average in this gustatory
desert"; however, there seems to be unanimous support
for the well-made, "tasty beers."

Mimosa S   – | – | – | M
*1849 Second St. (½ block north of Central Ave.), Highland
Park, 847-432-9770*
Kevin Schrimmer, the chef at the late, great Cafe Provençal,
is the chef-owner of this North Shore newcomer that's
viewed as both a "bit of sunny Italy" and a "sophisticated
bistro", suggesting the French/American/ Italian menu
defies easy categorization; however, there is a consensus
that this "pleasant" place "has caught on with reason."

Mirabell   ▽ 19 | 17 | 19 | $22
3454 W. Addison St. (bet. Kimball & St. Louis Aves.), 773-463-1962
◼ This "quaint" Northwest Side German-American has
made its reputation on an "authentic" menu that features
"very good sausages"; overall, it "tries really hard", and a
live oompah band lends spirit to special occasions.

Mity Nice Grill S   18 | 16 | 18 | $22
*Water Tower Pl., 835 N. Michigan Ave., mezzanine level
(bet. Chestnut & Pearson Sts.), 312-335-4745*
☑ "A mity nice retreat" for Water Tower Place shoppers and
"convenient" for a Near North rendezvous, this "'50s-type"
American offers "decent food for the nonventuresome",
including "good meat loaf"; while some say the fare is just
"average", most agree it's "an honest meal" and "a relief
after a long, happening day."

Mon Ami Gabi S   – | – | – | E
2300 Lincoln Park W. (Belden Ave.), 773-348-8886
Chef and managing partner Gabino Sotelino is the namesake
of this Lincoln Park Parisian-style bistro, which he
refashioned from his Un Grand Cafe space, adding a
reproduction turn-of-the-century bar to give the place a
new look; the revamped menu includes four versions of
steak frites that already have people talking.

Monastero's S   17 | 17 | 18 | $23
3935 W. Devon Ave. (Crawford Ave.), 773-588-2515
☑ "The best time to come" to this off-the-beaten-trail
Northwest Side Italian "is when there is singing" (Friday–
Saturday nights, but call to be sure), as it has become a
venue for operatic performers; applause is more scattered
for the cuisine: fans offer bravos for the "wonderful food",
including the "absolute best spinach lasagna", but there
are those who see "nothing extraordinary."

Mongolian Barbeque [S] 17 12 14 $17
3330 N. Clark St. (2 blocks north of Belmont Ave.), 773-325-2300
◪ "A good place to end a hunger strike" sums up this Wrigleyville "do-it-yourself" Asian where patrons help themselves to a prix fixe buffet of meats, veggies, starches and seasonings and hand it all over to a chef for a quick stir-fry; pros proclaim "I love adding my own touch to everything" (there are recipe cards for first-timers), while cons counter "if I wanted to cook, I would've stayed home."

MONTPARNASSE 25 22 23 $48
200 E. Fifth Ave. (1½ blocks east of Washington Blvd.), Naperville, 630-961-8203
■ "Special occasion restaurant" that some nominate as the "top French in the Western Suburbs"; "the area's prettiest room" features "absolutely outstanding food and service", leading loyalists to add that this gem "deserves more weekday patronage."

MORTON'S OF CHICAGO [S] 26 20 23 $49
Newberry Plaza, 1050 N. State St., lower level (Maple St.), 312-266-4820
9525 W. Bryn Mawr Ave. (River Rd.), Rosemont, 847-678-5155
1 Westbrook Corporate Ctr. (22nd St. & Wolf Rd.), Westchester, 708-562-7000
■ Suveryors once again have voted this trio "best steakhouse in Chicago"; a "meat lover's paradise", it's built its reputation on "quality, aged steaks", plus "very attentive" service that some consider "the most consistent" around; there are those who feel the decor "needs an update", but why mess with success?

Moti Mahal [S] 19 6 11 $14
2525 W. Devon Ave. (Western Ave.), 773-262-2080
1031-35 W. Belmont Ave. (Kenmore Ave.), 773-348-4392
■ These North Side and Wrigleyville Indians may be "lacking" in ambiance, but adherents say they do have "consistently good food" and a lunch buffet that "can't be beat"; "heavenly naans" and "the best chicken tikka masala" are on hand to neutralize swipes at the "dive" decor; N.B. the Belmont location is BYO.

Mrs. Levy's Delicatessen 14 11 13 $14
Sears Tower, 233 S. Wacker Dr., 2nd level (bet. Adams St. & Jackson Blvd.), 312-993-0530
◪ "If you are stuck in Sears Tower", this "decent deli" is "convenient"; but while "Mrs. Levy knows chicken noodle", most say the rest of the food is "ok but nothing special" and the service is "spotty."

Mrs. Park's Tavern ◗ⓢ   19 | 18 | 18 | $28

Doubletree Guest Suites Hotel, 198 E. Delaware Pl. (1 block east of Michigan Ave.), 312-280-8882

■ The downstairs neighbor to the Park Avenue Cafe is a "cozy" American bistro that serves until 1:30 AM, making it "perfect for after-hours fare" (one of the few such options in the Streeterville vicinity); regulars tout "creative" munchies like the salmon sandwich, and late-late-night revelers point out it's a "can't miss" breakfast hangout too.

My Favorite Inn ⓢ   21 | 12 | 20 | $25

11 Highwood Ave. (bet. Green Bay Rd. & Waukegan Ave.), Highwood, 847-432-5160

■ This veteran North Shore Italian may pay "perfunctory" attention to atmosphere, but the "old-fashioned and delicious" specialties trump any decor concerns; many diners single out "steak al forno to die for" as central to its appeal; now under new ownership, it has remained as "comfortable as an old shoe."

My π Pizza ◗ⓢ   17 | 14 | 16 | $14

2417 N. Clark St. (½ block north of Fullerton Pkwy.), 773-929-3380

■ Chicagoans of a certain age wax nostalgic about this circa-'70s Lakeview pizzeria, for many the site of "my first deep-dish" and then, as now, an apt date choice for anyone into the "cozy and collegiate" scene; most maintain the pies are still "good" and the "fireplace is a bonus in the winter."

Myron & Phil's Steakhouse ⓢ   21 | 14 | 20 | $28

3900 W. Devon Ave. (Crawford Ave.), Lincolnwood, 847-677-6663

■ An "old-time favorite for steaks, chopped liver and famous photos", this Northwest Side steak-and-seafooder is "a step into the past" that's "noisy and unhip"; however, it's "a good joint for padding your cholesterol numbers."

Nana's Cafe   ▽ 18 | 12 | 15 | $19

7 W. Kinzie St. (State St.), 312-527-0300

■ Tucked into a quiet River North street, this "basic" Italian with a "simple, unflashy" atmosphere finds favor with lunch workers seeking "great salads", "excellent meatball sandwiches" and "large portions" of pasta.

Nancy's Original Stuffed Pizza ⓢ   17 | 10 | 13 | $15

2930 N. Broadway (Wellington Ave.), 773-883-1977 ◗
3970 N. Elston Ave. (Irving Park Rd.), 773-267-8182

☑ These venerable North Siders specialize in stuffed pizza and their version is so dense that "it's a meal in a slice"; while there's "zero decor" and the "service won't break any records", they're still a "favorite", though maybe "not for trendy yuppies"; N.B. there's no alcohol permitted at the North Elston branch.

Narcisse ●⬛　　　　▽ 18 | 25 | 17 | $37
710 N. Clark St. (Superior St.), 312-787-2675
■ Offering tapas, caviar, cigars and fancy martinis, this "sexy" River North "singles bar" features "every trend in one place" and, not surprisingly, attracts a chic, "see-and-be-seen" crowd; though "very expensive for cocktails and dessert" and a "little intimidating" to some, it's still good "before or after the theater" or for "impressing a date."

New Japan ⬛　　　21 | 17 | 21 | $23
1322 Chicago Ave. (Dempster St.), Evanston,
847-475-5980
■ "Exceptional family-run service", "great sushi" and "terrific noodles and soups" make this "tranquil" Japanese a "very consistent" "Evanston favorite"; but those who don't get the minimalist thing find the "nice, clean" dining room a tad "sterile."

Next Door ⬛⇌　　　24 | 16 | 21 | $25
250 Skokie Blvd. (bet. Dundee & Lake Cook Rds.), Northbrook,
847-272-1491
■ The name refers to its being adjacent to its sister, Francesco's Hole in the Wall, and like its sibling, this North Suburban Italian bistro offers "always top-notch food" that has customers singing, and a no-reservations/no-plastic policy that leaves them grumbling; nonetheless, it's "always mobbed and loud" because diners can't help but return for the "best roast chicken in town."

Nick & Tony's ⬛　　　17 | 18 | 17 | $25
1 E. Wacker Dr. (bet. State St. & Wabash Ave.),
312-467-9449
◪ Whether the food at this near-Loop Italian is "solid" or "unremarkable" depends on which surveyor has your ear; despite being "inconsistent", it's a "good lunch spot" (especially for takeout) and "popular" as a pre-performance destination for those going to the Chicago Theater.

NICK'S FISHMARKET　　　24 | 23 | 24 | $48
1 First National Plaza, 79 W. Monroe St. (Clark St.),
312-621-0200
O'Hare International Ctr., 10275 W. Higgins Rd. (Mannheim Rd.),
Rosemont, 847-298-8200 ⬛
■ These Loop and airport-area, jacket-and-tie seafooders continue to be rated among the "tops in the city for fish" and "will wow you", even though they're "so expensive"; still, surveyors rationalize them as "anniversary restaurants" and "good for expense-account diners" looking for "swank" ambiance, "outstanding" service and a "black-and-blue ahi that will send you into orbit"; N.B. post-Survey, when the Loop branch relocated within the same plaza, it added a more casual grill.

94th Aero Squadron [S] 14 | 20 | 17 | $26
1070 S. Milwaukee Ave. (bet. Hintz & Palatine Rds.), Wheeling, 847-459-3700
◪ Aero-themed Northwest Suburban American alongside Palwaukee Airport that's a "must-see place" since it comes equipped with full-scale WWII planes, and allows patrons to listen to the control tower via tableside headsets while watching real takeoffs and landings; though "unique", with "great ambiance for a 16-year-old", gourmands gripe that the "average" cuisine never gets off the ground.

N. N. Smokehouse [S] 20 | 9 | 17 | $15
1465 W. Irving Park Rd. (bet. Ashland & Southport Aves.), 773-868-4700
■ A "pulled-pork paradise", this North Side BYO BBQ "hole-in-the-wall" does a "big take-out business" with locals and Cubs fans who love the "value" prices on "great smoked meats" and "awesome chicken"; from a theoretical standpoint it even appeals to vegetarians: "if I ate meat it would come from here – the smell is divine."

Nookies [S]⊄ 15 | 10 | 15 | $12
1746 N. Wells St. (Lincoln Ave.), 312-337-2454
Nookies Too [S] 17 | 9 | 15 | $12
2112 N. Halsted St. (bet. Dickens & Webster Aves.), 773-327-1400
Nookies Tree ◐[S]⊄ ▽ 14 | 10 | 15 | $12
3334 N. Halsted St. (Buckingham St.), 773-248-9888
■ Best known as "good breakfast joints" and as "great places to cure that Saturday night hangover", this North Side American trio caters to "young college grads" who swear by the "best fluffy omelets in town"; those less intoxicated say "standard diner fare"; N.B. Nookies Tree stays open from Friday morning–midnight Sunday.

North Pond Café [S] – | – | – | M
2610 N. Cannon Dr. (bet. Diversey & Fullerton Pkwys.), 773-477-5845
This Contemporary American featuring produce from the Midwest has what admirers think is "the prettiest location in the city", in the heart of Lincoln Park, adjacent to a tree-lined pond; it's a "terrific" newcomer with "innovative" food from Mary Ellen Diaz (ex Printer's Row); the only trouble is that reservations can take weeks to obtain.

Northside Cafe ◐[S] 14 | 16 | 15 | $17
1635 N. Damen Ave. (Milwaukee & North Aves.), 773-384-3555
◪ The "trendy bar food" and "people-watching" ambiance lead some to dub this "friendly" American "a little bit of Lincoln Park in Bucktown"; though some say the "bland", "totally average" food is nothing to get excited about, the general consensus is that it's "fun for drinks and hanging out", and the two-story glass atrium rises to the occasion "when you crave patio seating in February."

Nuevo Leon S　　　▽ 24 | 10 | 18 | $13
3657 W. 26th St. (bet. Central Park & Lawndale Aves.),
773-522-1515
1515 W. 18th St. (Ashland Ave.), 312-421-1517 ◑ 🏵
■ Relatively few respondents venture into these Pilsen
and Little Village Mexicans; however, those who do say
"don't let the locations scare you" away from "a great
Mexican dining experience" that includes "authentic"
food (including "terrific cheese enchiladas"), great prices
and "friendly service."

Oak Terrace S　　　▽ 21 | 23 | 22 | $29
Drake Hotel, 140 E. Walton St. (Michigan Ave.), 312-787-2200
■ This lesser-known restaurant in the Drake Hotel (the Cape
Cod Room is more renowned) is a "classy" American with
"great views" of Lake Michigan; while primarily known
for its "astounding breakfast buffets" and "over-the-top"
Sunday brunch, it's also "a treat" "for special occasions."

Oak Tree S　　　16 | 17 | 15 | $17
900 N. Michigan Ave., 6th level (bet. Pearson St. & Walton Pl.),
312-751-1988
☑ Popular for breakfast, this "upscale" American diner
located in a Gold Coast mall features an "extensive"
selection of dishes highlighted by "inventive omelets" and
"great salads"; though some find the food "ordinary" and
a "bit expensive for a coffee shop menu", a Michigan
Avenue view makes it a "pleasant refuge for shoppers"
and a nice choice for "lunch with Mom or the girls."

OCEANIQUE　　　24 | 18 | 22 | $40
505 Main St. (½ block east of Chicago Ave.), Evanston,
847-864-3435
■ "What a catch!" exclaim boosters of this French-
American seafooder, "one of the best" of its genre on the
North Shore with "fabulous food"; it's "more than a bit
pricey", but there's an "excellent wine list" and "exemplary"
service from a "knowledgeable" staff.

Old Barn, The S　　　19 | 20 | 20 | $25
8100 S. Parkside Ave. (bet. Central Ave. & 81st St.),
Burbank, 708-422-5400
☑ An "old-fashioned" "roadhouse classic" that's "been here
forever" (78 years), this South Side Traditional American
pleases "loyal followers" with its "still great" prime rib;
while sourpusses find it "bland" and lacking in imagination,
they concede that "it's the only decent place in that area."

Old Jerusalem S　　　18 | 7 | 14 | $13
1411 N. Wells St. (bet. Division St. & North Ave.), 312-944-0459
■ Old Towners laud this "good" Middle Easterner for serving
some of the "best hummus and falafel in town" at "great
prices"; however, it helps to overlook the "somewhat dumpy
room" – if you can't, opt for "takeout."

O'Neil's 🆂 | 21 | 18 | 20 | $27 |

1003 Green Bay Rd. (Scott Ave.), Winnetka, 847-446-7100

◾ This "comfortable" North Shore Italian seafooder offers "consistently" "well-prepared" cuisine that attracts a "young suburban crowd" and even a celeb or two; still, a few gripe about the "same menu all the time", "predictable" food and no reservations (except for parties of six or more).

one sixtyblue | – | – | – | E |

160 N. Loomis St. (Randolph St.), 312-850-0303

The worst-kept secret in town is that this West Side Contemporary American (just blocks from the United Center) has Michael Jordan as a silent partner; but don't look for basketball memorabilia here – instead, there's an Adam Tihany design and dishes with culinary and visual flash.

Oodles of Noodles 🆂 | 15 | 10 | 15 | $12 |

2540 N. Clark St. (2 blocks north of Fullerton Ave.), 773-975-1090

◾ "Fast, tasty, inexpensive" noodles are the name of the game at this Lakeview BYO Pan-Asian with portions that are "just what the name says"; some find it a "pleasant surprise", but critics counter it's "just another noodle shop."

Oo-La-La! Border Bistro 🆂 | 20 | 18 | 19 | $25 |

3335 N. Halsted St. (bet. Addison St. & Belmont Ave.), 773-935-7708

◾ "Oui, oui, oui" rave devotees of this Lakeview Franco-Italian whose menu consists of a "great mix of flavors and a wine list to go with it"; but if you can't make it in the evening, consider the "fun, fun, fun Sunday brunch"; P.S. the "boys' town" clientele makes this a "great place on Halloween."

Orbit ◗🆂   ▽ | 19 | 11 | 16 | $16 |

2948-54 N. Milwaukee Ave. (Central Park Ave.), 773-276-1355

◾ "Good food like Grandma's" – "the best pierogi" and "wonderful soups" – is the forte of this quintessential Polish-American in the heart of the Northwest Side's Little Warsaw district; the more reserved cite "weird" ambiance, but conclude "still ok for a meal out."

Original Gino's East 🆂 | 20 | 14 | 15 | $16 |

2801 N. Lincoln Ave. (Diversey Pkwy.), 773-327-3737
160 E. Superior St. (½ block east of Michigan Ave.), 312-943-1124
6156 95th St. (2 blocks east of Ridgeland Ave.), Oak Lawn, 708-598-5600
15840 S. Harlem Ave. (159th St.), Orland Park, 708-633-1300
1321 W. Golf Rd. (Algonquin Rd.), Rolling Meadows, 847-364-6644
9751 W. Higgins Rd. (bet. Mannheim & River Rds.), Rosemont, 847-698-4949
Tin Cup Pass Shopping Ctr., 1590 E. Main St. (Tyler Rd.), St. Charles, 630-513-1311
(Continues)

Original Gino's East (Cont.)
98 W. Main St. (bet. 1st St. & Rte. 72), West Dundee, 847-426-0500
☑ Whether you're debating the "dark, dingy" Streeterville original or the shiny suburban outposts, there are opinions aplenty about this deep-dish chain: many call it "the best pizza in Chi-town", with a cornmeal crust that's "worth the wait", but foes "can't stand the tourists" and "long lines."

Original Pancake House S⊅   21 13 17 $12
Village Ctr., 1517 E. Hyde Park Blvd. (bet. 51st St. & Lake Park Blvd.), 773-288-2323
22 E. Bellevue Pl. (¼ block east of Rush St.), 312-642-7917
2020 N. Lincoln Park W. (Armitage Ave. & Clark St.), 773-929-8130
5140 W. 159th St. (52nd Ave.), Oak Forest, 708-687-8282
■ These city and suburban flapjack parlors are "still unbeatable" for "lots of variety", including the "best Dutch baby pancakes on earth" and "apple pancakes made in heaven"; yet, griddle groupies should "get there early" or be prepared for a "brutal wait", as "many devoted followers" ensure "long lines."

Outback Steakhouse S   18 16 17 $21
720 W. Lake Cook Rd. (Arlington Hts. Rd.), Buffalo Grove, 847-541-4329
2005 River Oaks Dr. (Hwy. 94 & 159th St.), Calumet City, 708-862-0220
216 E. Golf Rd. (Roselle Rd.), Schaumburg, 847-843-8884
☑ Surveyors are divided over these suburban, Aussie-themed steakhouses, with enthusiasts extolling their "nice, quality steaks" at "fair prices" and the "can't-pass-it-up" 'bloomin' onion appetizer (the Outback version of onion rings); but cons contend that the quality is "not worth the wait" and "crowds."

Outpost, The S   22 16 19 $30
3438 N. Clark St. (Sheffield Ave.), 773-244-1166
☑ There are "great things going on inside" this "ambitious" Contemporary American, which has a "smart, inventive" menu of "quality cooking", an "extensive" selection of global wines by the glass, "attentive service" and "reasonable prices"; in short, "a most sophisticated corner bistro" that Wrigleyville hopes will "stay in the neighborhood."

Palette's S   16 22 17 $30
Newberry Plaza, 1030 N. State St. (bet. Maple & Oak Sts.), 312-440-5200
☑ The "spectacular ambiance" at this Rush Street–area Contemporary American consists of a dramatic, art-filled interior highlighted by an 11-foot statue of Icarus that dominates the dining room; despite compliments for the "very good steak and chops", some feel it "needs a better menu"; of course, even "if you don't like the food, the piano player [the estimable Dave Green] is great."

Palm, The 🅂　　　22　19　20　$46
Swissôtel, 323 E. Wacker Dr. (2 blocks east of Michigan Ave.),
312-616-1000
☑ While the nostalgic bemoan the "cold" interior and miss
"the charm of the original" setting in the defunct Mayfair
Regent, the new Swissôtel location of this NYC steak chain
is actually grander, with a patio offering a glimpse of Lake
Michigan; sentiment aside, surveyors, in this case mostly
"middle-aged men in suits" on "expense accounts", laud
the "obscene portions" of beef and lobster.

Panda Panda 🅂　　　17　14　16　$16
1825 Second St. (Central Ave.), Highland Park, 847-432-9470
☑ This North Shore Chinese spot gets mixed reviews, with
boosters singling out "the noodle dishes" and "hospitable
and accommodating" service, while the unimpressed find
the "typical" menu strictly "average"; your call.

Pane Caldo 🅂　　　21　19　19　$35
72 E. Walton St. (bet. Michigan Ave. & Rush St.), 312-649-0055
■ "Small, intimate and darn good", this "romantic" Italian
just steps from the Magnificent Mile has a big following for
its "scrumptious pasta dishes" and "fabulous desserts";
while a number find it "cramped" and "getting pricey", and
there are scattered complaints that the "attentive" staff
can be "snotty", it's still a "gem" for the "quality" food.

Papagus Greek Taverna 🅂　　　20　20　19　$25
Embassy Suites Hotel, 620 N. State St. (bet. Ohio & Ontario Sts.),
312-642-8450
Oakbrook Ctr., 272 Oakbrook Ctr. (bet. Rte. 83 & 22nd St.),
Oak Brook, 630-472-9800
☑ "Forget Greektown!" cry fans of these "cute" River North
and Oak Brook outposts, which some call "our best Greeks",
notwithstanding their connection to the Lettuce Entertain
You empire; naysayers dismiss the concept as "Walt Disney"
Greco, but converts insist the "melt-in-your-mouth braised
lamb" and "wonderful appetizers" speak for themselves.

Papa Milano 🅂　　　18　13　17　$20
951 N. State St. (Oak St.), 312-787-3710
☑ "Don't ever change" plead disciples of this "pure
nostalgia" Rush Street–area Italian that's thrived now for
47 years and counting as a "stereotypical red sauce slinger"
producing "great chicken parmigiana"; those in search of
a parental figure add "it's like I have an Italian mother."

Pappadeaux 🅂　　　–　–　–　M
798 W. Algonquin Rd. (Golf Rd.), Arlington Heights, 847-228-9551
921 Pasquinelli Dr. (Ogden Ave.), Westmont, 630-455-9846
Suburban outposts of this Houston Cajun seafood chain are
"wonderful spots" featuring "large portions" of "moderately
priced" fare and a "family-style ambiance"; some complain
about "long waits", but others happily reply "yum, yum."

Pappagallo's S   ▽ 18 | 17 | 17 | $24
246 Green Bay Rd. (north of Rte. 22), Highwood, 847-432-6663
■ Patrons of this North Shore Italian find it "charming and quiet" by day and crowded by night, especially weekends; "reliable food and service" pull them in, particularly for Sunday brunch and the "excellent early bird."

PARK AVENUE CAFE S   25 | 21 | 22 | $46
Doubletree Guest Suites Hotel, 199 E. Walton Pl. (Mies van der Rohe Way), 312-944-4414
■ Fanciers of Contemporary American fare say Chicago's Streeterville sibling of this NYC original is "superb", an "oasis of class and service" with an "eclectic" menu served amid collectible Americana; the food is "exquisite", desserts are "too pretty to eat" and the "spectacular dim sum–style brunch" is a "fresh change"; for those who need extra convincing, it's all complemented by a "primo vino selection."

Parthenon ◐S   20 | 16 | 18 | $21
314 S. Halsted St. (bet. Jackson Blvd. & Van Buren St.), 302-726-2407
◩ A "classic Greektown" whose "authentic" food – lamb that's "tender beyond belief" and "outstanding braised octopus" – and atmosphere draw birthday celebrants and other partyers; there are a few who say "ho-hum", but most everyone else cries "bring on the flaming cheese!"

Pasha ◐S   – | – | – | E
642 N. Clark St. (½ block north of Ontario St.), 312-397-0100
The current hot spot for River North night crawlers is this restaurant-cum-nightclub that swings with DJ music until 5 AM weekends; the kitchen stays open until 3 AM turning out French-Continental dishes (insiders tout the Black Passion dessert) with the occasional Italian influence.

Pasteur Cafe S   24 | 23 | 19 | $27
5525 N. Broadway (Bryn Mawr Ave.), 773-878-1061
■ Surveyors shout "welcome back!" to the top-rated Vietnamese in the *Survey* that's "better than ever" thanks to a "beautifully decorated", more spacious new Edgewater location that's reminiscent of "old French Saigon"; look for "superb", "perfectly prepared" cuisine that's so popular that regulars advise going "late to avoid the noisy" crowds.

Patrick & James S   21 | 23 | 21 | $31
368 Park Ave. (Vernon Ave.), Glencoe, 847-835-7000
■ This "gorgeous" Contemporary American, a "classy addition to the North Shore", earns plaudits for "eclectic furnishings", such as a stained-glass dome, a mahogany bar (once part of a riverboat) and other collectibles; chef Marshall Blair's efforts are equally "outstanding", and such friendly touches as complimentary soup and salad with entrees lead some to call it "a bargain"; it's a sibling to O'Neil's in Winnetka, but this one takes reservations.

Pegasus ◐ S   19 | 19 | 19 | $23
130 S. Halsted St. (bet. Adams & Monroe Sts.),
312-226-4666
■ This blue and white restaurant in Greektown is prized for
its "beautiful", warm weather rooftop garden ("best in the
Loop"), "friendly" staff and "solid" Greek cuisine featuring
"huge spanikopita" and "very good" barbecued lamb;
N.B. management provides customers with a free shuttle
bus to Bears and Blackhawks games.

Penny's Noodle Shop S ⌿   20 | 11 | 16 | $12
3400 N. Sheffield Ave. (Roscoe St.), 773-281-8222
950 W. Diversey Pkwy. (Sheffield Ave.), 773-281-8448
■ "Modern, clean" and "hopping student hangouts" in
Wrigleyville and the North Side with "cheap", "amazing,
fresh Thai" food, including lad nar chicken that "rocks"
and "yummy noodle dishes"; there are "long waits" for
tables, but once seated, service is "fast" and "efficient."

Pete Miller's Steakhouse ◐ S   20 | 20 | 19 | $33
1557 Sherman Ave. (Davis St.), Evanston, 847-328-0399
■ "Cozy" North Shore chophouse with "large portions"
of "high-quality aged steaks", the "best garlic mashed
potatoes" and "lots of cigar smoke"; those on a budget
recommend the adjacent pub for "great burgers" and live
jazz music every night.

Philander's Oak Park   21 | 19 | 21 | $34
Carleton Hotel, 1120 Pleasant St. (1 block east of Harlem Ave.),
Oak Park, 708-848-4250
☑ "Classy", 20-year-old American seafooder in the West
Suburbs showcasing a "wood-paneled" dining room that
"feels like a private club"; it may be "old-fashioned", but
"good fish" and live jazz every night ("makes the bar SRO")
fuel its reputation as a "classic spot."

Phoenix S   20 | 11 | 13 | $18
2131 S. Archer Ave. (Wentworth Ave.), 312-328-0848
■ A "wonderful selection" of "dynamite dim sum" is served
daily at this second-floor dining room in Chinatown, whose
large windows permit glimpses of Downtown; many
advise "go very early" on weekends, though midweek
tables are relatively easy to come by.

Pine Yard S   18 | 11 | 15 | $17
924 Church St. (Maple Ave.), Evanston, 847-475-4940
☑ North Shore Chinese that gets sweet and sour reviews:
while supporters say the preparations are definitely "above-
average" and single out "great moo shu" and egg rolls,
the less-convinced say "just your average Chinese", but
everyone agrees it's "not a bad bang for your buck."

Pizza Capri S   18 | 12 | 15 | $15
1716 W. Diversey Pkwy. (Halsted St.), 773-296-6000
1501 E. 53rd St. (Harper Ave.), 773-324-7777
1733 N. Halsted St. (Willow St.), 312-280-5700 ◗
5139 Main St. (Curtis St.), Downers Grove, 630-434-7777
■ City and suburban gourmet pizza chain with "frou-frou"
pies; while ratings-wise they're not quite up there with the
big boys, "awesome salads" and "great delivery service"
solidify their reputation as "sound neighborhood places."

Pizzeria Uno & Due ◗S   22 | 14 | 16 | $16
619 N. Wabash Ave. (Ontario St.), 312-943-2400
29 E. Ohio St. (Wabash Ave.), 312-321-1000
■ "The king" of deep-dish "still reigns" at these block-
apart River North "institutions" that "should be on the
Chicago Historical Society list" for their "outstanding
pizza year in and year out"; while regulars complain about
the tourists, "long waits on weekends" and warn that the
"original locations" in the city "are a class above" the
franchises, overall, "you can't go wrong."

P.J. Clarke's S   15 | 13 | 15 | $19
1204 N. State Pkwy. (Division St.), 312-664-1650
☑ "Classier than most Division Street bars", this "upscale"
pub "delivers on what it advertises": "excellent burgers,
Caesar salad" and "lots of yuppies" in a cheerfully "loud"
setting; if you expect fine cuisine, you'll be "disappointed."

Planet Hollywood S   12 | 20 | 14 | $19
633 N. Wells St. (Ontario St.), 312-266-STAR
☑ "Star power is wholly inedible" say surveyors heaping
scorn on Chicago's River North chapter of this International,
Hollywood-themed chain "for kids" looking "for the
props" ("cool stuff"); in terms of food, "if you stick to
simple, you'll survive."

Prairie S   22 | 22 | 21 | $36
Hyatt on Printer's Row, 500 S. Dearborn St. (Congress Pkwy.),
312-663-1143
■ "A Midwestern take on paradise" is how some view
this South Loop Regional American set amid Frank Lloyd
Wright–inspired decor; "wonderful ingredients" contribute
to "beautifully presented", "creative cooking" that may
even incorporate buffalo or ostrich; P.S. it's "convenient to
the Auditorium Theater."

Primavera Ristorante S   21 | 23 | 23 | $36
Fairmont Hotel, 200 N. Columbus Dr. (south of Wacker Dr.),
312-565-6655
■ For "a fun place for a special night out", it's tough to
beat this "very relaxing", East-of-Michigan hotel Italian
where the "talented" staff croons "operatic arias" and
popular tunes in a "classy", "elegant" setting; while the
food's second to the entertainment, it's still "good."

96

PRINTER'S ROW   25 | 21 | 23 | $40
550 S. Dearborn St. (Congress Pkwy.), 312-461-0780
■ Reviewers have only "superlatives" for this "resilient"
Contemporary American located south of the Loop and near
the Auditorium Theater; it's "always a pleasure" to wade
through Michael Foley's "innovative menu", especially for
one of his "superb game dishes" ("best venison in the
US"); an "attentive staff" contributes to an ambiance
that's "perfect for pampering on that special occasion."

Provence S   22 | 20 | 21 | $36
*64 Green Bay Rd. (½ block south of Winnetka Ave.),
Winnetka, 847-501-5505*
☑ Jacky Pluton's sunny touch of Southern France on the
North Shore is "reminiscent of travels to the region", and for
some, his "tasty" French bistro food, including "excellent
bouillabaisse", translates into the "best newcomer" in the
area; P.S. the early bird is "very reasonable."

P.S. Bangkok S   19 | 15 | 17 | $17
2521 N. Halsted St. (Fullerton Pkwy.), 773-348-0072
3345 N. Clark St. (bet. Addison St. & Belmont Ave.), 773-871-7777
■ "Sunday brunch is terrific" at these "cheap" Wrigleyville
and DePaul-area Thais known for an "enormous menu";
there's "great basil chicken" and the "best penang curry
west of Lake Michigan and the Andaman Sea" (look it up).

Public Landing S   ∇ 22 | 22 | 21 | $27
200 W. Eighth St. (State St.), Lockport, 815-838-6500
■ "Excellent American food in an historic setting" sums up
the appeal of this Southwest Suburban located in a restored
limestone building overlooking the I & M Canal; the
"gorgeous" atmosphere includes a "bright, airy", rustic
dining room with wooden rafters and old-fashioned quilts;
it's almost "as good as its sister [Tallgrass], at half the price."

Pump Room, The S   – | – | – | E
*Omni Ambassador East Hotel, 1301 N. State St. (Goethe St.),
312-266-0630*
One of Chicago's most famous dining rooms, this Gold Coast
legend has reopened following a change in management
and a $2 million redo; the new menu is French-accented
American with multicultural influences, and if it's more
contemporary than the former bill of fare, some traditions –
such as jackets required after 4 PM – remain.

Quincy Grille on the River   17 | 15 | 17 | $30
200 S. Wacker Dr. (Adams St.), 312-627-1800
☑ Surveyors say this American-seafood specialist, with a
view of the train tracks, is "handy" on Civic Opera House
nights and for "business lunches"; while the younger set
thinks the "standard" menu "needs flair" and finds the
atmosphere "too old boys' club" "stuffy", it's still "one of
the few nice spots in the Southwest Loop."

Rainforest Cafe S   13 | 22 | 15 | $19 |
605 N. Clark St. (bet. Grand Ave. & Ohio St.), 312-787-1501
121 Woodfield Mall (bet. Golf & Higgins Rds.), Schaumburg,
847-619-1900
▰ A contingent finds these River North and Northwest
Suburban eco-themed Americans "like Disneyland
without going there" and "tops for entertaining kids",
thanks to recreated rainstorms, robotic animals and live
cockatoos; but bashers call them a "tourist trap" with
"long waits", "crowds" and "mediocre" grub, insisting
the "novelty of the simulated atmosphere wears off."

Ranalli's   12 | 10 | 12 | $16 |
440 S. La Salle St., 2nd fl. (bet. Congress Pkwy. & Van Buren St.),
312-957-9600
138 S. Clinton St. (Adams St.), 312-258-8555 ◗ S
24 W. Elm St. (Dearborn St.), 312-440-7000 ◗ S
1925 N. Lincoln Ave. (Armitage Ave.), 312-642-4700 ◗ S
▰ Lincoln Park locals love the "super outdoor patios" at
the North Side links of this pizzeria chain, while the Loop
location draws a suit-and-tie lunch crowd; the verdict is
that the beer selection is "excellent", the pizza "notable"
and the salads "decent", but other items are "mediocre"
and it can seem like "every waitress has had a bad day."

Ravinia Bistro S   19 | 15 | 19 | $26 |
581 Roger Williams Ave. (bet. Green Bay Rd. & St Johns Ave.),
Highland Park, 847-432-1033
■ This "cute" North Shore bistro provides "gracious"
service and very good" French fare; depending on your
tolerance for crowds, some advise "don't go on a big
Ravinia night" when scores of pre-performance music
buffs fill the joint, while others, in harmony with the
entertainment, enthuse "nice before summer concerts."

Red Apple S⊄   16 | 10 | 14 | $11 |
6474 N. Milwaukee Ave. (bet. Devon & Nagle Aves.),
773-763-3407
3121 N. Milwaukee Ave. (Belmont Ave.), 773-588-5781
■ Belly up to the all-you-can-eat buffets at these Northwest
Side siblings that provide an "amazing array of decent
classic Polish food" at prices "cheaper than cooking at
home"; the "hearty" grub will most likely "hold you for
days", but as insurance, ice cream is included in the tab.

Redfish S   17 | 17 | 17 | $23 |
400 N. State St. (Kinzie St.), 312-467-1600
51 Town Sq. (Butterfield Rd.), Wheaton, 630-588-9158
▰ City and Suburban West Cajuns that play to mixed
reviews; boosters like the "fun", "lively" New Orleans
atmosphere, "strong drinks", "delicious crab cakes" and
"wonderful, redneck oysters Rockefeller"; detractors
declare that the food's "not authentic" ("another Heaven
on Seven knockoff") and "not quite there" yet.

Red Light 🅂   18 | 21 | 17 | $31
820 W. Randolph St. (1 block west of Halsted St.), 312-733-8880
▣ An "innovative" Pan-Asian sibling of neighboring Near
West Siders Marché and Vivo that's a "trendy hangout
for the young and beautiful", with "ultramodern" decor and
"very good" "exotic fusions", including a "don't-miss" whole
catfish; those not wearing black ask "what's the fuss?", find
the food "inconsistent" and strain to communicate over a
decibel level that "makes the NYC subway seem quiet."

Red Lion Pub 🅂   14 | 17 | 15 | $16
2446 N. Lincoln Ave. (Fullerton Pkwy.), 773-348-2695
▣ "Cheerio!" toast surveyors to this "fun" Lincoln Park
tavern that serves British pub grub, such as fish 'n' chips,
with warm Guinness ("like it's supposed to be"); while
"you'll feel like you're in London or Ireland", and it's a
"nice place to hangout", a few find the vittles just "average."

Red Tomato 🅂   17 | 15 | 16 | $23
3417 N. Southport Ave. (2 blocks north of Belmont Ave.),
773-472-5300
▣ "One of the first good neighborhood restaurants" in
Wrigleyville, this "cool", contemporary-looking pasta
emporium offers "dependable" Italian fare in a setting
"where you can wear a T-shirt"; while it still "has traces of
its glory days", a number think it "needs a shot in the arm."

Relish 🅂   21 | 18 | 20 | $31
2044 N. Halsted St. (bet. Armitage & Dickens Aves.), 773-868-9034
■ "Innovative" Lincoln Park American where chef Ron
Blazek's "unique menu" is chock-full of "super cuisine",
even if many are fixated on his "orgasm of chocolate"
dessert; there's a bargain prix fixe for the pre-theater
crowd, and insiders advise in summer sit in the "peaceful",
70-seat "fantastic outdoor garden with twinkling white
lights in the trees" – it's a "great date place."

Restaurant Okno ◗🅂   20 | 19 | 18 | $32
1332 N. Milwaukee Ave. (1½ blocks north of Division St.),
773-395-1313
■ A Wicker Park Eclectic that dazzles with "interesting
global food" served in a postmodern atmosphere that's "like
eating at the *Jetsons*" or "on the Enterprise"; "only the
hippest waiters and waitresses" attend the "pierced
crowd", so there's "great people-watching" everywhere you
turn, but the DJ-spun music has 'em begging "turn it down."

Retreat, The 🅂   ▽ 22 | 21 | 19 | $23
605 E. 111th St. (St. Lawrence Ave.), 773-568-6000
■ Located in an historic Pullman mansion, this Traditional
American "oasis on the South Side" has odd hours (call
ahead) that make it less accessible than some would like;
still, Southern specialties and "great grilled salmon" justify
the bother, and the place fills up for Sunday brunch.

Retro Bistro   23 | 18 | 21 | $30 |
Mt. Prospect Commons, 1746 W. Golf Rd. (Busse Rd.),
Mt. Prospect, 847-439-2424
■ While it might be a "half-step behind" D & J Bistro in
Lake Zurich, this strip mall Northwest Suburban French
sibling offers "consistently satisfying" food, "value wines", a
"super friendly" staff and a black-and-white setting with
"a nice city feel"; insiders add "don't miss the fabulous
prix fixe dinners."

Reza's ●S   18 | 15 | 17 | $19 |
5255 N. Clark St. (Berwyn Ave.), 773-561-1898
432 W. Ontario St. (Orleans St.), 312-664-4500
☑ "Wow, look at all this food!" exclaim delighted visitors
to these River North and Andersonville Persians where
"really good" vegetarian dishes, "the best lamb shank" and
dill rice "to die for" come at very "reasonable prices"; the
"large and busy" rooms don't score high on ambiance, but
what they lack in "atmosphere is compensated for in value";
N.B. the wine selection is surprisingly sophisticated.

Rhapsody S   23 | 24 | 21 | $35 |
CSO Symphony Ctr., 65 E. Adams St. (Wabash Ave.),
312-786-9911
■ Chef-partner Steven Chiappetti (Mango, Grapes) oversees
this "innovative" American located in the Loop's CSO
Symphony Center, where you can expect "beautiful
presentations that taste as good as they look" at a price
that's surprisingly affordable given the well-heeled and
semi-captive audience; while only an interior corridor
separates the dining room from the performance space,
this "is more than just a pre-symphony locale"; indeed,
given the early-bird crowds, you can best appreciate this
"fabulous addition" after the curtain goes up.

Rhumba S   20 | 22 | 20 | $29 |
3631 N. Halsted St. (Addison St.), 773-975-2345
■ Every day is carnival at this "kitschy" "but interesting"
Lakeview Brazilian that "appeals to all the senses"; the
"one-of-a-kind" atmosphere includes a Carmen Miranda
female impersonator ("worth dinner alone"), samba music,
dancing, a "not-for-the-timid" drink menu and "better-than-
you-would-expect" dishes, including chargrilled, skewered
meats; N.B. the restaurant morphs into a nightclub during
wee weekend hours.

Rico's S   21 | 17 | 18 | $24 |
626 S. Racine Ave. (Harrison St.), 312-421-7262
■ It's "hard to make a mistake" when choosing from the
menu of this "friendly", "well-run", family-owned Tri-Taylor
Italian with "terrific veal", a "spectacular stuffed artichoke"
and "fried calamari that's the best in the city"; to experience
this "hidden gem" more calmly, "don't get caught in the
pre-game" Bulls and Blackhawks dinner rush.

Rigoletto S　　　　　　　21 | 16 | 19 | $32
293 E. Illinois St. (bet. Green Bay Rd. & Western Ave.),
Lake Forest, 847-234-7675
■ While this "steady" North Shore veteran bills itself as
New American with Italian influences, most surveyors praise
the "imaginative" Northern Italian menu; overall, surveyors
say "we take friends and they want to go back."

Rinconcito Sudamericano S　▽ 20 | 10 | 18 | $19
1954 W. Armitage Ave. (Damen Ave.), 773-489-3126
■ "Be adventurous and you'll be glad" at this "no-decor"
Bucktown Peruvian offering a "consistently rewarding"
dining experience with "some of the most fascinating food in
Chicago" and very fair prices; a cadre of the culturally
curious asks: "do Peruvians eat this well every day?"

Ristorante DeMarco's　　　　– | – | – | M
5 N. 105 Rte. 53 (Lake Rd.), Itasca, 630-285-9200
Though this "great little storefront" in the Northwestern
'burbs has yet to be discovered by many, those who know
it praise the "superior traditional Italian" food, "nice
portions" and "reasonable prices"; the only gripe is that
already there are "long waits."

Ritz-Carlton Cafe ⵔS　　　22 | 22 | 22 | $30
Ritz-Carlton Hotel, 160 E. Pearson St. (Michigan Ave.),
312-573-5160
■ This informal, but still "expensive" Traditional American
companion to the acclaimed Dining Room is set next to a
sun-kissed lobby; it makes "a nice haven" for tired shoppers
and tourists looking for a "wide variety" of "simple but
excellent" sandwiches, salads and main courses; as
always, it remains a "classic" choice for "power breakfasts"
and an after-theater snack.

RITZ-CARLTON DINING ROOM S　27 | 27 | 27 | $59
Ritz-Carlton Hotel, 160 E. Pearson St. (Michigan Ave.),
312-573-5223
■ Chicago's highest-rated hotel restaurant (once again)
showcases chef Sarah Stegner's "perfect" Contemporary
French food and a cheese cart "so good it can't be legal";
factor in "outstanding service" that "will make you feel
like a millionaire" and "classy yet unpretentious" decor, and
it's no surprise that reviewers think dinner is akin to "a three-
hour vacation"; P.S Sunday brunch is "absolutely awesome."

Riva S　　　　　　　　21 | 23 | 19 | $38
Navy Pier, 700 E. Grand Ave. (Lake Shore Dr.), 312-644-7482
◪ "With the right table", dinner at this Navy Pier seafooder/
steakhouse includes "spectacular" views of the lake and
city skyline, undoubtedly part of its appeal; but supporters
also laud "very fresh fish" and "great pastas", outnumbering
those who carp about "tourist overload", "cold" service
and a "pricey" menu.

Rivers 19 | 18 | 18 | $30
Mercantile Bldg., 30 S. Wacker Dr. (bet. Madison & Monroe Sts.), 312-559-1515
◩ Steps away from the Civic Opera House, this New American is a handy pre-performance destination, as well as "a classy place for a business lunch" for Loop-area workers; reviewers say the crab cakes and corn chowder are standouts but that everything is "solid", including the outdoor terrace overlooking the Chicago River.

R.J. Grunts [S] 16 | 15 | 17 | $17
2056 N. Lincoln Park W. (Dickens Ave.), 773-929-5363
◩ The concept American that launched Rich Melman's Lettuce Entertain You empire nearly closed two years ago until popular sentiment (the public's and Melman's) kept it alive; a visit is "flashback time" to the '70s, but there's still a "huge salad bar" and the "best burger in town" and now with valet parking, business may boom again; but skeptics just grunt and call it a "dinosaur."

Robinson's No. 1 Ribs [S] 17 | 9 | 13 | $17
655 W. Armitage Ave. (Orchard St.), 312-337-1399
940 W. Madison Ave. (Clinton St.), Oak Park, 708-383-8452
◩ Lincoln Park and West Suburban ribberies that provoke extreme reactions; partisans point to "fall-off-the-bone" ribs, "wonderful BBQ chicken" and a "great pork sandwich"; detractors call the 'cue "just ok" and "maybe too sweet"; the decor rating isn't spectacular, but it's par for the genre.

Rock Bottom Brewery ☾ [S] 13 | 14 | 14 | $18
1 W. Grand Ave. (State St.), 312-755-9339
◩ Surveyors can't agree on whether this "loud" River North brewpub chain has "mediocre beer" and "pretty good food" or (except for "good mashed potatoes") "bland", "boring" grub and "great" suds; maybe it's just "a great place to meet for machos and beer" (no, that's not a typo).

Roditys ☾ [S] 20 | 15 | 18 | $20
222 S. Halsted St. (bet. Adams St. & Jackson Blvd.), 312-454-0800
◩ "Remodeling has helped" this "old- reliable", "above-average" Greektown "value" known for "generous portions" of "great taramasalata and calamari" and "excellent lamb"; however, service comments range from "indifferent" to "where else do they seem so glad to see you?"

Ron of Japan [S] 18 | 17 | 19 | $28
230 E. Ontario St. (Fairbanks Ct.), 312-644-6500
633 Skokie Blvd. (Dundee Rd.), Northbrook, 847-564-5900
◩ City and suburban Japanese steakhouses that are still a "fun" "diversion" for those who "aren't tired" of communal tables and flashing knives; the "awesome hibachi steak" wins some praise and for big spenders there's $150 kobe beef at the Downtown locale; still, some sharp-edged critics point out that the chefs "can't perform like Benihana's."

Rose & Crown [S] ▽ 19 | 20 | 20 | $15

420 W. Belmont Ave. (Lake Shore Dr.), 773-248-6654

◪ An authentic British pub with an "excellent beer selection" and that even rarer find, "great English food", this Lakeview tavern is the right spot for a pint of Guinness and a plate of "unbelievable" fish 'n' chips; however, the initially impressed say the bloom is off this rose and it "used to be better."

Rose Angelis [S] 21 | 20 | 21 | $24

1314 W. Wrightwood Ave. (bet. Racine & Southport Aves.), 773-296-0081

■ Enthusiasts "love everything about" this "inexpensive" DePaul/Lakeview Italian, "a great neighborhood cafe" whose small, interlinked dining rooms create an "intimate and romantic" ambiance; the "homestyle cooking" is a hit, from the "rich pastas" all the way down to the "excellent desserts", including an "out-of-this-world bread pudding" covered in caramel sauce; P.S. "long waits" on weekends make regulars moan "will the crowds ever go away?"

Rosebud Cafe [S] 22 | 17 | 19 | $28

1500 W. Taylor St. (2 blocks east of Ashland Ave.), 312-942-1117

Rosebud of Naperville [S] 18 | 18 | 15 | $24

48 W. Chicago Ave. (Main St.), Naperville, 630-548-9800

Rosebud on Rush [S] 21 | 17 | 19 | $30

720 N. Rush St. (Superior St.), 312-266-6444

◪ "After three or four days, I was hungry again" is the tongue-in-cheek assessment of these "traditional Italians" where the "very good food", including a "chicken Vesuvio to die for", comes in "gluttonous" portions; some huff about "condescending" service, and others find them "too noisy" and rushed", but all in all, "you get your money's worth"; those with a preference say the West Taylor Street original remains "the best of the group."

Roxy Cafe [S] 19 | 18 | 19 | $22

626 Church St. (Orrington St.), Evanston, 847-864-6540

◪ A "slick", "nice-looking" North Shore Italian-American that's "very cosmopolitan for a college town"; its "small but comprehensive menu" features "moderately innovative" dishes and it's a "reliable" choice if you're in the area.

Rudi Fazuli's [S] – | – | – | M

2442 N. Clark St. (bet. Arlington Pl. & Fullerton Pkwy.), 773-388-0100

This Italian offshoot of Clara's Pasta di Casa in the Western 'burbs moved in mid-'98 to more spacious Lakeview digs – a vintage building with gorgeous oak trim interior and a large, above-street-level outdoor patio; "great bread" and "fresh pasta" are the favorites of regulars who assure us "the food is much better than the name."

Rudi's Wine Bar & Cafe S   21 | 16 | 19 | $28
2424 N. Ashland Ave. (Fullerton Pkwy.), 773-404-7834
■ "Smoky" North Side French bistro that's "like a secret club" for its fans; they applaud whitefish that "will make you melt" and a "great wine list at terrific prices"; depending on your mood or your companion, the interior's either "sultry" and "seductive" or "too dark."

Rupert's for Steaks   ▽ 22 | 20 | 21 | $38
1701 W. Golf Rd. (west of Algonquin Rd.), Rolling Meadows, 847-952-8555
■ Tucked into an office complex, this Northwest Suburban outpost may have a "strange location", but devotees declare that it's the equivalent of a "very good" "Downtown steakhouse in the 'burbs"; with its "cozy, clubby" "paneled" room and "quiet, efficient service", it's an ideal "haven for the expense-account diner."

Russell's Barbecue S⊅   18 | 11 | 14 | $11
1621 N. Thatcher Ave. (North Ave.), Elmwood Park, 708-453-7065
■ Those in the mood for "an authentic trip back to 1940" head for this "cheap", "noisy" West Suburban ribhouse where barbecued beef and a pork sandwich that "rules" are "not bad for Yankees"; some have a look inside and "prefer to take out", though, in summer, the outdoor picnic tables are pleasant enough.

Russian Palace S   14 | 17 | 16 | $26
24-26 E. Adams St. (bet. State St. & Wabash Ave.), 312-629-5353
☑ A Loop Russian handy to Symphony Center and the Art Institute that has a few royalist backers who tactfully endorse it as a "different" kind of lunch spot; proles, however, think the "pricey" offerings are "just fair."

Russian Tea Time S   20 | 19 | 20 | $28
77 E. Adams St. (bet. Michigan & Wabash Aves.), 312-360-0000
■ The star of the Loop's Russians is this "gem" of a "family restaurant", which features an "incredible variety" of "delicious" dishes; regulars "crave the carrot salad", praise the potato latkes and note that "the seafood platter and a shot of vodka makes a trip to the Art Institute complete"; a "joyful place", it has a "beautiful", samovar-filled dining room staffed by "very knowledgeable waiters."

RUTH'S CHRIS STEAK HOUSE   25 | 20 | 23 | $40
431 N. Dearborn St. (Hubbard St.), 312-321-2725
■ Chicago chauvinism takes a beating when confronted with this New Orleans–based cow palace in River North that, in the eyes of many, "beats any local steakhouse" with its "mouthwatering" porterhouse coated with melted butter and served on oven-hot platters ("love the sizzle"); there's also abundant appreciation for "great side dishes", "decadent desserts" and "top-notch" service.

Sabatino's ◗ S   20 | 17 | 20 | $26
4441 W. Irving Park Rd. (bet. Cicero Ave. & Pulaski Rd.), 773-283-8331
☒ A "cozy", "quiet", decades-old Northwest Sider that looks "the way an Italian restaurant is supposed to be", i.e. sporting a "big-booth setting" with a "nice piano bar"; the food's "old-fashioned but well prepared", especially the "wonderful veal", and there's "always something appealing on the menu"; dissenters, perhaps looking for some razzle-dazzle, find it "tired."

Sai Cafe S   23 | 14 | 17 | $25
2010 N. Sheffield Ave. (Armitage Ave.), 773-472-8080
☒ This Lincoln Park Japanese gets lots of votes for being among the "best in town" with a "standout", "inventive" sushi bar that's so popular regulars advise arriving "at least 90 minutes before you're really hungry"; the "very crowded and claustrophobic" interior may seem less than ideal, in which case "get it delivered or take out."

Salbute   – | – | – | M
20 E. First St. (bet. Garfield & Washington Sts.), Hinsdale, 630-920-8077
Diners say there are "nice presentations" of "unusual", "interesting Mexican" fare at this "quaint storefront", a West Suburban BYO yearling with a colorfully decorated dining room; the early reports are that it's "worth a trip", even if they "need to improve service."

Saloon, The S   20 | 18 | 19 | $36
Seneca Hotel, 200 E. Chestnut St. (1 block east of Michigan Ave.), 312-280-5454
☒ Opinions diverge on this Streeterville steakhouse, with fans finding it a pleasantly "quiet place for a good piece of meat", and critics countering that it's "so-so" and "expensive for what it is"; it does pull in a sizable convention crowd who apparently lean in its favor.

Salpicón S   22 | 17 | 20 | $33
1252 N. Wells St. (1½ blocks north of Division St.), 312-988-7811
■ "For exotic tequilas, this is your place" say cheerful disciples of this Old Town Mexican, a "colorful room" with "creative cuisine" that some say ranks "just below Frontera Grill", thanks to chef Priscila Satkoff, half of the husband-and-wife owner team; if the "beautiful", "tasty" food and "intimate atmosphere" aren't enough, there's also an award-winning wine list.

Salvatore's Ristorante S   18 | 17 | 17 | $26
525 W. Arlington Pl. (Clark St.), 773-528-1200
■ "Romantic" Italian, tucked into a "picturesque" Lincoln Park side street, that features "lovely, light creations with homemade pastas", a "quiet and inviting" atmosphere and live entertainment on weekends.

Santorini ◐ S
| 21 | 19 | 19 | $27 |

800 W. Adams St. (Halsted St.), 312-829-8820

■ This seafooder "with a Greek accent" gets plenty of support as "one of Greektown's best" for "unbelievable" red snapper and grilled octopus, and meat eaters can order up "superb lamb chops"; the "very pretty interior" – country decor with a wood-burning hearth – is a crowd-pleaser too.

Sarkis Grill S ⇄
| 15 | 9 | 18 | $10 |

2632 Grosse Point Rd. (Central Ave.), Evanston, 847-328-9703

■ The personable and outrageous owner Sarkis "is the show" at this venerable North Shore "dive with personality"; a "coming-of-age spot", it serves "great omelets" to "post-party" college students among others.

Savannah's
| 19 | 17 | 19 | $30 |

1156 W. Grand Ave. (Halsted St.), 312-666-9944

■ "Low country, high performance" is the verdict on this Southern stop on the Near West Side where the specialty is Carolina coastal cuisine served in a "fetching, comfortable room" with a cigar-friendly area in back; it may be "a repeat restaurant" if "inconsistency" issues can be resolved.

Savoy Truffle ⇄
| 22 | 12 | 19 | $26 |

1466 N. Ashland Ave. (bet. Division St. & North Ave.), 773-772-7530

■ "It feels like you're eating in someone's home" at this North Side BYO Eclectic, "a scruffy storefront" "oasis of fine cuisine" with a "lovable" chef-owner; it's "a real sleeper" and perhaps that's just as well, given the difficulty of getting a reservation; those who've sampled every dish say it "needs more frequent menu changes."

Sayat Nova S
| 19 | 15 | 18 | $21 |

157 E. Ohio St. (bet. Michigan Ave. & St. Clair St.), 312-644-9159
20 W. Golf Rd. (Mt. Prospect Ave.), Des Plaines, 847-296-1776

■ City and Northwest Suburban Middle Easterns with "the best lamb chops", "exotic couscous dishes" and lots of "vegetarian favorites served with special care"; prices are so low by Michigan Avenue standards that one devotee dubs the location "the jewel of the Mile."

Schulien's S
| 18 | 19 | 20 | $25 |

2100 W. Irving Park Rd. (Hoyne Ave.), 773-478-2100

■ North Side German-American "Chicago legend", in business for 112 years, where "old-fashioned" specialties such as Wiener schnitzel and planked whitefish are "always good", but probably secondary to the tableside magician who performs on request at the end of the meal; although the prestidigitator "can't make the tab disappear", he's an "entertaining" feature, especially "for the kids."

Scoozi! 🅂　　　20 20 19 $28
410 W. Huron St. (1½ blocks west of Orleans St.),
312-943-5900
☑ "Chicago's original yuppie Italian restaurant" is a "big
barn" in River North that "cranks the tourists through" on
weekends, plays to families on Sundays and pulls in young
professionals during the week; fans "love the antipasti
bar", "great people-watching" and "consistent-as-ever"
kitchen; naysayers dis it as "noisy" and "tired."

SEASONS 🅂　　　27 26 27 $59
Four Seasons Hotel, 120 E. Delaware Pl., 7th fl. (bet.
Michigan Ave. & Rush St.), 312-649-2349
■ "You feel you've arrived" when dining at this "lots of
moolah" Michigan Avenue hotel room where "wonderful
service", "beautiful decor" and Mark Baker's "delicious",
"innovative" New American food add up to a "first-class"
experience; while it makes a "wonderful anniversary
restaurant", surveyors say don't overlook the awe-inspiring
brunch that's among "the best in Chicago."

Seasons Cafe ◑🅂　　　24 23 24 $31
Four Seasons Hotel, 120 E. Delaware Pl., 7th fl. (bet.
Michigan Ave. & Rush St.), 312-649-2349
■ This nonsmoking adjunct to Seasons has a more casual
American menu, but the food is still "wonderful" and,
relatively speaking, represents a "good value"; surveyors
say the "comfy setting" is a "delightful refuge from the city's
bustle" or from high-powered shopping; it's also "a nice
place to have lunch with Mom", among other sweethearts.

1776　　　▽ 24 15 20 $34
397 Virginia St./Rte. 14 (bet. Dole & McHenry Aves.),
Crystal Lake, 815-356-1776
■ A "gourmet outpost in the Far Northwest suburbs" that
specializes in game and seafood, this Contemporary
American is labeled "a great surprise" that locals "should
thank their lucky stars" for; a "super" 5,000-bottle wine
inventory is impressive and better still, "the owner has the
knowledge to back it up"; while ambiance isn't a strong suit,
the "wonderful, wonderful" food more than compensates.

Shark Bar 🅂　　　▽ 17 19 15 $26
212 N. Canal St. (Lake St.), 312-559-9057
☑ While some opine that the "emphasis is on the bar and
[live] music" at this "cool", "funky", Southern–Soul Food
City West import and think an "upgrade in food caliber is
needed", pros protest, citing "decent", all-around vittles
highlighted by "fabulous sweet potato pie" and "great",
honey-dipped fried chicken.

SHAW'S CRAB HOUSE & BLUE CRAB LOUNGE S
| 23 | 19 | 21 | $35 |

21 E. Hubbard St. (½ block east of State St.), 312-527-2722

Shaw's Seafood Grill S | 20 | 15 | 19 | $28 |

660 W. Lake Cook Rd. (west of Waukegan Rd.), Deerfield, 847-948-1020

■ Surveyors applaud the "excellent fish", "orgasmic" lobster club sandwich, "great crab cakes" and "clubby atmosphere" of this Near North seafooder, saying it's among the "best" in the city; a boisterous contingent prefers the "fun" raw bar in the lounge to anything in the dining room; scores are lower for the North Suburban sequel, and some find the menu "too limited", but it's a "better value" than its sibling, especially the "bargain early bird."

Shiroi Hana S   ▽ | 21 | 10 | 17 | $18 |

3242 N. Clark St. (Belmont Ave.), 773-477-1652

■ "Don't tell anyone" beg fans of this Wrigleyville Japanese known for "very good sushi kept simple and inexpensive"; the "top-notch quality" means that, despite "run-down" surroundings, it gets "super crowded" with "long waits."

Shish Kabab House S | – | – | – | I |

9250 S. Harlem Ave. (92nd Pl.), Bridgeview, 708-599-4011

While it won't win any awards for speed, this dependable Suburban Southwest Middle Eastern offers juicy kebabs at a very attractive price; overall, a big plus for the area.

SIGNATURE ROOM AT THE 95TH S | 18 | 25 | 19 | $39 |

John Hancock Ctr., 875 N. Michigan Ave., 95th fl. (bet. Chestnut St. & Delaware Ave.), 312-787-9596

☑ Since, "on a clear day", they're probably heading to the observation deck of the Hancock anyway, "bring out-of-towners for lunch" (specifically, the "bargain buffet") to this recently renovated 95th-floor New American; while others favor Sunday brunch as "the best time to go", most see more in the "glorious" view than in the food.

Singha S | 17 | 13 | 16 | $15 |

340 N. Clark St. (Kinzie St.), 312-467-0300

■ This River North Thai is a popular lunch destination for Loop office workers who appreciate the "amazingly speedy service" and "cheap" prices; while the "good", if "typical", renditions don't make anyone gush, the feeling is that it's a reliable place to go to when the boss is watching the clock.

Sixty-Five S | 18 | 7 | 13 | $16 |

336 N. Michigan Ave. (Wacker Dr.), 312-372-0306
2414 S. Wentworth Ave. (24th Pl.), 312-225-7060

☑ There are mixed feelings among surveyors about these Chinatown and Loop spots, which get plaudits for "top-notch Chinese seafood", but demerits for "no atmosphere at all" and a "not-too-friendly" staff; N.B. the Downtown location is primarily a carry-out/delivery option.

Slice of Life S🚭 | 16 | 13 | 17 | $17 |

4120 W. Dempster Ave. (1½ blocks west of Crawford Ave.), Skokie, 847-674-2021

■ "The only kosher restaurant I've ever found with portobellos" is this North Suburban with "exceptionally friendly waitresses" and a "wide menu" ranging from fish, pizza, pasta and veggie options to the occasional Tex-Mex interpretations.

Smith & Wollensky S | – | – | – | E |

318 N. State St. (Chicago River), 312-670-9900

An important New York import that's already hitting the high-water mark in River North, thanks to aged-on-the-premises meat, a winning wine list and a beautiful riverside location; on hand is veteran Chicago chef Hans Aeschbacher and S&W's highly acclaimed signature crackling pork shank.

Smoke Daddy ●S | – | – | – | M |

1804 W. Division St. (bet. Ashland & Damen Aves.), 773-772-6656

"Finger lickin' good" rave fans of this West Side rib shack, which a few consider "the best BBQ in town"; no-cover blues and jazz is a big plus as well, but "huge portions" of 'cue are what bring the crowds by.

Sorriso | – | – | – | M |

321 N. Clark St. (Kinzie St.), 312-644-0283

A visit to this River North Italian "always impresses visitors", particularly if you snag an outdoor table on the riverside patio; while the food gets a few nods ("great for lunch") and some say it's "romantic" inside, it's the "great views" outside that garner the most attention.

Souk ●S | – | – | – | M |

1552 N. Milwaukee Ave. (bet. Damen & North Aves.), 773-227-9110

Not your ordinary hummus hut, this newcomer features what the owner calls "tribal cuisine", which encompasses Middle Eastern, North African and Eastern Mediterranean dishes; the nomads of Wicker Park and neighboring Bucktown seem happy to have this oasis around.

SOUL KITCHEN S | 23 | 20 | 18 | $28 |

1576 N. Milwaukee Ave. (Damen Ave.), 773-342-9742

■ "Trendy", "funky" Southern-accented Wicker Parker whose motto – 'loud food, spicy music' – "sums it up very well"; expect an eclectic crowd encompassing everyone from theater directors to "dyed-hair boys in skirts"; yet, even with all the characters, it's Monique King's "vibrant" food that steals the show; some wail "if only they took reservations", but if you can't stand the wait (up to two hours on weekends), stay out of the kitchen.

South Gate Cafe S　　　　18 | 18 | 18 | $25
655 Forest Ave. (Deer Path Rd.), Lake Forest, 847-234-8800
☑ "You'll feel like you're at a country inn" at this North
Shore American, a charming Downtown Lake Forest spot
whose traditional menu makes room for "imaginatively
prepared food", particularly "great desserts"; some maintain
that it's "losing ground", though optimists note it "still offers
a nice outdoor setting" via its tree-filled patio.

Southport City Saloon S　　　15 | 15 | 16 | $17
2548 N. Southport Ave. (Fullerton Pkwy.), 773-975-6110
☑ "Don't challenge the chef – stick with the burgers" at
this DePaul-area pub where "the outdoor garden" in
summer and the "fireplace in winter" are both appealing.

SPAGO S　　　　　　　24 | 22 | 22 | $42
520 N. Dearborn St. (Grand Ave.), 312-527-3700
☑ Chicagoans have embraced Wolfgang Puck's satellite
operation and say it "actually deserves its hype", thanks
to "puckishly delightful" (ouch) Californian cuisine and
"excellent service with no attitude"; insiders advise "try
the smoked salmon pizza" (it isn't always on the menu, but
you can order it) and other "witty, wood-fired" pies, and
check out the grill room, which has a less pricey menu, but
offers Puck signatures such as meat loaf; the main dining
room is "beautiful" and a "great show", but very "noisy."

Spasso S　　　　　　▽ 21 | 19 | 20 | $32
*614 W. Liberty St./Rte. 176 (1 block west of Rte. 12),
Wauconda, 847-526-4215*
■ Wauconda say this Far Northwest outpost is "proof that
the suburbs can deliver good Italian cooking", especially
the "wonderful" signature dish, *bocconcini alla florentina*
(crêpes with spinach and ricotta, topped with mozzarella);
tough to please Chicagoans begrudgingly admit it's "pretty
good for being almost in Wisconsin."

Spavone Seven Hills S　　▽ 22 | 19 | 22 | $25
222 Greenwood Rd. (Milwaukee Ave.), Glenview, 847-967-1222
■ A 35-year-old North Suburban favorite, this local Sicilian
offers "reliable" food and a "lively" ambiance that includes a
karaoke bar, making it "great for parties or showers."

SPIAGGIA S　　　　　　25 | 26 | 24 | $52
*One Magnificent Mile Bldg., 980 N. Michigan Ave., 2nd fl.
(Oak St.), 312-280-2750*
■ Scores are as high as the cost of entrees at this luxury
Italian that's "by far the city's best"; Paul Bartolotta's
pastas are "phenomenal" ("the tortellini can make you cry"),
but you "can't get a bad meal" regardless of what you order;
the "romantic", "vibrant dining room" is "beautiful", as are
its "spectacular views" of the lake and Michigan Avenue;
add "exquisite service" that is "dedicated to detail" and you
have "a great place to impress whomever you're with."

SPRUCE　　　　　　　　　23　23　23　$49
230 E. Ontario St. (bet. Fairbanks & St. Clair Sts.), 312-642-3757
☑ The departure in mid-'98 of award-winning chef Keith
Luce from this well-received Streeterville Contemporary
American leaves surveyors hoping the "innovative" and
"artful" food will continue; the "gorgeous room" and
remarkable wine list remain unchanged, of course,
and the minority who found Luce's cooking "contrived"
may be eager for a fresh face.

Standard India 🅂　　　　▽ 15　5　11　$14
917 W. Belmont Ave. (Clark St.), 773-929-1123
■ "Try to ignore the decor" ("bubblegum pink arches")
when dining at this North Side BYO Indian that offers
"good", "bargain-priced buffets" at lunch and dinner;
transplanted New Yorkers say it "reminds me of Sixth Street."

Stanley's Kitchen & Tap 🅂　　16　13　15　$16
1970 N. Lincoln Ave. (Armitage Ave.), 312-642-0007
■ Those who dismiss this Lincoln Parker's offerings as mere
"bar food" are drowned out by others who appreciate
American "comfort" fare at "ridiculously cheap prices"; the
"great brunch" draws "a wonderful mix" of "singles,
families" and "baseball hat–wearing college grads."

Starfish Cafe & Raw Bar 🅂　　21　18　19　$32
1856 W. North Ave. (Wolcott Ave.), 773-395-3474
☑ This "exposed brick" Bucktown seafooder, with Southern,
Californian and Caribbean influences, attracts "trendy
thirtysomethings" with "innovative" dishes and "fabulous"
desserts; despite a good rating, there are scattered gripes
about "arrogant" service, and Saturdays tend to be hectic.

Star of Siam 🅂　　　　　19　14　16　$16
11 E. Illinois St. (State St.), 312-670-0100
☑ A "cheap", "very good and reliable" River North Thai
with a "convenient location" and "quick lunch" service to
handle the "busy" crowds; if you're chained to your desk,
there's "excellent delivery."

Stefani's 🅂　　　　　　21　16　20　$28
1418 W. Fullerton Pkwy. (Southport Ave.), 773-348-0111
☑ Dining on the "terrific" outdoor patio is "like Italy in the
summer", only this "reliable Italian eatery" is in the DePaul
area; recommended on the "broad menu" are homemade
pastas and the chicken Vesuvio.

Stevie B's 🅂　　　　　▽ 19　7　13　$18
*1953 N. Clybourn Ave. (bet. Armitage & Racine Aves.),
773-327-7750*
■ "It's true – great ribs can be found at a strip mall" marvel
surveyors over this Clybourn Corridor rib house; "arrive
famished" to take full advantage of the portions or take
them home and "be as messy as you want"; either way,
you'll fill up: "I credit Stevie B's for the size of my thighs."

Stir Crazy Cafe S
17 | 17 | 16 | $17

186 N. Northbrook Ct. Mall (bet. Skokie Blvd. & Waukegan Rd.), Northbrook, 847-562-4800
105 Oak Brook Ctr. Mall (Rte. 83 & 22nd St.), Oak Brook, 630-575-0155

☒ "Some people are artists at loading their bowl" at these North and West Suburban, serve-yourself Asian stir-fries that offer a "wonderful choice of sauces" in a "fun, if somewhat chaotic", atmosphere; boosters observe that mall locations make them handy "after shopping or a movie", while dissenters say "cute idea" but "disappointing" quality.

Strega Nona S
18 | 17 | 17 | $26

3747 N. Southport Ave. (Addison St.), 773-244-0990

☒ A "noisy", "bustling", "see-and-be-scene" Wrigleyville-area Italian (named for the grandmother/witch of children's stories) that "tries to be different" with "eclectic" pastas; surveyors are in accord about the "great bruschetta", but otherwise there are "hits and misses" (menu "reads much better than it tastes") and "uneven service"; N.B. scenes from *My Best Friend's Wedding* were filmed here.

Su Casa S
15 | 16 | 16 | $20

49 E. Ontario St. (1½ blocks west of Michigan Ave.), 312-943-4041

☒ While it "still hangs in there", this near–Magnificent Mile Mexican, which benefits from "a fortunate location" ("good lunchtime place"), earns few raves for its "generic" food; however, "after a golden margarita, who cares?"

Sunset S
– | – | – | M

1520 N. Damen Ave. (bet. Milwaukee & North Aves.), 773-772-7414

This sister property to Jane's in Bucktown brings a touch of Californian cuisine to its Wicker Park neighborhood; the simple but artfully decorated storefront is part of a small shopping center so it offers something even more rare in this part of town – free parking.

Suntory S
▽ 21 | 22 | 20 | $36

11 E. Huron St. (bet. State St. & Wabash Ave.), 312-664-3344

☒ At lunch and dinner, this River North Japanese pulls in a male-dominated business clientele that's drawn to "excellent food", "knowledgeable servers" and an atmosphere that evokes "elegance in every respect"; but a few refuse to bow – "not worth the price."

Suprarossa S
16 | 14 | 15 | $18

210 E. Ohio St. (1 block east of Michigan Ave.), 312-587-0030
4256 N. Central Ave. (bet. Irving Park Rd. & Montrose Ave.), 773-736-5828
7309 W. Lawrence Ave. (1 block west of Harlem Ave.), Harwood Heights, 708-867-4641 ☾

Suprarossa (Cont.)
6913 N. Milwaukee Ave. (bet. Devon & Touhy Aves.), Niles,
847-647-0036
6301 Purchase Dr. (Rte. 53), Woodridge, 708-852-1000
☑ City and suburban spots with full-scale Italian menus,
though most focus on the "excellent wood-oven pizzas"
and "substantial portions" ("salad comes in a big bowl");
bashers say other than pies, "nothing special" here.

Sylviano's Ristorante   ▽ 19 20 20 $29
2809 Butterfield Rd. (Myers Rd.), Oak Brook, 630-571-3600
☑ Located in the back of an office complex, this "hard to
find" "West Suburban gathering spot" is dubbed the area's
"best Northern Italian" by business lunchers on expense
accounts, and a "beautiful retreat" by after-fivers who
like the "sexy atmosphere."

Szechwan East S   19 16 16 $21
340 E. Ohio St. (bet. Fairbanks & McClurg Cts.), 312-255-9200
☑ "Very good" East of Michigan Avenue Chinese with a
"lavish" lunch buffet that fans think is "the best deal in
town"; while dissenters tag it as "average", in an area
with few Chinese options, this is one of the better ones.

Szechwan House S   ▽ 19 17 17 $24
625 N. Michigan Ave. (Ontario St.), 312-642-3900
■ For the benefit of surveyors who "find all the Szechwan
locations confusing", this is the below-street-level Michigan
Avenue spot that's "dependable"; it offers "large servings"
and a lunch buffet with a "good range of choices."

Szechwan North S   ▽ 17 14 14 $18
Glenbrook Mktpl. Shopping Ctr., 2857 Pfingsten Rd.
(Willow Rd.), Glenview, 847-272-0007
☑ North Suburban Chinese that's a "surprise in suburbia"
to those who insist the "good quality" food allows them to
"taste all the ingredients"; naysayers think "it seems to be
coasting" and find it "just ok."

Szechwan Palace S   ▽ 17 15 17 $18
1629 Chicago Ave. (bet. Church & Davis Sts.), Evanston,
847-475-2500
☑ North Shore regional Chinese drawing mixed comments:
"better-than-average" vs. "run-of-the-mill"; it's yet another
choice for a "luncheon buffet at reasonable prices."

Szechwan Restaurant S   ▽ 16 15 14 $24
Olympia Fields Shopping Ctr., 3452 E. Vollmer Rd.
(Governor's Hwy.), Olympia Fields, 708-481-1770
☑ A handy location at a busy Southwest Suburban
intersection boosts attendance at this regional Chinese,
though the "friendly staff" and "broad selection" of dishes
certainly help too; regulars recommend the lunch buffet
over a "sort of tired" dinner menu, and some gripe "they
haven't changed anything since they opened."

Tagine S   – – – M
1629 N. Halsted St. (½ block north of North Ave.), 312-573-1515
Moroccan newcomer that adds a bit of exotic flavor to the
Halsted Street theater district; the lavishly decorated space
features a lounge and bar on the first floor (close enough for
an intermission gulp) and a smoke-free dining room upstairs.

Taj Mahal S   – – – M
*Dania Ctr., 14812 S. La Grange Rd. (bet. 148th & 149th Sts.),
Orland Park, 708-460-5800*
This little-known Suburban Southwest Indian may make a
bigger splash now that it has a liquor license (wine and beer
only); the few surveyors who've visited find it "excellent",
appreciate its budget-friendly lunch and dinner menus and
say "too bad it's so far out."

TALLGRASS S   28 23 26 $58
1006 S. State St. (10th St.), Lockport, 815-838-5566
■ "Charming [Victorian] period decor" and "service so
unobtrusive it's almost scary" are two highlights of this
far-flung New French, the sophisticated sibling of Public
Landing in historic Lockport; while it's a "long drive",
Robert Burcenski's "outstanding" cooking is "creativity
personified" and so, as "the suburban [restaurant
equivalent of] Everest", it's "worth the trip."

Tanglewood S   17 18 17 $31
*Laundry Mall, 566 Chestnut St. (Spruce St.), Winnetka,
847-441-4600*
☑ Devotees of this North Shore American bistro "can't
understand why it isn't busier" given chef Daniel Kelch's
cooking and a "pleasant atmosphere" that includes a "nice
outdoor patio"; those who shrug "just so-so", with decor
that "lacks pizazz", think they know, but the converted are
content to keep this "sleeper" to themselves.

Tania's ●S   ▽ 16 19 17 $26
*2659 N. Milwaukee Ave. (bet. Diversey Pkwy. & Kedzie Ave.),
773-235-7120*
■ A Northwest Side supper club that surveyors recommend
primarily "for dancing" – the "fast" salsa music is ideal
for working off the "diverse menu" of Cuban and Spanish
cuisine; if you don't care to shake it on a full stomach, the
kitchen is open into the wee hours on weekends.

Tapas Barcelona S   18 17 16 $23
*1615 Chicago Ave. (bet. Church & Davis Sts.), Evanston,
847-866-9900*
☑ North Shore diners appreciate this Evanston Spanish as
"a good choice for tapas without having to go Downtown"
and "a fun place to people-watch"; tapas fans counter –
"predictable" and "not as interesting" as competitors.

Tarantino's 🅂   18 │ 19 │ 18 │ $26 │
1112 W. Armitage Ave. (Seminary St.), 773-871-2929
■ "Convenient", "comfortable" Lincoln Park Italian from a
former partner in the now defunct Jim & Johnny's that's
"rapidly becoming a favorite" as a "nice spot for dinner"
in the nabe; the "very good" offerings include "great"
grilled calamari and risotto.

Tavern in the Town   ▽ 23 │ 24 │ 23 │ $35 │
519 N. Milwaukee Ave. (bet. Cook & Lake Rds.), Libertyville,
847-367-5755
■ Considered by some "the most romantic restaurant in the
Chicago area", this Northwest Suburban Contemporary
American is a "real sleeper" that combines "classy", "old-
world" "Victorian charm" with "outstanding" food and
"the best wine list in the 'burbs"; P.S. you get a "great
lunch for the money" here too.

Tavern on Rush ◑🅂   ‒ │ ‒ │ ‒ │ E │
1031 N. Rush St. (Bellevue Pl.), 312-664-9600
This Rush Street steakhouse is a step-sibling to other Phil
Stefani ventures (Tuscany, Riva, Lino's), but it's the beef,
not the pedigree, that keeps the two-story, clubby space
packed daily; in summer, the outdoor cafe (great people-
watching) may be your best bet.

Taylor Brewing Company 🅂   ▽ 14 │ 16 │ 15 │ $18 │
200 E. Fifth Ave. (Washington Ave.), Naperville, 630-717-8000
▣ Most think this "casual", "interesting-looking" West
Suburban brewpub offers solid suds and "excellent ribs";
however, there are scattered complaints that the much-
acclaimed hamburgers are "good" but a tad overhyped.

Taza 🅂⊅   ▽ 16 │ 11 │ 12 │ $10 │
39 S. Wabash Ave. (Monroe St.), 312-425-9988
■ "What fast food should be" is how surveyors summarize
this Loop International whose specialty is marinated-and-
grilled chicken; it's a "healthy alternative" with "high-
quality" offerings, including the "town's best mashed
potatoes"; the easily bored think it "needs to expand its
menu for repeaters."

Tecalitlan ◑🅂   19 │ 15 │ 19 │ $16 │
1814 W. Chicago Ave. (bet. Ashland & Damen Aves.),
773-384-4285
■ For "cilantro-heavy", "killer burritos" and "real spicy
salsa" at "cheap prices", step up to this Ukrainian Village–
area Mexican storefront that's a "neighborhood favorite."

Thai Borrahn 🅂   ‒ │ ‒ │ ‒ │ I │
(fka Thai Room)
16 E. Huron St. (State St.), 312-440-6003
A cramped but prettily decorated River North Thai serving
better-than-average spicy fare; it's a handy lunch spot for
area office workers, though evenings are less crowded.

Thai Classic 🅂 ▽ 21 | 15 | 18 | $17
3332 N. Clark St. (bet. Belmont Ave. & Roscoe St.), 773-404-2000
■ Cognoscenti think "'Classic' was a good choice for the name" of this "dependable" Wrigleyville BYO Thai where "you can sit on the floor" (or in chairs) and enjoy "great deal" weekend buffets at lunch and dinner; "street parking may be impossible", but the food is "worth the exercise."

Thai 55th 🅂 ▽ 15 | 7 | 11 | $12
1607 E. 55th St. (Lake Park Ave.), 773-363-7119
☑ "When you work on the South Side and feel like Thai, this works" say resigned patrons of this "good value" BYO; detractors think "dreary institutional decor" and "poor service" mean it "would never survive out of Hyde Park."

Thai Little Home Cafe 🅂 ▽ 21 | 9 | 19 | $17
4747 N. Kedzie Ave. (Lawrence Ave.), 773-478-3944
■ An "always-satisfying" Albany Park Thai short on looks but long on value, offering "a great deal and a great meal" at lunch and a staff that's "very accommodating to special requests"; N.B. dinner is served Friday–Saturday only.

Thai Star Cafe 🅂 19 | 9 | 14 | $14
660 N. State St. (Erie St.), 312-951-1196
■ "Ignore the Formica" and focus on the "authentic" food at this "shabby" BYO Thai with "excellent soups and pad Thai"; it's "reliable" for Near North workers and take-out types looking for "solo dining in front of the TV."

Three Happiness ◗🅂 18 | 10 | 14 | $17
2130 S. Wentworth Ave. (Cermak Rd.), 312-791-1228
209 W. Cermak Rd. (Wentworth Ave.), 312-842-1964
☑ "Chinatown's cornerstones" are "huge", sprawling ventures that get raves for their "very crowded" dim sum brunch ("arrive early"); the rest of the menu is characterized as just "adequate" and some argue they "need a broom."

302 West ▽ 25 | 23 | 23 | $46
302 W. State St. (3rd St.), Geneva, 630-232-9302
■ Located in a "lovely" refurbished bank building, this "outstanding" Far West Suburban New American offers a "sophisticated menu" of "innovative cooking", a massive choice of desserts made on premises and an award-winning wine list; live music and the "watchful eye of hostess/co-owner Catherine Findlay" add to the atmosphere; overall, "bank on good food and an empty piggy bank."

312 Chicago 🅂 – | – | – | M
Hotel Allegro, 136 N. La Salle St. (Randolph St.), 312-696-2420
Handsome, Italian-accented hotel dining room that's a capable Loop newcomer; its talented chef (Dean Zanella, ex Grappa) and budget-friendly menu pulls in a financial-district crowd at lunch and a pre-theater throng at night; N.B. the brunch menu on Saturday and Sunday is an unusual feature for the area.

Thyme 🅂   – | – | – | M
464 N. Halsted St. (bet. Grand & Milwaukee Aves.),
312-226-4300
Chef-partner John Bubala formerly manned the stove at
Marché and much of that restaurant's see-and-be-seen
crowd has taken a shine to his West-of-Loop effort – a
regional French with Spanish influences that also offers a
plant-filled outdoor patio in summer; trendies also slink over
to Thyme's attached Sinabar lounge for dessert.

Tien Tsin 🅂   ▽ 18 | 14 | 17 | $17
7018 N. Clark St. (Touhy Ave.), 773-761-2820
☑ "Throwback" Chinese on the Far North Side whose
supporters find it "great for a BYO", although many miss
the defunct North Shore location; critics say it "needs a
little fine tuning" and that quality "varies."

Tiffin 🅂   ▽ 22 | 20 | 18 | $20
2536 W. Devon Ave. (3 blocks west of Western Ave.),
773-338-2143
■ The few surveyors who know this Devon-district Indian
located on a decor-challenged restaurant row call it a "style
contender" with a "terrific, upscale setting"; "excellent"
food, including a "wonderful cheap lunch buffet", and
"attentive" service "with extra touches" make this
operation a "favorite."

Tilli's 🅂   14 | 18 | 15 | $20
1952 N. Halsted St. (½ block south of Armitage Ave.),
773-325-0044
☑ This "yuppie spot in the 'hood" (that's the Lincoln Park
'hood) has an Eclectic menu with a "wide, if not bizarre,
range" of global eats and a "hip" but "cozy" atmosphere
("nice fireplace"); while the food rating seems to support
those who think it's "ambitious, but lacking", a handful of
comments indicate there are some "tasty" choices.

Timbers Charhouse 🅂   16 | 16 | 17 | $24
Crossroads Shopping Ctr., 295 Skokie Valley Rd. (bet.
Clavey & Lake Cook Rds.), Highland Park, 847-831-1400
☑ A "decent" North Shore seafooder/steakhouse where
diners go "for the fish and generous portions and not the
decor or style"; naysayers say "nothing is better than good
here" and find it "overpriced", though some concede it's
"ok for what it's supposed to be."

Tokyo Marina 🅂   ▽ 20 | 13 | 17 | $18
5058-60 N. Clark St. (Carmen Ave.), 773-878-2900
■ "Relaxed neighborhood" Japanese in Edgewater that's
barely on the radar screen of most surveyors; those who
have it in scope declare it "highly reliable" for "good
tempura", "super sushi" and "udons that are udicious",
which we interpret as a compliment.

Tomboy [S] 21 | 17 | 20 | $28
5402 N. Clark St. (Balmoral Ave.), 773-907-0636
■ Andersonville BYO Eclectic that serves a "hip crowd" so diverse that "watching the clientele is a kick"; the "ambitious kitchen" is pretty lively too, turning out "offbeat" dishes, such as "delightful" porcupine shrimp, proffered by "witty servers" who contribute to the "cheerful, relaxed" atmosphere; some quibble that it's "not spectacular" and "not quite there", but fans insist it's "trying hard" and "sure to be a winner."

Tommy Nevin's Pub ☾ [S] 16 | 16 | 17 | $18
1450 Sherman Ave. (Lake St.), Evanston, 847-869-0450
■ To "fill a void for the old country", head to this North Shore Irish-American where "good burgers", "great salmon salad" and "the best corned beef in town" combine with Gaelic "warmth and open arms" to create a "fun place to visit" no matter where your grandparents hailed from; its proximity to Northwestern means it's "teeming with college kids" – especially "in mid-March" and when there's live entertainment.

Tony Spavone's Ristorante [S] ▽ 20 | 17 | 19 | $26
266 W. Lake St. (Springfield Dr.), Bloomingdale, 630-529-3154
◪ "Go to hear Tony sing" is the recommendation from those who applaud the crooning owner of this Suburban Northwest Italian where a "fun evening" includes serenades and "good, old-fashioned" food prepared with a "heavy garlic hand"; however, those not so in tune with the kitchen's handiwork appraise it as "average."

Topo Gigio Ristorante [S] 21 | 18 | 19 | $27
1516 N. Wells St. (1 block south of North Ave.), 312-266-9355
■ "As close to Italy as you can get without buying a ticket" rave supporters of this "consistently fine" Old Town trattoria with "perfectly textured" pastas and a garden so pretty that some declare "outdoors, si – indoors, grazie, no"; it's "a favorite with the twentysomething crowd" and those heading to Second City a block away.

TOPOLOBAMPO 27 | 24 | 25 | $43
445 N. Clark St. (bet. Hubbard & Illinois Sts.), 312-661-1434
■ Rick Bayless' dressier, pricier sibling of the Frontera Grill (in the same River North building) is "reason enough to live in Chicago" say civic-boosting boasters who are proud to call this "best Mexican in the country" their own; a recent expansion has relieved the "cramped space" somewhat, but made it no easier to secure reservations for a "great experience" that "never disappoints" locals or their "out-of-town guests"; for those who "can't wait to go back", much of the menu changes bi-weekly.

Toque ◑ 🔄   – | – | – | E
816 W. Randolph St. (½ block west of Halsted St.), 312-666-1100
A noisy, stylish yearling on the West Randolph Street corridor that offers skillful French-accented Contemporary American cooking by Mark Chmielewski; while you may get trampled by the crowds before a Bulls game, other times are less hectic; P.S. everybody orders the warm chocolate cake.

Toulouse on the Park   20 | 23 | 21 | $40
2140 N. Lincoln Park W. (bet. Dickens St. & Webster Ave.), 773-665-9071
☑ The "beautiful", Versailles-inspired decor "outshines the food" at this Lincoln Park French that gets votes for "the most romantic restaurant in town", even if minimalists think the gilt and mirrors are "a tad overboard"; feelings are split over the kitchen as well – "wonderful" and "excellent" vs. "average" and "overpriced"; however, don't Toulouse faith, because everyone agrees its Cognac Room next door is a "great piano bar" and there's no cover for dinner guests.

Trader Vic's 🔄   17 | 21 | 18 | $29
Palmer House, 17 E. Monroe St. (bet. State St. & Wabash Ave.), 312-726-7500
☑ This "touristy" Polynesian chain's Loop link inside the Palmer House offers an "average" buffet, but froufrouphiles love the "mai tais that lure you back" and think a visit makes a "great change of pace."

Trattoria Dinotto · 🔄   20 | 15 | 20 | $26
163 W. North Ave. (Wells St.), 312-787-3345
■ "Great things do come in small packages" assure appreciators of this Old Town Italian, a "friendly storefront" with "excellent pastas" and a "terrific" staff; but what some say is "cozy and charming", others call "cramped"; we hear the Valentine's Day decor is a sight to behold.

Trattoria Gianni 🔄   21 | 15 | 19 | $28
1711 N. Halsted St. (1 block north of North Ave.), 312-266-1976
■ Recent remodeling hasn't improved the decor scores at this Halsted Italian, indicating, perhaps, that surveyors are too busy enjoying Gianni Delisi's "tasty" preparations to notice; it's "always a pleasant experience" for pre-theater diners headed for the Steppenwolf or Royal George.

Trattoria No. 10   23 | 21 | 21 | $34
10 N. Dearborn St. (bet. Madison & Washington Sts.), 312-984-1718
☑ "You'll impress your clients" at this Loop Italian that pulls in a professional clientele at lunch and a big pre-theater throng in the early evening; despite scattered gripes that it's "still a basement", most think the dining room is a "subterranean delight" that serves as home to the "best" raviolis, including a "to-die-for" butternut squash version; P.S. bar flies recommend the "awesome happy hour fare."

Trattoria Parma S
| 19 | 17 | 20 | $30 |

400 N. Clark St. (Kinzie St.), 312-245-9933
☑ The jury's still out on this rustic Italian, a River North sibling of Vinci; supporters call it a "rising star" that serves a "yummy garlic spread" and an "interesting variety" of dishes so "everyone will find something they like"; the more cautious venture that "the potential seems to be there."

Trattoria Pizzeria Roma S
| 20 | 15 | 18 | $25 |

1535 N. Wells St. (½ block south of North Ave.), 312-664-7907
☑ Chicago's first trattoria still packs them into close quarters in Old Town, indicating that it remains an "excellent value" 12 years after opening; while the Italian menu is not as modern as it once seemed, the food is still "really tasty."

Tre Kronor S⛶
| ▽ | 24 | 17 | 23 | $16 |

3258 W. Foster Ave. (bet. Kedzie & Kimball Aves.), 773-267-9888
■ Albany Park BYO Scandinavian that's "just plain delightful" for an "intimate" breakfast, lunch or dinner, though the morning is a favorite because of the "best Swedish pancakes in town"; admirers add: "don't miss the meatball sandwich" or the lemon tart and custard.

TRIO S
| 27 | 25 | 27 | $67 |

1625 Hinman Ave. (Davis St.), Evanston, 847-733-8746
■ This "amazing" North Shore Eclectic provides "one of the greatest culinary experiences you will ever have" thanks to "outstanding" service, "continually creative" cooking and artistic presentations so "visually striking" they look like "Cirque du Soleil on a plate"; a few claim that it's "fading from glory", but the majority thinks it's still a surefire "winner" "for special occasions", and if you can handle the "expensive" tab, try the "to-die-for" dégustation menu.

Trocadero S
| – | – | – | M |

1750 N. Clark St. (½ block north of La Salle St.), 312-932-1750
The sibling of Hudson Club, this Lincoln Park newcomer resembles a European cafe, from its Parisian Metro stop entrance to its Continental bistro menu; with 38 wines by the glass, it's no surprise that patrons like to sit and sip here.

Tsunami S
| 21 | 21 | 16 | $31 |

1160 N. Dearborn St. (½ block south of Division St.), 312-642-9911
☑ Near North Japanese that wows the younger crowd (and irks traditionalists) with its nightclubby, "sleek, stark decor" that includes a "chic sake bar" upstairs; beyond the "great" ambiance is a "solid" sushi menu.

Tucci Benucch S
| 18 | 19 | 18 | $22 |

900 N. Michigan Ave., 5th level (Walton St.), 312-266-2500
☑ Shop-'til-you-drop types are grateful for this "cute", "Disneyland"-ish Italian in a Michigan Avenue mall; most think the menu's "a whole step up from fast food", with "superb pizzas" and "great angel hair pasta", but bashers think, other than "convenient" location, it's "nothing special."

Tufano's Vernon Park Tap [S] ⊄ 20 | 12 | 18 | $19
1073 W. Vernon Park Pl. (Taylor St.), 312-733-3393
■ This "down-to-earth spot" in the Tri-Taylor area is "the way Italian restaurants should be", assuming your definitive version includes "good, homestyle cooking", "reasonable prices" and a "fun" crowd", with "cops, hockey players and [owner] Joey keeping everyone moving", especially before United Center events.

Tuscany [S] 23 | 19 | 19 | $31
3700 N. Clark St. (Waveland Ave.), 773-404-7700
1014 W. Taylor St. (Morgan St.), 312-829-1990 ◐
1415 W. 22nd St. (Rte. 83), Oak Brook, 630-990-1993
■ "Huge portions of extremely well-prepared food" are the draw at this city and suburban troika of rustic Italians, which are aided by smart locations – one store is near United Center, another is steps from Wrigley Field and the third sits in the less-competitive western 'burbs; insiders recommend "anything from the wood-burning oven."

Twilight ◐ [S] ⊄ ▽ 17 | 8 | 12 | $17
1924 W. Division St. (Damen Ave.), 773-862-8757
■ Wicker Park American that pulls in locals who appreciate the "casual attitude" and Katherine August's "imaginative cooking"; some gripe that the menu is too "limited" and that the decor "could use serious help", but wait-times suggest August is doing something right; a liquor license is in the works, but as of press time it was still BYO.

Twin Anchors ◐ [S] 21 | 13 | 17 | $21
1655 N. Sedgwick St. (1 block north of North Ave.), 312-266-1616
■ Surveyors swear by the ribs ("would make a vegetarian think twice") and swear at the long waits – "get there early" or "get takeout" – at this "crowded" Old Town "grungy bar" that's been a barbecue "favorite" for over 60 years; P.S. don't forget to crank up the "great jukebox."

Twisted Lizard [S] 16 | 15 | 14 | $17
1964 N. Sheffield Ave. (Armitage Ave.), 773-929-1414
◪ A Lincoln Park Tex-Mex stop that gets as many comments for its "intriguing basement setting" and "lively", "cheery atmosphere" as it does for its "average" food; it's a local haven that some deride as a "yuppie kennel", but "if you can stomach the J. Crewsers", this "fun, little hideout" with "killer margaritas" just might be your cup of tequila.

Il Jack's Italian [S] ▽ 21 | 19 | 18 | $29
(fka Colucci's)
1758 W. Grand Ave. (bet. Ashland & Damen Aves.), 312-421-7565
■ Formerly known as Colucci's, this East Village Italian (with an emphasis on steaks) strikes some as "a gem and a treat"; while others "can't understand all the fuss", they will allow "it's surely consistent."

Udupi Palace S
∇ | 21 | 10 | 14 | $13 |

2543 W. Devon Ave. (3 blocks west of Western Ave.),
773-338-2152

■ The word 'Palace' might be stretching things in describing this "unassuming" Indian-Vegetarian where it's best to "ignore the decor [and] focus on the samosas" and "heavenly dosai"; it gets some votes for best Indian on the Devon Avenue strip, but others warn that the "enchanting food" is "for spice lovers only."

Uncle Julio's Hacienda S
| 17 | 18 | 16 | $21 |

855 W. North Ave. (Clybourn Ave.), 312-266-4222

☑ Kids "watch the tortilla machine for hours" at this "large, commercial" Clybourn Corridor Tex-Mex serving "generous portions" of "simple, straightforward" food at "reasonable prices"; while many prefer to hang at the bar for the "great frozen swirl drinks" and chips and salsa, on super-crowded Fridays you may have no choice – there's no reserving.

Uncle Tannous S
| 17 | 13 | 17 | $23 |

2626 N. Halsted St. (Wrightwood Ave.), 773-929-1333

☑ Waiters at this Lakeview Middle Eastern "describe the food in the most mouthwatering way" and the "always-on-stage" "owner makes customers feel important"; but while fans single out the lamb and advise "taste everything", foes feel that the fare is "overrated."

Un DiAmo Ristorante S
∇ | 20 | 16 | 19 | $28 |

1617 N. Wells St. (½ block north of North Ave.), 312-337-8881

☑ Though located across the street from Second City, this "little" Italian largely remains an "Old Town secret", despite being "quaint, romantic" and ideal "for a date"; those not in love sigh "pretty good, but not out of this world."

VA PENSIERO
| 25 | 22 | 23 | $39 |

Margarita Inn, 1566 Oak Ave. (Davis St.), Evanston,
847-475-7779

■ "Yesterday's ambiance, tomorrow's food" is one way of summing up Peggy Ryan's highly rated North Shore Italian, an "exquisite gem" serving "innovative, delicious" cuisine in an "understated" and "romantic" environment; the low-key location may explain why "it's the least famous of the top-tier restaurants, yet one of the best" – it's "the place to take people you want to impress."

Via Emilia Ristorante S
| 19 | 17 | 19 | $30 |

2119 N. Clark St. (Dickens Ave.), 773-248-6283

☑ Those giving thumbs up to this Lincoln Park Italian call it "a welcome neighborhood addition" and praise the "warm" atmosphere, "authentic" waiters with "thick accents" and "delicious" Bolognese dishes, including freshly made pasta that "will melt in your mouth"; on the flip side is a contingent that says "uneven" and "nothing special."

Via Veneto S
19 | 14 | 19 | $24

3449 W. Peterson Ave. (Kimball Ave.), 773-267-0888

■ "What a find!" exclaim fans of this "well-priced", "good neighborhood" Italian on the Far Northwest Side, where adventurous diners will find "solid" food and service and an affordable wine list; the sidewalk cafe tables are "excellent on a summer night", and even skeptics who consider the fare "common" concede that it's "the best in its area."

Viceroy of India S
19 | 14 | 16 | $18

2520 W. Devon Ave. (bet. California & Western Aves.), 773-743-4100
19W 555 Roosevelt Rd. (Highland Ave.), Lombard, 630-627-4411

■ Devon corridor and West Suburban Indians that receive plaudits for "spicy yet flavorful food", including "tandoori that kicks butt"; aggressiveness aside, these are "reliably good" spots that differ little from their nearby competitors, but please most patrons.

Village, The ●S
18 | 20 | 18 | $25

71 W. Monroe St. (bet. Clark & Dearborn Sts.), 312-332-7005

■ The rustic member of the Italian Village troika in the Loop boasts a theatrical country setting, including twinkling lights and secluded, grotto-like booths that are "a must for ultimate privacy"; the "old-fashioned" menu is "reliable" and "quick service" makes it a popular pre-theater destination.

Vinci S
23 | 20 | 21 | $32

1732 N. Halsted St. (Willow St.), 312-266-1199

■ "One of the top three or four Italians in Chicago", this Lincoln Parker is "great at everything", from "thrilling" polenta con funghi to "divine" ravioli with brown-butter sauce; its proximity to the Steppenwolf and Royal George theaters is another plus, but the "well-thought-out menu", "always-attentive service" and "beautiful decor" would be hits in any location.

Vivaldi Trattoria S
– | – | – | M

5141 Main St. (Curtis St.), Downers Grove, 630-434-7700
144 S. Oak Park Ave. (Lake St.), Oak Park, 708-848-8885

These suburban West trattorias stick to the basics of straightforward pastas and simple salads and appetizers, with the occasional fish special tossed in; they won't win awards for originality, but capably cooked Italian fare at modest prices still counts for something, as the weekend throngs will attest.

Vivere
22 | 24 | 22 | $38

71 W. Monroe St. (bet. Clark & Dearborn Sts.), 312-332-4040

■ A "classy" Loop member of the Italian Village family where "creative, upscale" dishes resembling a "party on a plate" are served amidst "surreal", "eye-catching" decor; factor in a "fantastic wine list" and it's clear why most think it's an "outstanding" dining experience.

Vivo 🅂   21 | 20 | 18 | $32

838 W. Randolph St. (1 block west of Halsted St.), 312-733-3379
📧 Those hip to this "trendy" Near West Italian find it a "classy, dressy" "place to be seen", but detractors deride a "too dark", "overcrowded" setting with a "high decibel" level; there is more agreement on the food, which is generally "terrific", as is the "romantic" upstairs table – a private spot built into an old elevator shaft.

Voila   15 | 17 | 15 | $27

33 W. Monroe St. (bet. Dearborn & State Sts.), 312-580-9500
📧 This "stylish" French bistro, located across the street from the Loop's Shubert Theater, is endorsed as a "good pre-theater" option and a "welcome" choice for Downtowners who appreciate its "business lunch" potential and "broad menu"; however, those not concerned with "convenience" say the food's "nothing special" and "could be improved."

Volare 🅂   ▽ 21 | 17 | 19 | $30

201 E. Grand Ave. (St. Clair St.), 312-410-9900
◼ "Watch this new spot" say devotees of this Streeterville Italian yearling, which is largely undiscovered by surveyors, but possessed of a loyal following that praises its "hearty pasta servings", "great mixed seafood appetizer" and "value" prices; those who dub it "relaxing and quiet" apparently don't visit on weekends.

Walker Bros. 🅂   22 | 17 | 19 | $13

825 W. Dundee Rd. (bet. Arlington Hts. Rd. & Rte. 53),
Arlington Heights, 847-392-6600
1615 Waukegan Rd. (2 blocks north of Lake Ave.),
Glenview, 847-724-0220
620 Central Ave. (4 blocks east of Green Bay Rd.),
Highland Park, 847-432-0660
153 Green Bay Rd. (bet. Central & Lake Aves.), Wilmette,
847-251-6000
◼ North and Northwest Suburban pancake chain that "destroys all willpower" with the "best breakfast – bar none", including "hard-to-beat" omelets, "great" pecan waffles and a "don't-miss" apple pancake that's the "highlight of the menu"; it may be the "butter capitol of Chicago", but kids of all ages "always clean their plates here", possibly because "long lines" ensure that people are starving when they finally do eat (visit very early or midweek to dine in "relative peace").

Walter's   ▽ 23 | 21 | 22 | $35

28 Main St. (1 block east of Cumberland Rd.), Park Ridge,
847-696-2992
📧 "A great new menu" – try to save room for the "amazing dessert variety" – has North suburbanites cheering this Eclectic as "a fine place to enjoy a fine meal when in the area"; "calm and attentive" service means there's "no big hoopla."

Washington Gardens S | 18 | 12 | 18 | $23 |
(fka Alex's Washington Gardens)
*256 Green Bay Rd. (Highwood Ave.), Highwood,
847-432-0309*
☑ Venerable North Shore Italian noted for its "great
treatment of seafood" and "reliable thin-crust pizza"; factor
in an "always trying to please" owner and "comfortable"
surroundings and its appeal is clear; however, foes feel the
food is "predictable" and it's "coasting on its reputation."

Waterford   ▽ | 22 | 22 | 20 | $40 |
*Oak Brook Hills Hotel & Conference Ctr., 3500 Midwest Rd.
(Rte. 31), Westmont, 630-850-5555*
■ The pricey dining room of the Oak Brook Hills Hotel in the
West Suburbs presents an American-Continental menu in
"elegant" surroundings worthy of its crystal-clear name; it's
a "special occasion spot" for a meal "with your in-laws",
assuming you like them that much.

Wayside Manor   ▽ | 21 | 21 | 23 | $39. |
1216 Main St. (Linden Ave.), Crete, 708-672-8080
■ Few surveyors manage the long drive to this Far South
Suburban housed in a "beautiful" Victorian mansion, but
those who do report "terrific" Classic French cuisine, "good
service" and a "romantic" atmosphere; a trip makes a
"wonderful splurge", especially at Christmas.

Weber Grill S | 18 | 15 | 17 | $25 |
*920 N. Milwaukee Ave. (2 blocks north of Lake Cook Rd.),
Wheeling, 847-215-0996*
☑ Novel Northwest Suburban American that cooks its food
on Weber kettle grills; there's "great barbecue" and "good
steaks and seafood" "without the charcoal smell"; while
"grilled food in the winter is a real treat", predictably there
are those who sniff "my Weber at home is just as good."

Weeghman Park
Restaurant & Brewery S | – | – | – | M |
3535 N. Clark St. (Addison St.), 773-248-3535
Weeghman Park was the original name for Wrigley Field,
and this brewpub draws Cub fans on game days with its
handcrafted beers and traditional tavern menu.

Wildfire S | 19 | 19 | 19 | $28 |
*159 W. Erie St. (bet. LaSalle & Wells Sts.), 312-787-9000
Oak Brook Shopping Ctr., 232 Oak Brook Ctr., Oak Brook,
630-586-9000*
■ These "spacious" River North and West Suburban
Traditional Americans prepare everything from "superb
chicken on a spit" and wood-oven pizzas to seafood and
steaks cooked over open flames; "if you like smoky treats"
they're a "good concept", though the open kitchen's roaring
fire makes some diners "smell like a campfire" at meal's end.

Wild Onion 🅂　　　　17 | 15 | 17 | $21
3500 N. Lincoln Ave. (Cornelia Ave.), 773-871-5555
◪ North Sider whose American menu morphed into European bistro fare post-*Survey*; the "artsy"-looking space is still home to the "world's best onion soup" and the "very good" Sunday brunch remains some diners' "best-kept secret"; so for those who thought it was previously "nothing to write home about", it might be time for a letter.

Windows of Cuisine 🅂　　　　20 | 14 | 17 | $20
1636 Old Deerfield Rd. (Richfield Rd.), Highland Park,
847-831-3155
◼ Even though this North Shore Chinese is located in an "out-of-the-way" spot, it's "easy to park" there; once you do, you can enjoy "always good" food in a "relaxing" ambiance.

Wishbone 🅂　　　　21 | 15 | 17 | $18
1800 W. Grand Ave. (west of Ashland Ave.), 312-829-3597
1001 W. Washington Blvd. (west of Halsted St.),
312-850-2663
◼ A touch of "down-home on the West Side", these "bustling" but "amiable" Southern outposts, with Cajun-Creole/Soul Food specialties, are revered for their "outrageous amounts" of "vibrant vittles" at a "terrific" "bargain" breakfast and "amazing" brunch, which can seem like a "zoo, but it's fun"; to avoid "long lines" on weekends, some prefer going off-peak or for dinner; N.B. the Washington Boulevard location has lots more space.

Wonton Club ➊　　　　18 | 20 | 16 | $24
661 N. Clark St. (1 block north of Ontario St.), 312-943-6868
◪ This "trendy" River North Pan-Asian draws a split decision: some judges give high marks for the "great, funky decor", "cute atmosphere" and "tasty noodle dishes", but others note "average sushi" and too much "attitude."

Woo Lae Oak 🅂　　　　▽ 19 | 20 | 19 | $25
30 W. Hubbard St. (bet. Dearborn & State Sts.), 312-645-0051
◼ Boosters claim this River North spot, part of a Seoul-based chain, offers the "best Korean food" in Chicago; it's certainly an "upscale", "high-end" concept featuring beautiful "traditional decor", a "helpful staff" and spicing that's "toned down" for novices.

Work of Art Café　　　　▽ 21 | 14 | 20 | $22
1332 N. Halsted St. (4 blocks south of North Ave.), 312-280-1718
◼ "The prices are great and the food is too" say fans of this "artful" North Side French-Vietnamese BYO, whose "beautifully executed" cuisine is almost "too pretty to eat" and easily outshines the ambiance ("dimming the lights would improve the atmosphere"); the "out-of-the-way location" means it may need to draw "a larger crowd to fly", but insiders wouldn't mind if it remained undiscovered.

Yoshi's Cafe S
23 | 18 | 21 | $34
3257 N. Halsted St. (Belmont Ave.), 773-248-6160

■ Star chef "Yoshi [Katsumura] is still performing" to raves at this French-Asian fusion in Lakeview; while nostalgists miss "the old, formal" Yoshi's that occupied the same location and find this "enlarged", "noisier" space "bland", they welcome the "lower prices" and agree the food's "still amazing" and the staff "knowledgeable" and "attentive."

Yvette ● S
18 | 18 | 18 | $31
1206 N. State Pkwy. (Division St.), 312-280-1700

◪ Live piano-bar music accompanies dinner every night at this Gold Coast French, a "pretty, cozy, upscale neighborhood" spot; though some say they'd like it better if the "decent food" improved, it's a place to remember when you want to "dine late" and dance too.

Yvette Wintergarden
17 | 18 | 17 | $31
311 S. Wacker Dr. (Jackson Blvd.), 312-408-1242

◪ This French bistro resembles its sibling Yvette, but it's in the Loop, attracting a steady lunch clientele with its "sun-drenched atrium" and the dinner-and-dancing set by night; though critics carp about "inconsistent" performance, "if you order right, you can have a good meal."

Zarrosta Grill S
18 | 17 | 17 | $24
1045 N. Rush St. (bet. Bellevue Pl. & Cedar St.), 312-642-1500
118 Oak Brook Ctr. (Cermak Rd./22nd St. & Rte. 83),
Oak Brook, 630-990-0177

◪ Here's a switch – a California-style concept that made its mark in a suburban mall, then opened a sequel in the city; whether in the Rush Street–area or the Western 'burbs, these "casual", "upbeat" hangouts offer among the "best of the designer pizzas" and earn extra applause for their "fabulous, big salads" and "great wine flights."

Zaven's S
22 | 20 | 22 | $38
260 E. Chestnut St. (bet. DeWitt Pl. & Lake Shore Dr.),
312-787-8260

■ "Take your mistress" to this "quiet and romantic" Streeterville Continental that attracts "regular followers" for its signature rack of lamb, "out-of-this-world fish specials" and "the most congenial host" in town (Zaven himself); even if the "menu is not particularly creative", it's "dependable."

Zealous
24 | 18 | 22 | $42
174 N. York Rd. (1 block south of North Ave.), Elmhurst,
630-834-9300

■ Acolytes say this New American "real find in the Western suburbs" is "aptly named", since chef-owner Michael Taus "keeps outperforming himself" with "innovative", "strongly flavored" food and "amazing presentations"; though there's "not much ambiance" in the "small" storefront setting, it's "the place to go if you think no one's doing anything new."

Zia's Trattoria S | ▽ | 26 | 19 | 23 | $31 |
6699 N. Northwest Hwy. (bet. Harlem & Touhy Aves.),
773-775-0808

■ Not everyone has discovered this "small, intimate" Far Northwest Side Italian seafooder, but those who have declare it their "new favorite" due to "excellent food" from a seasonal menu that might include the likes of butternut squash ravioli.

ZINFANDEL | 23 | 20 | 21 | $33 |
59 W. Grand Ave. (bet. Clark & Dearborn Sts.), 312-527-1818

☑ A kissing cousin to Frontera Grill and Topolobampo, this River North all-American delights devotees with rotating menus that focus on a new region each month; "the concept itself deserves praise" and Susan Goss' execution results in dishes so "wonderful" and "intriguing" that some are tempted to "eat the plate too"; despite occasional barbs that it's "uneven" and "a little too precious", most agree "there's nothing else quite like it."

Zofia's S | ▽ | 18 | 13 | 18 | $17 |
310 W. Rand Rd. (4 blocks northwest of Arlington Hts. Rd.),
Arlington Heights, 847-259-5050

☑ Suburban Northwest Polish that dishes out "stick-to-your-ribs food" in "super-huge portions", which distracts some diners from the "tacky decor"; a few old-timers maintain it "used to be better" at its original Milwaukee Avenue site, but most find it tough to argue with the "reasonably priced" fare.

Zum Deutschen Eck S | 18 | 19 | 18 | $23 |
2924 N. Southport Ave. (Lincoln Ave.), 773-525-8389

■ "For the occasional Germanic fix", you "gotta love the oompah music" and "very good", if "heavy", "traditional food" at this Lakeview Teutonic; "take your extroverted friends" or "group parties" for the "big menu, big portions and big atmosphere."

Indiana

Top Food
26 La Salle Grill
25 Miller Bakery Cafe
   Clayton's

Top Service
25 La Salle Grill
24 Clayton's
23 Miller Bakery Cafe

Top Decor
27 Clayton's
23 Louis' Bon Appetit
   La Salle Grill

Top Value
Jalapeño's Hottest
Strongbow Inn
Pump's on 12

F	D	S	C

Antoinette's S

–	–	–	M

13231 Wicker Ave. (133rd St.), Cedar Lake, 219-374-5000
A Cedar Lake Italian that's "a great find" for those who
enjoy the "warm and friendly" staffers and "congenial bar";
while the food may be more sophisticated than the down-
home decor might suggest, some say that it's just "ok."

Basil's S

19	18	17	$27

521 Franklin Sq. (bet. 5th & 6th Sts.), Michigan City, 219-872-4500
◪ "Very upscale for an area [filled] with mall food", this
Italian-French makes "a nice place for lunch" for shoppers
at the nearby Lighthouse Place Outlet Center; though
some damn it with faint praise ("not bad for Michigan
City"), others maintain it's "a real treat."

Cafe Venezia

22	16	20	$28

*Ross Plaza Shopping Ctr., 405 W. 81st Ave. (½ mi. west of
I-85 on Hwy. 30), Merrillville, 219-736-2203*
▪ Some say that "the best Italian food in Indiana" – "the
place for pasta" and "great raviolis" – is tucked into a
small shopping center along a busy highway; a "polished
staff" and proximity to cultural events (Northwest Indiana
Symphony, Star Plaza) are other pluses.

Clayton's S

25	27	24	$34

*66 W. Lincoln Way (bet. Lafayette & Washington Sts.),
Valparaiso, 219-531-0612*
▪ Devotees decree that "Chicago's restaurants should
take notice and learn" from this Valparaiso Eclectic;
it may be "out there in farm country", but it earns
stratospheric scores for its "excellent", "creative" food
and "New York atmosphere"; insiders tout the three-
course prix fixe dinner on Tuesday and Thursday.

129

Jalapeño's Hottest Mexican Restaurant S
14 | 22 | 16 | $17

200 Hwy. 41 (bet. Main & Woodhole Sts.), Schererville, 219-864-8862

◪ This Schererville Mexican's long-winded name is intended to differentiate it from a similarly monikered chain; while the "pleasant", "south-of-the-border" decor earns compliments, there's less consensus on the food, which some claim is "too greasy" and "not very special"; take this as a warning or an endorsement: "the food is really hot."

La Salle Grill
26 | 23 | 25 | $37

115 W. Colfax Ave. (Main St.), South Bend, 219-288-1155

■ Chicagoans heading to South Bend for Notre Dame games have this "cosmopolitan" American option for "beautifully presented" offerings that are "worth the drive" regardless of who the Irish are playing; stogie aficionados say "check out the cigar room" as well.

Louis' Bon Appetit S
23 | 23 | 23 | $39

302 S. Main St. (Walnut St.), Crown Point, 219-663-6363

■ Another "best-kept secret", this one's in a "beautiful old mansion" with Victorian decor that's a fine setting for chef Louis' "wonderful Classic French" cooking; it's "great for special occasions", especially those evenings when live piano or classical guitar music are featured; P.S. check out the Bastille Day celebration, which draws a huge crowd.

Miller Bakery Cafe S
25 | 18 | 23 | $30

555 S. Lake St. (4 blocks north of Hwys. 12 & 20), Gary, 219-938-2229

■ "Hard-to-find" "haven" of "superbly presented" New American cuisine in Gary's snazzy Miller Beach area that's "one of the best in Northwest Indiana"; while a few think it benefits from an "otherwise bland restaurant" scene, the majority says "you'd better believe it – worth a road trip."

Phil Smidt's S
20 | 14 | 19 | $27

1205 N. Calumet Ave. (Indianapolis Blvd.), Hammond, 219-659-0025

◪ "Decade after decade", this Hammond seafooder brings in the crowds for "wonderful" lake perch and "the best" frogs' legs swimming in so much butter that "it will raise your cholesterol to new heights"; decor is "a throwback" to the '40s or earlier – so much so that "you expect to see your grandmother"; critics counter: "prices up, quality down."

Pump's on 12 S
15 | 16 | 15 | $19

3085 W. Dunes Hwy. (Hwy. 12, 2½ mi. west of Hwy. 421), Michigan City, 219-874-6201

◪ Dunes-area roadhouse featuring a "nice selection" of "good" American pub grub; a "new, expanded menu" with more pasta and salad offerings may up ratings, but "some changes don't sit well with the regulars."

Strongbow Inn [S] 23 | 20 | 21 | $23

2405 Hwy. 30 (Hwy. 49), Valparaiso, 219-462-5121

■ A Valpo American classic that's made a name for itself by specializing in one item – turkey – in various guises, including an "outstanding" roast version, a "great pot pie" and "the world's best club sandwich"; it's "a terrific tribute to my favorite bird", thus customers can be seen gobblin' at the "excellent Sunday brunch" as well.

Tandoor [S] ▽ 18 | 12 | 18 | $18

1535 Hwy. 41 (30th St.), Schererville, 219-865-9511

◪ Sophisticated Schererville Indian in a shopping center offering "an incredible bargain" daily lunch buffet; while "unexciting" to some, it's "essential" to others since it's "the only restaurant of its type in the area."

Michigan

Top Food
22 Jenny's
   Grande Mere Inn
21 Tosi's

Top Service
23 Grande Mere Inn
22 Tosi's
   Restaurant Toulouse

Top Decor
24 Restaurant Toulouse
22 Grande Mere Inn
21 Miller's Country House

Top Value
Redamak's
Hyerdall's Cafe
Blue Plate Cafe

F	D	S	C

Bill Knapp's S
16 | 14 | 18 | $16

848 Ferguson St. (Hwy. 39 & I-94), Benton Harbor, 616-925-3212
■ Vacationing families take note, this "clean", "quick" and "quiet" Benton Harbor link in a Traditional American chain is a "dependable" option "when you're on the road and hungry", since the tab won't "put you in the poor house"; critics counter "only if you'd otherwise starve."

Blue Plate Cafe S⊘
18 | 14 | 15 | $16

15288 Red Arrow Hwy. (Warren Woods Rd.), Union Pier, 616-469-2370
■ You'll "dream about the pancakes" at this "cute" breakfast and lunch hangout, with fresh-squeezed juices, organic coffee and baked-from-scratch goodies; not surprisingly, the "great brunch" on Sundays is popular, particularly if taken on the lovely outdoor patio.

Chequers S
19 | 20 | 17 | $22

220 Culver St. (Main St.), Saugatuck, 616-857-1868
■ Saugatuck English-style pub that gets "very cramped" but is "worth the wait" for "excellent fish 'n' chips", shepherd's pie and lots of ales.

Fanny's Famous S
– | – | – | M

Gordon Beach Inn, 16220 Lakeshore Rd. (Townline Rd.), Union Pier, 616-469-0900
The original Fanny's, a 40-year fixture in Evanston that closed in '87, has been re-created at this dinner-only Italian-American, a 110-seater inside the Gordon Beach Inn; Fanny's son provided the recipe for the famous spaghetti, and mementos from the original decorate the walls.

Global Bar & Grill S
▽ 14 | 13 | 16 | $16

215 Butler St. (Mason St.), Saugatuck, 616-857-1555
■ Offering an International menu, this Saugatuck stop has "above-average food" "for a bar" and a "fun atmosphere" that frequently includes live music; just "stick to the basics" ("love the roasted chicken") and you'll do ok.

Grande Mere Inn   22 | 22 | 23 | $30
5800 Red Arrow Hwy. (I-94, exit 22), Stevensville, 616-429-3591
■ This lakeside seafooder with "top-notch" food, including a signature lake perch dish, is "recommended", especially if you secure a window table for the "wonderful sunsets" and view of Lake Michigan; as the rating attests, management pays "close attention to service."

Hannah's S   17 | 17 | 19 | $22
115 S. Whittaker St. (I-94, exit 1), New Buffalo, 616-469-1440
◪ A "huge" old house (1890) is the setting for this New Buffalo Eclectic with everything from BBQ to Bohemian-style roast duck; comments also range widely, from "a favorite" "after Christmas tree hunting" for "very good food" to "dark, dismal" place with "lots of mediocre" grub; you decide.

Hyerdall's Cafe S⇄   18 | 12 | 17 | $14
9673 Red Arrow Hwy. (Lake St.), Bridgman, 616-465-5546
◪ Long-standing, "little roadside" Bridgman American offering "home country" cooking, such as stewed chicken and "great pies and baked goods"; it's also favored for the signature Swedish pancakes served at breakfast.

Jenny's S   22 | 20 | 20 | $31
15460 Red Arrow Hwy. (Warren Woods Rd.), Lakeside, 616-469-6545
■ The recent move by Jennifer Smith's Eclectic has excited fans who found the old Union Pier space "too noisy", but think the "new digs suit them well"; moreover, the food still makes for "the best dinner in Harbor Country", especially for those who order the "wonderful sea bass."

Kent's S   – | – | – | M
203 W. Buffalo St. (Rte. 12, 2 blocks east of Whittaker St.), New Buffalo, 616-469-6255
Kent Buell, formerly chef at Betise on the North Shore, is cooking on the New Buffalo side of Lake Michigan these days; it's "a real find" say vacationing Chicagoans who rave about the "great" Eclectic food, fine wine and service and "unpretentious" setting.

Miller's Country House S   20 | 21 | 19 | $30
16409 Red Arrow Hwy. (Community Hall Rd.), Union Pier, 616-469-5950
■ Frequent travelers to and through the Union Pier area "would never miss stopping" at this "excellent country restaurant" with two distinct dining areas: a cozy pub with burgers and other bar fare and a "lovely" formal dining room with an Eclectic menu; in sum, a "warm, welcoming oasis" that's "popular with the elderly set" and just about anyone else who stops by.

Redamak's 🅂⌀   16 | 13 | 15 | $13
616 E. Buffalo St. (Red Arrow Hwy.), New Buffalo, 616-469-4522
■ When "you've gotta have that greasy cheeseburger",
onion rings and a milk shake, many turn to this New Buffalo
roadhouse for a satisfying fix of "good lousy-for-you food";
it's "a great place for kids after you've been in the car",
but summer crowds make it "unbearable on hot days."

Red Arrow Roadhouse 🅂   17 | 15 | 16 | $17
15710 Red Arrow Hwy. (Townline Rd.), Union Pier, 616-469-3939
■ "Spartan atmosphere" is just part of the charm of this
"sanitized" Union Pier roadhouse with "much-better-than-
average food", including (wonder of wonders) a "great
veggie chile", ribs, burgers and other American staples;
it's "unpretentious" and "family-friendly", though the no-
reservations policy ("bummer") can mean a long wait for
those with unlucky timing.

Restaurant Su Casa 🅂⌀   – | – | – | I
306 W. Main St. (Hwy. 19), Fennville, 616-561-5493
An East-of-Saugatuck Mexican that doesn't look like
much from the outside and, ok, isn't much on the inside,
either, but the authentic and inexpensive food makes it
worth seeking out.

Restaurant Toulouse 🅂   21 | 24 | 22 | $30
248 Culver St. (Griffith St.), Saugatuck, 616-857-1561
☑ "Very capable", "beautiful" French bistro sibling of
Chequer's that devotees dub "probably the best" in town;
however, snobs sniff it's "Saugatuck's idea of fine dining."

Skip's Other Place 🅂   17 | 13 | 17 | $21
16710 Lake Shore Rd. (Red Arrow Hwy.), Union Pier, 616-469-3330
■ A Union Pier American that could be more accurately
called "Skip's Only Place", but whatever the name and
despite the "dowdy" decor, people "love it" for "great
prime rib", burgers or "just a drink."

Sole Mio East 🅂   – | – | – | M
16038 Red Arrow Hwy. (Union Pier Rd.), Union Pier, 616-469-9636
Chicagoans saddened at the loss of Sole Mio in Lincoln
Park can now cheer up because Dennis Terczak has
re-established his French-accented Italian on the well-
traveled Red Arrow Highway in Union Pier; indeed, with
about 140 seats, there's twice as much room as before.

Tosi's   21 | 19 | 22 | $28
4337 Ridge Rd. (1 mi. west of Red Arrow Hwy.),
Stevensville, 616-429-3689
☑ This Harbor Country Italian still serves "the best
minestrone" around, as demonstrated by the fact that
returning Chicagoans often order some to take home;
while a few think the food "has slipped", it remains "an
oasis off I-94" with "excellent service."

Wisconsin/Milwaukee

Top Food
29 Sanford
27 Rist. Bartolotta
Grenadier's
25 River Lane Inn
Boulevard Inn

Top Service
28 Sanford
26 Grenadier's
25 Rist. Bartolotta
Immigrant Room
24 Heaven City

Top Decor
24 Immigrant Room
Rist. Bartolotta
English Room
Boulevard Inn
Karl Ratzsch's

Top Value
Ed Debevic's
Buca di Beppo
Historic Turner Rest.
Elsa's on the Park
Rist. Bartolotta

F | D | S | C

Bartolotta's Lake Park Bistro [S] — | — | — | M
3133 E. Newberry Blvd. (Lake Dr.), Milwaukee, 414-962-6300
Joseph Bartolotta, brother of Paul Bartolotta of Spiaggia in Chicago, is no slouch with the pots and pans either, judging by this effort, a 150-seat bistro in a turn-of-the-century park pavilion on a bluff overlooking Lake Michigan; but there's also the original Ristorante Bartolotta, plus his his newest venture, Nonna Bartolotta's.

Beans & Barley [S] ▽ 19 | 15 | 15 | $12
1901 E. North Ave. (Oakland Ave.), Milwaukee, 414-278-7878
■ This Eclectic health fooder shares space with a grocery, giving customers one-stop shopping for dining in and taking home; it's a "comfy spot" for "good vegetarian" dishes, which are rare north of the Cheddar Curtain.

Boulevard Inn [S] 25 | 24 | 23 | $29
925 E. Wells St. (Prospect Ave.), Milwaukee, 414-765-1166
◪ Valet parking makes this Continental a popular destination for Milwaukee suits in search of a "great spot for a business lunch"; it's also a "romantic and elegant" evening option accompanied by piano music.

Brett Favre Steakhouse [S] — | — | — | E
500 N. Water St. (Clybourn St.), Milwaukee, 414-276-4444
A paen to the touchdown-throwing quarterback for the Green Bay Packers, this massive steakhouse has room for nearly 400 fans in a boisterous, brick-walled space decorated with pictures, jerseys and other memorabilia of you-know-who; the classic steak menu is augmented with Cajun dishes and specialties from Favre's native Mississippi.

Buca di Beppo S   17 | 21 | 19 | $19
1233 N. Van Buren Ave. (Juneau Ave.), Milwaukee, 414-224-8672
☑ The Milwaukee link of this Minneapolis-based theatrical
Italian offers "big portions" of "family-style fare for the
masses" in an atmosphere that includes old-fashioned
twinkling Christmas lights and a shrine to Frank Sinatra;
"it's definitely a place to go with a group", the better to
endure the "long waits" and "noisy" surroundings.

Cafe at the Pfister S   17 | 17 | 17 | $23
Pfister Hotel, 424 E. Wisconsin Ave. (Jefferson St.),
Milwaukee, 414-273-8222
☑ Casual cafe in the elegant Pfister Hotel offering three
meals a day; while some think it's "better for breakfast",
they feel the eating experience in general isn't up to the
decor of this "stunning hotel."

China Gourmet S   – | – | – | I
330 E. Kilbourn Ave. (Milwaukee Ave.), Milwaukee,
414-272-1688
Diners will always find a bargain at this Downtown regional
Chinese owned in part by Chicago restaurateur Austin
Koo; there's a lunch buffet daily ($7.25), a dinner version
Friday–Saturday ($12.95) and an all-you-can-eat Sunday
brunch ($9.95); in sum, "excellent for Milwaukee."

Chip and Py's S   ▽ 24 | 22 | 19 | $24
East Towne Sq., 1340 W. Towne Sq. Rd. (Port Washington Rd.),
Mequon, 414-241-9589
■ Respondents regard this "artsy" Continental a half-
hour north of Milwaukee as a subdued place that's "perfect
for a ladies' luncheon" – try the "excellent seafood";
it's a bit livelier on weekend evenings when live jazz
adds to the ambiance.

Coerper's 5 O'Clock Club S   ▽ 28 | 19 | 23 | $28
2416 W. State St. (24th St.), Milwaukee, 414-342-3553
■ Now a more than a half-century old, this seafooder/
steakhouse with "*77 Sunset Strip* decor" pulls in an
eclectic crowd, lured by "huge portions of great steaks"
that are "absolutely the best in town"; it's definitely "worth
the drive", even if some gibe "arrive by air" to avoid the
"hostile neighborhood"; N.B. reservations are required.

Crawdaddy's   ▽ 23 | 18 | 20 | $20
6501 W. Greenfield Ave. (65th St.), West Allis, 414-778-2228
■ A "delightful" Cajun-Creole in West Allis that recently
moved across the street and doubled its seating capacity,
to the relief of regulars who've had to contend with long
waits; it's "sometimes too noisy" (sometimes?), but the
"great food" is ample compensation.

Dancing Ganesha [S] — | — | — | I

1692-94 N. Van Buren St. (Brady St.), Milwaukee, 414-220-0202

Don't look for undistinguished buffets and Far East knickknacks at this rule-bending East Indian whose modestly priced regional fare is prepared by two female chefs; its contemporary good looks rely on rotating artwork by local and Chicago artists.

Ed Debevic's [S] 15 | 19 | 16 | $14

780 N. Jefferson St. (bet. Mason & Wells Sts.), Milwaukee, 414-226-2200

◪ This Milwaukee outpost of a Chicago-based chain is known for its '50s look and wisecracking waiter–shtick; while the diner-style vittles are "good", some suggest going "for the fun, not the food" ("kids love to go here after school dances"), otherwise it's "not worth the wait."

Eddie Martini's [S] 25 | 22 | 23 | $39

8612 Watertown Plank Rd. (bet. 84th & 87th Sts.), Wauwatosa, 414-771-6680

■ Set in an "elegant, clubby" space, this '40s-style supper club has been around for all of four years but has the retro look down pat, including an "exceptional staff" of white-jacketed waiters fetching "huge drinks" for an "always-packed" crowd; surveyors add that the steak-and-seafood menu is "surprisingly sophisticated", offering "great ostrich" in addition to the usual suspects.

Elm Grove Inn ▽ 19 | 21 | 19 | $24

13275 Watertown Plank Rd. (124th St.), Elm Grove, 414-782-7090

■ Suburban Milwaukee Continental with "quality service" and a "good overall menu", including fresh fish, veal and steak; it's in a landmark building that can be tricky to find, but apparently the effort is rewarded.

Elsa's on the Park ☾ [S] 20 | 21 | 17 | $21

833 N. Jefferson St. (bet. Kilbourn & Wells Aves.), Milwaukee, 414-765-0615

■ An "in-spot for late dining", this Milwaukee American may be better known as a place "where the beautiful people hang" than for its food, but "fantastic burgers and sandwiches" await those who can stop people-watching long enough to dine; it's a "very pretty place for a date", just don't let your eyes wander.

English Room, The [S] 23 | 24 | 23 | $40

Pfister Hotel, 424 E. Wisconsin Ave. (Jefferson St.), Milwaukee, 414-273-8222

■ The Pfister Hotel's "very comfortable" fine dining room combines a "classical" setting of "old-time elegance" with "beautiful presentations" of "excellent" Contemporary American food; overall, a "delightful" experience.

Golden Mast Inn S　　　– – – M
*1270 Lacy Ln. (west of Hwy. 100, just off Hwy. 16), Okauchee,
414-567-7047*
Lakeside Teutonic seafooder whose Friday fish fry is a "best
bet"; but what really draws the fans, by car and by boat,
is the "gorgeous setting" with a "charmingly theatrical
atmosphere" and views that promote "romantic dining."

Grenadier's　　　27 21 26 $43
747 N. Broadway (Mason St.), Milwaukee, 414-276-0747
■ Highly rated French-accented American featuring Charles
Weber's "wonderful and creative" cuisine; service takes
a hit or two for being "rather pretentious", but overall the
experience is "superior in all aspects" and "can compare
with Chicago's best."

Heaven City S　　　22 23 24 $34
*S91 W27850 National Ave. (Fox River), Mukwonago,
414-363-5191*
■ Tucked into a riverside lodge rumored to be "a Capone
haunt", this New American jazzes up its Midwestern menu
with promotions (from 'Tapas Tuesdays' to 'May Mushroom
Madness') and live entertainment five nights a week; locals
are pleased with the "unusual dishes with exotic sauces",
though they caution that due to Friday and Saturday crowds,
it's "best on weekdays."

Historic Turner Restaurant S　　　18 18 19 $20
1034 N. Fourth St. (State St.), Milwaukee, 414-276-4844
■ "Milwaukee's ethnic history in a nutshell" is on display
at this decades-old German-American, even though some
surveyors are still griping about a 1995 remodeling that
"emasculated" the atmosphere; count on crowds "if
there's an event at the Bradley Center" nearby because
ticket-holders storm in for the "great pre-game fish fry."

Immigrant Room　　　25 24 25 $44
*American Club, Highland Dr. (bet. Orchard & School Sts.),
Kohler, 920-457-8888*
■ The "very classy" fine dining room of the acclaimed
American Club resort gets some votes as "the best dining
experience in Wisconsin", thanks to "truly fine" New
American food and "unbelievable service"; however, a
few proles find it a tad "pretentious."

Karl Ratzsch's S　　　24 24 22 $29
*320 E. Mason St. (bet. Broadway & Milwaukee St.),
Milwaukee, 414-276-2720*
■ "Best German restaurant in a city full of them" is what
surveyors say about this 95-year-old "incredible step back in
time" serving "great sauerbraten, potato pancakes"
and the "best stuffed pork chops in the Midwest"; it's an
"all-time favorite" that's "worth the drive every time" when
seeking an example of "old-world perfection."

Kilbourn Cafe S   ▽ 15 | 14 | 15 | $26
Wyndham Milwaukee Ctr. Hotel, 139 E. Kilbourn Ave., 2nd fl. (Water St.), Milwaukee, 414-291-4793
◪ Reviewers' responses indicate that it's best to visit this Milwaukee hotel dining room during daylight hours for the "great pasta bar" at lunch Monday–Friday or the wide-ranging Sunday brunch buffet; otherwise, only "adequate."

King and I, The S   20 | 18 | 18 | $22
823 N. Second St. (Wells St.), Milwaukee, 414-276-4181
◼ Though those who dub this reliable Downtown ethnic spot "the best Thai in the Midwest" may need to get out more, there's no doubt that it's "authentic" and pleases the majority of its patrons, except for the sometimes "smoky" atmosphere.

Louisa's Trattoria S   19 | 20 | 18 | $22
801 N. Jefferson St. (Wells St.), Milwaukee, 414-273-4224
◪ Some find this Downtown Italian's food "above average", some "below", but the place is usually "hopping" with "noisy", young professionals and it's a popular pre-theater destination as well, suggesting it has more going for it than just "to-die-for focaccia."

Mader's German Restaurant S   21 | 22 | 20 | $26
1037 N. Old World Third St. (Highland Ave.), Milwaukee, 414-271-3377
◪ Out-of-town visitors arrive by the busload at this "Bavarian rhapsody" of "good", "hearty" food and decor "that takes you back to Germany"; try the "nice sampler plates" for a quick Teutonic tour, but also know that detractors think it's "too commercial" and "overrated."

Mangia Trattoria S   23 | 18 | 22 | $29
5717 Sheridan Rd. (58th St.), Kenosha, 414-652-4285
◼ Kenosha Italian "sleeper" that's close to the outlet malls and is a sister property to Mantuano Mediterranean Table in Chicago; it draws as many patrons from the North Suburbs as it does from Milwaukee and some find it "a good meeting place" between the two cities; but the "halfway location" aside, the "delicious" cooking and "ever-changing" menu are what keeps everyone, including families, coming back.

Mimma's Cafe S   24 | 23 | 21 | $27
1307 E. Brady St. (Arlington Pl.), Milwaukee, 414-271-7337
◼ More than 50 pasta dishes, along with veal and seafood offerings, are available on this Milwaukee Italian's "huge menu" that also accommodates a 500-bottle wine list; the "food is great, the wait is not", so call ahead.

Nonna Bartolotta's S   – | – | – | M

17700 W. Capital Dr. (Calhoun Rd.), Brookfield, 414-790-7005
Joseph Bartolotta's latest offering is a casual, rustic Italian in
an old farmhouse in Brookfield; look for panini, individual
pizzas from a wood-burning oven, pastas, roasted-meat
specials and a choice of three dining rooms.

Osteria del Mondo S   22 | 21 | 21 | $32

*Knickerbocker Hotel, 1028 E. Juneau Ave. (bet. Astor & N.
Prospect Sts.), Milwaukee, 414-291-3770*
■ A "very modern" Italian that offers "totally terrific
presentations" of "interesting" fare according to the few
reviewers who commented on it; it seems worth a try.

Pandl's in Bayside S   18 | 18 | 18 | $24

8825 N. Lake Dr. (Brown Deer Rd.), Bayside, 414-352-7300
☑ "Return to old Milwaukee charm" at this "dependable"
German-American, a "cozy" standby for more than 30
years that's prized "for good whitefish" and a Sunday
brunch that's "one of [the city's] finest."

Pasta Tree, The S   – | – | – | M

1503 N. Farwell Ave. (Albion St.), Milwaukee, 414-276-8867
Three guesses what the specialty is at this "tiny", local
Italian that's acquired a liquor license since the last
Survey; complimentary salads make a visit a "good value"
and while there's "tight seating", that adds to the "quaint"
charm for admirers.

Red Rock Cafe S   21 | 12 | 17 | $22

4022 N. Oakland Ave. (Capital Ave.), Shorewood, 414-962-4545
☑ Since the food rating is close to double that of the decor
score, you know people aren't coming to this "crowded and
noisy" sea shanty for its looks, but for the "good seafood" –
the owner is a fish wholesaler.

Ristorante Bartolotta   27 | 24 | 25 | $29

7616 W. State St. (76th St.), Wauwatosa, 414-771-7910
■ Combine "Wisconsin portions and European ideas"
with "great attention to detail" and you have this "always
fun" Milwaukee-area Italian whose chef-owner Joseph
Bartolotta is the brother of Paul Bartolotta of Chicago's
Spiaggia; a few sniff that it "doesn't stand up" to his frère's
fare, but more say it's "one of the best in the Midwest"
and agree that the state "needs more of these."

River Lane Inn   25 | 19 | 21 | $26

4313 W. River Ln. (Brown Deer Rd.), Brown Deer, 414-354-1995
☑ With the same chef for 18 years and the same manager
for nine, it's no surprise that consistency is the hallmark of
this suburban Milwaukee Cajun-influenced seafooder with
"the best swordfish" and "special" calamari; canoodling
couples also consort in the "quaint", "romantic atmosphere."

Riversite, The   _ | _ | _ | M

1120 N. Cedarburg Rd. (Mequon Rd.), Mequon, 414-242-6050
Casually elegant Regional American in Mequon that
overlooks the Milwaukee River (everybody vies for a
window table); the menu is divided among fish, meat and
game dishes and makes use of local ingredients; though the
name is the same as that of a long-shuttered restaurant
that previously occupied this site, there's no other
relationship between the two.

Rudy's Mexican Restaurant S   _ | _ | _ | I

627 S. Fifth St. (National Ave.), Milwaukee, 414-291-0296
While loyalists "love the enchiladas and the setting" of
this Downtown Milwaukee Mexican and consider it a
"good" choice for large groups, the jaded sigh it's "like a
number of other places."

Sanford   29 | 24 | 28 | $56

1547 N. Jackson St. (Pleasant St.), Milwaukee, 414-276-9608
■ Surveyors say that "the best reason to go to Milwaukee"
is Sanford D'Amato's "small, exclusive" Contemporary
French, which has "incredible", "original" cuisine and
"fabulous" service; it's "hard to equal" for "special occasion
dining" and while "very expensive", it's clearly "worth it";
it may be "almost on a par with Charlie Trotter's – wow!"

Saz's S   18 | 16 | 17 | $20

5539 W. State St. (Hawley Rd.), Milwaukee, 414-453-2410
■ This "Milwaukee landmark" is a "good old-fashioned,
blue-collar bar" that's frequently crowded thanks to
"great atmosphere" and "super ribs" that are "worth the
two-and-a-half-hour drive from Chicago"; leave work
early if you want to make the "memorable Friday happy
hour" and "think about bringing home some sauce."

Steven Wade's Cafe   ▽ 23 | 20 | 24 | $43

17001 W. Greenfield Ave. (170th St.), New Berlin, 414-784-0774
▣ Devotees deem this New Berlin Gallic specialist "second
best [to Sanford's] for French accents" (we assume they
mean the food, not the conversation); it's no place for
bargain-hunters, but places with award-winning wine
lists seldom are.

Three Brothers S⇄   ▽ 21 | 14 | 18 | $22

2414 S. St. Clair St. (Russell Ave.), Milwaukee, 414-481-7530
■ The "funky, old-time feel" of this Milwaukee Serbian
"landmark" is so homespun that a meal here "feels like
you're intruding on a family dinner", complete with "large
portions" of "simple" but tasty ethnic food.

Indexes to Restaurants

Special Features and Appeals

TYPES OF CUISINE*

American (New)
Bandera
Blackbird
Blue Plate Cafe/M
Brasserie T
Cafe Absinthe
California Cafe B&G
Celebrity Cafe
Chaplin's on Church
Charlie Trotter's
Cielo
Club Macanudo
Courtright's
Crofton on Wells
Daily B&G
Daniel J's
Earth
Elaine & Ina's
English Room/W
erwin
Flat Top Grill
Fresh Starts
Goose Island
Gordon
Green Dolphin St.
Grenadier's/W
Harvest on Huron
Heaven City/W
Hubbard St. Grill
Hudson Club
Immigrant Room/W
Iron Mike's Grille
Jack's American
Jane's
Jilly's Cafe
John's Place
Leo's Lunchroom
Lucca's
Madam B
Mango
Manhattan's
Marché
Mashed Potato Club
Michael Jordan's
Miller Bakery Cafe/I
Mimosa
Mrs. Park's Tavern
North Pond Café
Oceanique
one sixtyblue

Outpost
Palette's
Park Ave. Cafe
Patrick & James
Planet Hollywood
Printer's Row
Pump Room
Relish
Rhapsody
Rigoletto
Rivers
Seasons
1776
Signature Room
Spruce
Tanglewood
Tavern in the Town
302 West
312 Chicago
Toque
Twilight
Wild Onion
Zealous

American (Regional)
Blackhawk Lodge
Daniel J's
Entre Nous
Fireside Beverly
Flatlander's
Heaven City/W
Meritage Cafe
Prairie
Riversite/W
Savannah's
Zinfandel

American (Traditional)
Allgauer's
America's Brewpub
Ann Sather
Ann Sather Cafe
Ann Sather Express
Barn of Barrington
Bill Knapp's/M
Breakfast Club
Buckingham's
Cafe at Pfister/W
Cafe Selmarie
Charlie's Ale Hse.

---

* All restaurants are in the Chicago area unless otherwise indicated
  (I=Indiana, M=Michigan and W=Wisconsin).

Cheesecake Factory
Cité
Claim Company
Clubhouse
Cornelia's Roosterant
Daily B&G
Dave & Buster's
Dick's Last Resort
Don Roth's
Ed Debevic's
Ed Debevic's/W
Eli's
Elsa's on the Park/W
Fanny's Famous/M
Fog City Diner
Founders Hill
Four Farthings
Gale St. Inn
Gary Barnett's
Genesee Depot
Green Door Tavern
Hackney's
Hard Rock Cafe
Harry Caray's
Historic Turner/W
Houston's
Hyerdall's Cafe/M
Johnny Rockets
Kilbourn Cafe/W
La Salle Grill/I
Lawry's
Lloyd's
Lou Mitchell's
Lou Mitchell's Exp.
Medici
Medici on 57th
Miller's Pub
Mill Race Inn
Millrose Brewing Co.
Mirabell
Mity Nice Grill
Mrs. Park's Tavern
94th Aero Squadron
Nookies
Nookies Too
Nookies Tree
Northside Cafe
Oak Terrace
Oak Tree
Old Barn
Orbit
Original Pancake Hse.
Pandl's in Bayside/W
Philander's
P.J. Clarke's

Public Landing
Pump's on 12/I
Quincy Grille
Rainforest Cafe
Red Arrow Roadhse./M
Retreat
Ritz-Carlton Cafe
R.J. Grunts
Rock Bottom Brew.
Roxy Cafe
Sarkis Grill
Saz's/W
Seasons Cafe
Skip's Other Place/M
South Gate Cafe
Southport City
Stanley's Kitchen
Strongbow Inn/I
Taylor Brewing Co.
Tommy Nevin's
Walker Bros.
Waterford
Weber Grill
Weeghman Park
Wildfire

Argentinean
El Nandu

Asian
Big Bowl
Hi Ricky
Lan's Bistro Pacific
LuLu's
Madam B
Mongolian BBQ
Oodles of Noodles
Red Light
Stir Crazy Cafe
Wonton Club
Yoshi's Cafe

Austrian
Edelweiss Bistro

Bakeries
Corner Bakery
Lutz Continental

Bar-B-Q
Barry's Ribs
Bones
Brother Jimmy's
Carson's Ribs
Dick's Last Resort
Famous Dave's

145

Fireplace Inn
Hickory Pit
Joe's Be-Bop Cafe
N. N. Smokehse.
Robinson's Ribs
Russell's BBQ
Saz's/W
Smoke Daddy
Stevie B's
Twin Anchors
Weber Grill

Brazilian
Rhumba

Cajun/Creole
Club Creole
Crawdaddy Bayou
Crawdaddy's/W
Davis St. Fishmkt.
Dixie Kitchen
Heaven on Seven
Heaven on Seven/Rush
House of Blues
Jackson Harbor Grill
Louisiana Kitchen
Maple Tree Inn
Pappadeaux
Redfish
River Lane Inn/W
Wishbone

Californian
California Pizza Kit.
Deleece
Spago
Sunset
Zarrosta Grill

Caribbean
Havana Café
Julio's Latin Cafe

Chinese
August Moon
Ben Pao
Best Hunan
China Gourmet/W
Chinoiserie
Dee's
Emperor's Choice
Furama
Hi Howe
Hong Min
Jia's
Mandar Inn

Panda Panda
Phoenix
Pine Yard
Sixty-Five
Szechwan East
Szechwan House
Szechwan North
Szechwan Palace
Szechwan Rest.
Three Happiness
Tien Tsin
Windows of Cuisine

Coffee Shops/Diners
Chicago Diner
Ed Debevic's
Ed Debevic's/W
Heaven on Seven
Heaven on Seven on Rush
Manny's Coffee Shop
Nookies
Nookies Two
Nookies Tree
Sarkis Grill

Continental
Biggs
Boulevard Inn/W
Cafe La Cave
Ceiling Zero
Chip and Py's/W
Elm Grove Inn/W
Golden Mast Inn/W
La Strada
Lutnia
Lutz Continental
Pasha
Trocadero
Waterford
Zaven's

Cuban
Club Macanudo
Cohiba
Havana Café
Mambo Grill
Tania's

Czech
Bohemian Crystal
Czech Plaza

Delis/Sandwich Shops
Bagel
Belden Deli
Chicago Flat Sammies

Manny's Coffee Shop
Max's Deli
Mrs. Levy's Deli

Dim Sum
Furama
Hong Min
LuLu's
Phoenix
Szechwan East
Three Happiness

Eclectic/International
Bacchus Nibbles
Beans & Barley/W
Bite Cafe
Blind Faith Cafe
Bluepoint Oyster
Brett's
Clayton's/I
Con Fusion
Deleece
Dellwood Pickle
Feast
56 West
foodlife
Global B&G/M
Hannah's/M
Hopcats Brewing Co.
Jack's American
Jenny's/M
Jerome's Red Ginger
John's Place
Kent's/M
Kerouac Jack's
Leo's Lunchroom
Lucky Platter
Mango
Mashed Potato Club
M Cafe
Merlot Joe
Miller's Country Hse./M
Planet Hollywood
Restaurant Okno
Savoy Truffle
Slice of Life
Taza
Tilli's
Tomboy
Trio
Walter's

English
Chequers/M
Red Lion Pub
Rose & Crown

Ethiopian
Addis Abeda
Ethiopian Village
Mama Desta's

Fondue
Fondue Stube
Geja's Cafe

French
Basil's/I
Cafe 36
Fond de la Tour
Gabriel's
Le Français
Les Nomades
Louis' Bon Appetit/I
Montparnasse
Pasha
Steven Wade's/W
Toulouse on the Park
Wayside Manor

French Bistro
Albert's Café
Bank Ln. Bistro
Barrington Country
Bartolotta's Lake Park/W
Betise
Bistro Banlieue
Bistro 110
Bistrot Zinc
Bistro Ultra
Brasserie Jo
Burgundy Bistro
Cafe Bernard
Cafe Central
Cafe Matou
Cafe Pyrenees
Cafe 36
Clark St. Bistro
Cyrano's Bistrot
D & J Bistro
Dionne's Cafe
Fifth Ave. Bistro
Froggy's
Julie Mai's
KiKi's Bistro
La Crêperie
La Sardine
Le Bouchon
Le Loup Cafe
Marché
Mon Ami Gabi
Oo-La-La!
Provence

Ravinia Bistro
Rest. Toulouse/M
Retro Bistro
Rudi's Wine Bar
Voila
Yoshi's Cafe
Yvette
Yvette Wintergarden

French (New)

Ambria
Aubriot
Carlos'
Everest
Gilles
Green Dolphin St.
Le Titi de Paris
Le Vichyssois
Lucca's
Mimosa
Oceanique
Pump Room
Ritz-Carlton Din. Rm.
Sanford/W
Tallgrass
Thyme
Work of Art Café

German

Berghoff
Edelweiss Bistro
Fritzl's
Genesee Depot
Golden Ox
Historic Turner/W
Karl Ratzsch's/W
Mader's German/W
Mirabell
Pandl's in Bayside/W
Schulien's
Zum Deutschen Eck

Greek

Athenian Room
Costa's
Cross-Rhodes
Grecian Taverna
Greek Islands
Papagus
Parthenon
Pegasus
Roditys
Santorini

Hamburgers

Bones
Boston Blackie's

Charlie Beinlich's
Claim Company
Dick's Last Resort
Ed Debevic's
Ed Debevic's/W
Gold Coast Dogs
Hackney's
Hard Rock Cafe
Johnny Rockets
Medici
Medici on 57th
Miller's Country Hse./M
Pete Miller's
P.J. Clarke's
Redamak's/M
R.J. Grunts
Southport City
Taylor Brewing Co.
Tommy Nevin's

Health Food

Beans & Barley/W
Chicago Diner

Hot Dogs

Fluky's
Gold Coast Dogs

Indian

Bukhara
Dancing Ganesha/W
Gaylord India
Indian Garden
Jaipur Palace
Klay Oven
Moti Mahal
Standard India
Taj Mahal
Tandoor/I
Tiffin
Udupi Palace
Viceroy of India

Indonesian

August Moon

Irish

Fadó Irish Pub
Irish Oak
Tommy Nevin's

Italian

(N=Northern; S=Southern;
N&S=Includes both)
Adagio (N&S)
Angelina Rist. (S)
Anna Maria (N&S)

Antoinette's/I (N&S)
a tavola (N&S)
Babaluci (S)
Bacchanalia (N&S)
Bar Louie (S)
Basil's/I (N)
Basta Pasta (S)
Bella Notte (S)
Bella Vista (N&S)
Bice Grill (N)
Bice Rist. (N)
Bruna's Rist. (N&S)
Buca di Beppo (S)
Buca di Beppo/W (N&S)
Cafe Borgia (N)
Cafe Luciano (N&S)
Cafe Med (N&S)
Cafe Spiaggia (N&S)
Cafe Venezia/I (N&S)
Campagnola (N&S)
Capriccio's (N&S)
Carmine's (S)
Carpaccio Rist. (N)
Centro Rist. (S)
Chicago Pizza (N&S)
Ciao Tutti (N&S)
Clara's Pasta (N&S)
Clark St. Bistro (N)
Club Lucky (S)
Coco Pazzo (N)
Coco Pazzo Cafe (N)
Como Inn (N&S)
Convito Italiano (N&S)
Cornelia's Roosterant (N&S)
Cucina Bella (N&S)
Cucina Paradiso (N&S)
Cucina Roma (N&S)
D'Agostino's (N&S)
Da Nicola (N&S)
Daniello's (S)
Dave's Italian (S)
Del Rio (N)
EJ's Place (N&S)
Erie Cafe (N)
Fanny's Famous/M (N&S)
Filippo's (N&S)
Fly Me to the Moon (N&S)
Francesca's by River (N&S)
Francesca's North (N&S)
Francesca's on Taylor (N&S)
Franceseo's (S)
Franconello's (N&S)
Gabriel's (N)
Giannotti Steak Hse. (N&S)
Gilardi's (N&S)

Graziano's (N&S)
Gusto Italiano (N&S)
Harry Caray's (S)
La Bocca Verità (N&S)
La Borsa (N)
La Cantina (N&S)
La Donna (N&S)
La Gondola (N&S)
La Rosetta (S)
La Sorella (N&S)
Lino's Rist. (N&S)
Louisa's Trattoria/W (N&S)
Madison's (N&S)
Maggiano's (S)
Mangia Trattoria/W (N&S)
Marcello's (N&S)
Mia Cucina (N&S)
Mia Francesca (N)
Mimma's Cafe/W (N&S)
Mimosa (N&S)
Monastero's (N&S)
My Favorite Inn (N&S)
Nana's Cafe (N&S)
Next Door (N&S)
Nick & Tony's (S)
Nonna Bartolotta's/W (N)
O'Neil's (N)
Oo-La-La! (N&S)
Osteria del Mondo/W (N&S)
Pane Caldo (N)
Papa Milano (S)
Pappagallo's (N)
Pasta Tree/W (N&S)
Primavera Rist. (N)
Red Tomato (N&S)
Rico's (N)
Rigoletto (N)
Rist. Bartolotta/W (N)
Rist. DeMarco's (N&S)
Rose Angelis (N&S)
Rosebud Cafe (S)
Rosebud/Naperville (S)
Rosebud/Rush (S)
Roxy Cafe (N&S)
Rudi Fazuli's (N&S)
Sabatino's (N)
Salvatore's Rist. (N)
Scoozi! (S)
Sole Mio East/M (N&S)
Sorriso (N&S)
Spasso (N)
Spavone Seven (N&S)
Spiaggia (N&S)
Stefani's (N)
Strega Nona (N&S)

Suprarossa (N&S)
Sylviano's Rist. (N)
Tarantino's (N&S)
Tony Spavone's (N)
Topo Gigio (N&S)
Tosi's/M (N)
Tratt. Dinotto (N&S)
Tratt. Gianni (N&S)
Tratt. No. 10 (N&S)
Tratt. Parma (N&S)
Tratt. Pizzeria Roma (N&S)
Tucci Benucch (N&S)
Tufano's Vernon Park (S)
Tuscany (N)
Il Jack's (N&S)
Un DiAmo Rist. (N&S)
Va Pensiero (N&S)
Via Emilia (N)
Via Veneto (N&S)
Village (N&S)
Vinci (N&S)
Vivaldi Trattoria (N)
Vivere (N&S)
Vivo (S)
Volare (N&S)
Washington Gardens (N&S)
Zia's Trattoria (N&S)

Japanese
Akai Hana
Benihana
Cocoro
Daruma
Happi Sushi
Hatsuhana
Itto Sushi
Kamehachi
Kuni's
Kyoto
Matsuya
New Japan
Ron of Japan
Sai Cafe
Shiroi Hana
Suntory
Tokyo Marina
Tsunami

Jewish
(*Kosher)
Bagel
Bones
Manny's Coffee Shop
Slice of Life*

Korean
Bando
Woo Lae Oak

Mediterranean
Boulevard
Cafe Med
Cuisines
Gilles
Grapes
Le Loup Cafe
Mantuano
Souk

Mexican/Tex-Mex
Abril
Blue Agave
Campeche
Don Juan
El Jardin
El Presidente
El Tipico
Fernando's
Frida's
Frontera Grill
Hacienda Tecalitlan
Jalapeño's Hottest/I
Julio's Latin Cafe
La Canasta
Las Bellas Artes
Las Fuentes
Las Palmas
Lindo Mexico
Lupita's
Mambo Grill
Mi Casa Su Casa
Nuevo Leon
Rest. Su Casa/M
Rudy's Mexican/W
Salbute
Salpicón
Su Casa
Tecalitlan
Topolobampo
Twisted Lizard
Uncle Julio's

Middle Eastern
A La Turka
Cousin's
Hashalom
Old Jerusalem
Reza's
Sayat Nova
Shish Kabab Hse.
Souk
Uncle Tannous

Moroccan
L'Olive
Tagine

Noodle Shops
Hi Ricky
Oodles of Noodles
Penny's Noodle Shop

Persian
Cy's Crab House
Reza's

Peruvian
Machu Picchu
Rinc. Sudamericano

Pizza
Aurelio's
Bacino's
Bertucci's
Bricks
California Pizza Kit.
Carmen's
Chicago Pizza
Edwardo's
Father & Son Pizza
Giordano's
Graziano's
Leona's
Leona's Neighborhood
Leona's on Taylor
Leona's Sons
Lou Malnati's
Marcello's
My π Pizza
Nancy's
Original Gino's
Pizza Capri
Pizzeria Uno & Due
Ranalli's
Suprarossa
Tratt. Pizzeria Roma
Zarrosta Grill

Polish
Lutnia
Orbit
Red Apple
Zofia's

Polynesian
Trader Vic's

Romanian
Little Bucharest

Russian
Russian Palace
Russian Tea Time

Scandinavian
Tre Kronor

Scottish
Duke of Perth
Earl of Loch Ness

Seafood
Bluepoint Oyster
Bob Chinn's
Bubba Gump Shrimp
Cape Cod Room
Catch 35
Coerper's/W
Cy's Crab House
Davis St. Fishmkt.
Don's Fishmarket
Dover Straits
Eddie Martini's/W
Golden Mast Inn/W
Grande Mere Inn/M
Half Shell
Joe's Crab Shack
J.P.'s Eating Place
King Crab
Magnum's
Myron & Phil's
Nick's Fishmarket
Oceanique
O'Neil's
Pappadeaux
Philander's
Phil Smidt's/I
Quincy Grille
Red Rock Cafe/W
Riva
River Lane Inn/W
Shaw's Crab Hse.
Shaw's Seafood
Starfish Cafe
Timbers Charhse.
Zia's Trattoria

Serbian
Three Brothers/W

South American
Julio's Latin Cafe
Machu Picchu
Mambo Grill
Rinc. Sudamericano

Southern/Soul
Army & Lou's
Biloxi Grill
Brother Jimmy's
Dixie Kitchen

Gladys Luncheonette
House of Blues
Jackson Harbor Grill
Savannah's
Shark Bar
Soul Kitchen
Wishbone

Southwestern
Blue Mesa
Dish

Spanish
Arco de Cuchilleros
Cafe BaBaReeba!
Cafe Iberico
Emilio's Tapas Bar
Granada
Mesón Sabika
Tania's
Tapas Barcelona

Steakhouses
Bogart's
Brett Favre Steakhse./W
Buckingham's
Butcher Shop
Capital Grille
Carmichael's
Chicago Chop Hse.
Coerper's/W
Cy's Steak
Eddie Martini's/W
EJ's Place
Erie Cafe
Gene & Georgetti
Giannotti Steak Hse.
Gibsons Steakhse.
Gino's Steak Hse.
Hickory Pit
Iron Mike's Grille
Jack Gibbons Garden
Jimmy's Charhse.
Jimmy's Steakhse.
Kinzie Chophse.
Lone Star Steakhse.
Madison's
Magnum's
Millennium Steaks
Morton's
Myron & Phil's
Outback Steakhse.
Palm
Pete Miller's
Riva
Rupert's

Ruth's Chris
Saloon
Smith & Wollensky
Tavern on Rush
Timbers Charhse.

Swedish
Ann Sather
Ann Sather Cafe
Ann Sather Express
Tre Kronor

Tapas
Cafe BaBaReeba!
Cafe Iberico
Emilio's La Perla
Emilio's Tapas Bar
Granada
Mesón Sabika
Narcisse
Tapas Barcelona

Thai
Arun's
Bangkok
Bangkok Star
Dao
King and I/W
Penny's Noodle Shop
P.S. Bangkok
Singha
Star of Siam
Thai Borrahn
Thai Classic
Thai 55th
Thai Little Home
Thai Star Cafe

Turkish
A La Turka
Cousin's

Vegetarian
(Most Chinese, Indian and
Thai restaurants)
Beans & Barley/W
Blind Faith Cafe
Chicago Diner
Heartland Cafe
Udupi Palace

Vietnamese
Julie Mai's
Le Colonial
Pasteur Cafe
Work of Art Café

NEIGHBORHOOD LOCATIONS

CHICAGO

City Northwest

Abril
Arun's
Babaluci
Bando
Bar Louie
Basta Pasta
Cafe Matou
Con Fusion
Don Juan
El Tipico
Fondue Stube
Frida's
Giordano's
Hi Howe
Indian Garden
Julio's Latin Cafe
Le Bouchon
Lutnia
Lutz Continental
Meritage Cafe
Merlot Joe
Mirabell
Monastero's
Moti Mahal
N. N. Smokehse.
Orbit
Red Apple
Rinc. Sudamericano
Sabatino's
Suprarossa
Tania's
Thai Little Home
Tiffin
Tre Kronor
Udupi Palace
Via Veneto
Viceroy of India
Zia's Trattoria

City South

Army & Lou's
August Moon
Bacchanalia
Bruna's Rist.
Dixie Kitchen
Edwardo's
Emperor's Choice
Fireside Beverly
Franconello's
Furama

Giordano's
Gladys Luncheonette
Gold Coast Dogs
Hickory Pit
Jackson Harbor Grill
LuLu's
Mandar Inn
Manny's Coffee Shop
Medici on 57th
Nuevo Leon
Original Pancake Hse.
Phoenix
Pizza Capri
Retreat
Rico's
Rosebud Cafe
Sixty-Five
Thai 55th
Three Happiness

City West

a tavola
Bella Notte
Bite Cafe
Blackbird
Bluepoint Oyster
Breakfast Club
Cafe Absinthe
Cafe Med
Carmichael's
Club Lucky
Como Inn
Costa's
El Nandu
Feast
Flat Top Grill
Francesca's on Taylor
Giordano's
Greek Islands
Hacienda Tecalitlan
Hi Ricky
Hong Min
Jane's
La Borsa
La Sardine
Leona's Neighborhood
Leona's on Taylor
Leo's Lunchroom
Madison's
Marché
Millennium Steaks

Northside Cafe
one sixtyblue
Parthenon
Pegasus
Red Light
Restaurant Okno
Roditys
Santorini
Savannah's
Savoy Truffle
Shark Bar
Smoke Daddy
Souk
Soul Kitchen
Starfish Cafe
Sunset
Tecalitlan
Thyme
Toque
Tufano's Vernon Park
Tuscany
Twilight
Il Jack's
Vivo
Wishbone

Diversey to Howard
(Bounded by I-90/94
to the West)
Addis Abeda
A La Turka
Angelina Rist.
Anna Maria
Ann Sather
Ann Sather Cafe
Ann Sather Express
Arco de Cuchilleros
Bagel
Bangkok
Bangkok Star
Belden Deli
Bella Vista
Bistrot Zinc
Brett's
Cafe Selmarie
Campeche
Carmen's
Carson's Ribs
Chicago Diner
Cornelia's Roosterant
Cousin's
Cy's Crab House
Cy's Steak
Daily B&G
Da Nicola

Daniel J's
Deleece
Dellwood Pickle
Dish
Edwardo's
El Jardin
erwin
Ethiopian Village
Fernando's
Fluky's
Fly Me to the Moon
Furama
Gale St. Inn
Genesee Depot
Grecian Taverna
Half Shell
Hashalom
Heartland Cafe
Hi Ricky
Irish Oak
Jack's American
Julie Mai's
Kerouac Jack's
La Bocca Verità
La Crêperie
La Donna
Le Loup Cafe
Leona's
Leona's Sons
Little Bucharest
L'Olive
Lucca's
Machu Picchu
Madam B
Mama Desta's
Matsuya
Mia Francesca
Mi Casa Su Casa
Mongolian BBQ
Moti Mahal
Nancy's
Nookies Tree
Oo-La-La!
Outpost
Pasteur Cafe
Penny's Noodle Shop
Pizza Capri
P.S. Bangkok
Red Tomato
Rhumba
Rose & Crown
Rose Angelis
Schulien's
Shiroi Hana
Standard India

Strega Nona
Thai Classic
Tien Tsin
Tokyo Marina
Tomboy
Tuscany
Weeghman Park
Wild Onion
Yoshi's Cafe
Zum Deutschen Eck

Downtown/Loop

Bacino's
Bandera
Benihana
Ben Pao
Berghoff
Bertucci's
Bice Grill
Bice Rist.
Big Bowl
Bistro 110
Boston Blackie's
Boulevard
Brasserie Jo
Bubba Gump Shrimp
Buckingham's
Bukhara
Butcher Shop
Cafe Iberico
California Pizza Kit.
Capital Grille
Carson's Ribs
Catch 35
Celebrity Cafe
Centro Rist.
Charlie's Ale Hse.
Chicago Chop Hse.
Cielo
Cité
Club Creole
Coco Pazzo
Coco Pazzo Cafe
Cocoro
Corner Bakery
Crofton on Wells
Cuisines
Cyrano's Bistrot
Dao
Dick's Last Resort
Earth
Ed Debevic's
Edwardo's
Elaine & Ina's
Entre Nous

Everest
Fadó Irish Pub
56 West
Fog City Diner
Frontera Grill
Gaylord India
Gene & Georgetti
Giordano's
Gold Coast Dogs
Gordon
Grapes
Green Door Tavern
Hard Rock Cafe
Harry Caray's
Harvest on Huron
Hatsuhana
Havana Café
Heaven on Seven
Heaven on Seven/Rush
House of Blues
Houston's
Hubbard St. Grill
Hudson Club
Indian Garden
Jaipur Palace
Joe's Be-Bop Cafe
Joe's Crab Shack
Kinzie Chophse.
Klay Oven
La Cantina
Lan's Bistro Pacific
La Rosetta
La Strada
Lawry's
Les Nomades
Lino's Rist.
Lloyd's
Lou Malnati's
Lou Mitchell's
Maggiano's
Magnum's
Mambo Grill
Mango
Manhattan's
Mantuano
Mashed Potato Club
Michael Jordan's
Miller's Pub
Mrs. Levy's Deli
Nana's Cafe
Narcisse
Nick & Tony's
Nick's Fishmarket
Original Gino's
Palm

Papagus
Pasha
Pizzeria Uno & Due
Planet Hollywood
Prairie
Primavera Rist.
Printer's Row
Quincy Grille
Rainforest Cafe
Ranalli's
Redfish
Reza's
Rhapsody
Riva
Rivers
Rock Bottom Brew.
Ron of Japan
Rosebud/Rush
Russian Palace
Russian Tea Time
Ruth's Chris
Sayat Nova
Scoozi!
Singha
Sixty-Five
Smith & Wollensky
Sorriso
Spago
Spruce
Star of Siam
Su Casa
Suntory
Suprarossa
Szechwan East
Szechwan House
Taza
Thai Borrahn
312 Chicago
Topolobampo
Trader Vic's
Tratt. No. 10
Tratt. Parma
Village
Vivere
Voila
Volare
Wildfire
Wonton Club
Woo Lae Oak
Yvette Wintergarden
Zinfandel

Near North/Gold Coast
(Chicago Ave. on South,
to North Ave. on North,
to I-90/94 on West)
Albert's Café
Bar Louie
Big Bowl
Biggs
Bistrot Zinc
Blackhawk Lodge
Blue Agave
Cafe Luciano
Cafe Spiaggia
California Pizza Kit.
Cape Cod Room
Carmine's
Cheesecake Factory
Chicago Flat Sammies
Club Macanudo
Corner Bakery
Edwardo's
Eli's
Erie Cafe
Fireplace Inn
foodlife
Gibsons Steakhse.
Jia's
Kamehachi
KiKi's Bistro
Le Colonial
Lucky Platter
Marcello's
M Cafe
Mity Nice Grill
Mrs. Park's Tavern
Oak Terrace
Oak Tree
Old Jerusalem
Original Pancake Hse.
Palette's
Pane Caldo
Papa Milano
Park Ave. Cafe
P.J. Clarke's
Pump Room
Ranalli's
Ritz-Carlton Cafe
Ritz-Carlton Din. Rm.
Saloon
Salpicón
Seasons
Seasons Cafe
Shaw's Crab Hse.
Signature Room
Spiaggia

Tagine
Tavern on Rush
Thai Star Cafe
Topo Gigio
Tratt. Dinotto
Tratt. Pizzeria Roma
Tsunami
Tucci Benucch
Yvette
Zarrosta Grill
Zaven's

Near North/Lincoln Park
(North Ave. on South,
to Diversey on North,
to I-90/94 on West)
Adagio
Ambria
Ann Sather Express
Athenian Room
Aubriot
Bacino's
Bistro Ultra
Blind Faith Cafe
Blue Mesa
Bricks
Brother Jimmy's
Buca di Beppo
Cafe BaBaReeba!
Cafe Bernard
Charlie's Ale Hse.
Charlie Trotter's
Chicago Pizza
Clark St. Bistro
Cohiba
Cousin's
Cucina Bella
D'Agostino's
Dave & Buster's
Dee's
Duke of Perth
Earl of Loch Ness
Edwardo's
El Presidente
Emilio's Tapas Bar
Father & Son Pizza
Filippo's
Flat Top Grill
Four Farthings
Geja's Cafe
Giordano's
Golden Ox
Goose Island
Green Dolphin St.
Hopcats Brewing Co.

Iron Mike's Grille
Itto Sushi
Jerome's Red Ginger
Jia's
Johnny Rockets
John's Place
J.P.'s Eating Place
King Crab
Kyoto
La Canasta
La Gondola
Las Fuentes
Lindo Mexico
Louisiana Kitchen
Max's Deli
Medici
Mon Ami Gabi
Morton's
My π Pizza
Nookies
Nookies Too
North Pond Café
Oodles of Noodles
Original Gino's
Original Pancake Hse.
Penny's Noodle Shop
Pizza Capri
P.S. Bangkok
Ranalli's
Red Lion Pub
Relish
Reza's
R.J. Grunts
Robinson's Ribs
Rudi Fazuli's
Rudi's Wine Bar
Sai Cafe
Salvatore's Rist.
Southport City
Stanley's Kitchen
Stefani's
Stevie B's
Tarantino's
Tilli's
Toulouse on the Park
Tratt. Gianni
Trocadero
Twin Anchors
Twisted Lizard
Uncle Julio's
Uncle Tannous
Un DiAmo Rist.
Via Emilia
Vinci
Work of Art Café

Suburban North

Akai Hana
Allgauer's
Bagel
Bank Ln. Bistro
Bella Notte
Bertucci's
Betise
Blind Faith Cafe
Bones
Brasserie T
Cafe Central
Cafe Luciano
Campagnola
Capriccio's
Carlos'
Carmen's
Carson's Ribs
Ceiling Zero
Chaplin's on Church
Charlie Beinlich's
Chicago Diner
Chinoiserie
Claim Company
Convito Italiano
Corner Bakery
Cross-Rhodes
Cucina Roma
Daruma
Dave's Italian
Davis St. Fishmkt.
Del Rio
Dixie Kitchen
Don's Fishmarket
Ed Debevic's
Edelweiss Bistro
Edwardo's
EJ's Place
El Tipico
Flatlander's
Flat Top Grill
Francesca's North
Francesco's
Froggy's
Gabriel's
Gary Barnett's
Giannotti Steak Hse.
Gilles
Giordano's
Gusto Italiano
Hackney's
Happi Sushi
Jilly's Cafe
Jimmy's Charhse.
Jimmy's Steakhse.

Kuni's
Las Palmas
Lindo Mexico
Lou Malnati's
Lucky Platter
LuLu's
Lupita's
Maggiano's
Max's Deli
Mesón Sabika
Mimosa
My Favorite Inn
Myron & Phil's
New Japan
Next Door
Oceanique
O'Neil's
Panda Panda
Pappagallo's
Patrick & James
Pete Miller's
Pine Yard
Provence
Ravinia Bistro
Rigoletto
Ron of Japan
Roxy Cafe
Sarkis Grill
Shaw's Seafood
Slice of Life
South Gate Cafe
Spavone Seven
Stir Crazy Cafe
Szechwan North
Szechwan Palace
Tanglewood
Tapas Barcelona
Timbers Charhse.
Tommy Nevin's
Trio
Va Pensiero
Walker Bros.
Washington Gardens
Windows of Cuisine

Suburban Northwest

Bacchus Nibbles
Barn of Barrington
Barrington Country
Barry's Ribs
Benihana
Best Hunan
Biloxi Grill
Bob Chinn's
Buca di Beppo

Cafe La Cave
Cafe Pyrenees
California Cafe B&G
Carpaccio Rist.
Carson's Ribs
Corner Bakery
Crawdaddy Bayou
D & J Bistro
Daniello's
Daruma
Don Roth's
Dover Straits
Fritzl's
Gale St. Inn
Gilardi's
Graziano's
Hackney's
Indian Garden
Joe's Crab Shack
Las Palmas
Le Français
Le Titi de Paris
Le Vichyssois
Lou Malnati's
Lou Mitchell's Exp.
Maggiano's
Mia Cucina
Millrose Brewing Co.
Morton's
Nick's Fishmarket
94th Aero Squadron
Original Gino's
Outback Steakhse.
Pappadeaux
Rainforest Cafe
Retro Bistro
Rist. DeMarco's
Rupert's
Sayat Nova
1776
Spasso
Suprarossa
Tavern in the Town
Walker Bros.
Walter's
Weber Grill
Zofia's

Suburban South
Aurelio's
Bogart's
Burgundy Bistro
Cafe Borgia
Fresh Starts
Gino's Steak Hse.

Hackney's
Jack Gibbons Garden
Maple Tree Inn
Old Barn
Original Gino's
Original Pancake Hse.
Outback Steakhse.
Wayside Manor

Suburban Southwest
Courtright's
Dionne's Cafe
Public Landing
Shish Kabab Hse.
Szechwan Rest.
Taj Mahal
Tallgrass

Suburban West
Allgauer's
America's Brewpub
Bacino's
Benihana
Bertucci's
Bistro Banlieue
Bohemian Crystal
Buca di Beppo
Cafe 36
California Pizza Kit.
Carson's Ribs
Ciao Tutti
Clara's Pasta
Clubhouse
Corner Bakery
Costa's
Cucina Paradiso
Cucina Roma
Czech Plaza
Dave & Buster's
Emilio's La Perla
Emilio's Tapas Bar
Famous Dave's
Fifth Ave. Bistro
Fond de la Tour
Founders Hill
Francesca's by River
Giannotti Steak Hse.
Giordano's
Granada
Greek Islands
Joe's Crab Shack
Las Bellas Artes
La Sorella
Las Palmas
Leona's
Lone Star Steakhse.

Maggiano's
Magnum's
Mesón Sabika
Mill Race Inn
Montparnasse
Morton's
Original Gino's
Papagus
Pappadeaux
Philander's
Pizza Capri
Redfish
Robinson's Ribs
Rosebud/Naperville
Russell's BBQ

Salbute
Stir Crazy Cafe
Suprarossa
Sylviano's Rist.
Taylor Brewing Co.
302 West
Tony Spavone's
Tuscany
Viceroy of India
Vivaldi Trattoria
Waterford
Wildfire
Zarrosta Grill
Zealous

INDIANA

Antoinette's
Basil's
Cafe Venezia
Clayton's
Jalapeño's Hottest
La Salle Grill

Louis' Bon Appetit
Miller Bakery Cafe
Phil Smidt's
Pump's on 12
Strongbow Inn
Tandoor

MICHIGAN

Bill Knapp's
Blue Plate Cafe
Chequers
Fanny's Famous
Global B&G
Grande Mere Inn
Hannah's
Hyerdall's Cafe
Jenny's

Kent's
Miller's Country Hse.
Redamak's
Red Arrow Roadhse.
Rest. Su Casa
Rest. Toulouse
Skip's Other Place
Sole Mio East
Tosi's

WISCONSIN/MILWAUKEE

Bartolotta's Lake Park
Beans & Barley
Boulevard Inn
Brett Favre Steakhse.
Buca di Beppo
Cafe at Pfister
China Gourmet
Chip and Py's
Coerper's
Crawdaddy's
Dancing Ganesha
Ed Debevic's
Eddie Martini's
Elm Grove Inn
Elsa's on the Park
English Room
Golden Mast Inn
Grenadier's
Heaven City
Historic Turner
Immigrant Room

Karl Ratzsch's
Kilbourn Cafe
King and I
Louisa's Trattoria
Mader's German
Mangia Trattoria
Mimma's Cafe
Nonna Bartolotta's
Osteria del Mondo
Pandl's in Bayside
Pasta Tree
Red Rock Cafe
Rist. Bartolotta
River Lane Inn
Riversite
Rudy's Mexican
Sanford
Saz's
Steven Wade's
Three Brothers

SPECIAL FEATURES AND APPEALS

Brunch
(Best of many)
Aubriot
Barn of Barrington
Betise
Bistro 110
Blackhawk Lodge
Blue Plate Cafe/M
Boulevard Inn/W
Brett's
California Cafe B&G
Celebrity Cafe
Cité
Clark St. Bistro
Deleece
erwin
Feast
Frontera Grill
Hannah's/M
House of Blues
Hyerdall's Cafe/M
Jalapeño's Hottest/I
John's Place
Louis' Bon Appetit/I
Mader's German/W
Medici
Medici on 57th
94th Aero Squadron
North Pond Café
Northside Cafe
Oak Terrace
Oo-La-La!
Osteria del Mondo/W
Pandl's in Bayside/W
Park Ave. Cafe
Pump Room
Retreat
Ritz-Carlton Din. Rm.
R.J. Grunt's
Saz's/W
Seasons
Tavern on Rush
312 Chicago
Thyme
Wild Onion
Wishbone

Buffet Served
(Check prices, days
and times)
Barn of Barrington
Best Hunan

Boulevard
Cafe La Cave
Celebrity Cafe
China Gourmet/W
Cielo
Cité
Dick's Last Resort
El Jardin
Flat Top Grill
Gaylord India
Grenadier's/W
Indian Garden
Jaipur Palace
Jerome's Red Ginger
Jia's
Joe's Be-Bop Cafe
Klay Oven
La Cantina
Le Loup Cafe
Lindo Mexico
Mader's German/W
Miller's Country Hse./M
Moti Mahal
My π Pizza
94th Aero Squadron
Oak Terrace
Pandl's in Bayside/W
Pappagallo's
Primavera Rist.
P.S. Bangkok
Retreat
Rivers
Seasons
Signature Room
Standard India
Stanley's Kitchen
Strongbow Inn/I
Szechwan East
Szechwan House
Szechwan Palace
Szechwan Rest.
Taj Mahal
Tandoor/I
Tania's
Thai Borrahn
Thai Classic
Tiffin
Tratt. Gianni
Tratt. Pizzeria Roma
Viceroy of India
Village
Vivere
Wild Onion

Business Dining

Ambria
Bank Ln. Bistro
Barn of Barrington
Barrington Country
Bella Vista
Ben Pao
Betise
Bice Rist.
Bill Knapp's/M
Bistro 110
Blackhawk Lodge
Bob Chinn's
Boulevard
Boulevard Inn/W
Brasserie Jo
Brasserie T
Buckingham's
Butcher Shop
Cafe Venezia/I
Cape Cod Room
Capital Grille
Catch 35
Centro Rist.
Charlie Trotter's
Chicago Chop Hse.
Chip and Py's/W
Coco Pazzo
Coco Pazzo Cafe
Como Inn
Courtright's
Crofton on Wells
Cyrano's Bistrot
Don Roth's
Eddie Martini's/W
Eli's
Elm Grove Inn/W
Entre Nous
Erie Cafe
Everest
Gene & Georgetti
Gibsons Steakhse.
Gordon
Grapes
Grenadier's/W
Hannah's/M
Harry Caray's
Harvest on Huron
Hatsuhana
Hubbard St. Grill
Immigrant Room/W
Iron Mike's Grille
Karl Ratzsch's/W
KiKi's Bistro
Kilbourn Cafe/W

King and I/W
Kinzie Chophse.
La Strada
Lawry's
Le Colonial
Le Français
Les Nomades
Lino's Rist.
Lloyd's
Louisa's Trattoria/W
Mader's German/W
Madison's
Maggiano's
Magnum's
Mangia Trattoria/W
Mantuano
Marché
Miller Bakery Cafe/I
Mimma's Cafe/W
Morton's
Mrs. Park's Tavern
Nick & Tony's
Nick's Fishmarket
Old Barn
Osteria del Mondo/W
Palm
Pandl's in Bayside/W
Pane Caldo
Papagus
Park Ave. Cafe
Pasta Tree/W
Phil Smidt's/I
Prairie
Primavera Rist.
Printer's Row
Pump Room
Quincy Grille
Rhapsody
Rist. Bartolotta/W
Ritz-Carlton Cafe
Ritz-Carlton Din. Rm.
River Lane Inn/W
Rivers
Rosebud/Rush
Rupert's
Ruth's Chris
Saloon
Sayat Nova
Saz's/W
Scoozi!
Seasons
Shaw's Crab Hse.
Signature Room
Smith & Wollensky
Spago

Spiaggia
Spruce
Steven Wade's/W
Tandoor/I
Tavern on Rush
312 Chicago
Topolobampo
Tosi's/M
Trader Vic's
Tratt. No. 10
Tratt. Parma
Tuscany
Va Pensiero
Village
Vivere
Vivo
Voila
Walter's
Waterford
Yvette Wintergarden

BYO
Bagel
Bite Cafe
Chinoiserie
Dellwood Pickle
Genesee Depot
Hashalom
Hong Min
Le Loup Cafe
Leo's Lunchroom
L'Olive
Moti Mahal
N. N. Smokehse.
Old Jerusalem
Oodles of Noodles
Penny's Noodle Shop
Salbute
Savoy Truffle
Standard India
Steven Wade's/W
Thai Classic
Thai 55th
Thai Star Cafe
Tien Tsin
Tomboy
Tre Kronor
Twilight
Work of Art Café

Caters
(Best of many)
Angelina Rist.
Army & Lou's
a tavola

Babaluci
Bacchus Nibbles
Biloxi Grill
Blind Faith Cafe
Blue Plate Cafe/M
Cafe BaBaReeba!
Cafe Borgia
Cafe Luciano
Carmine's
Centro Rist.
Clara's Pasta
Clayton's/I
Convito Italiano
Corner Bakery
Cucina Bella
Daily B&G
Da Nicola
Daniello's
Del Rio
Don Juan
Eddie Martini's/W
El Jardin
Elm Grove Inn/W
Erie Cafe
erwin
Feast
Flat Top Grill
Fond de la Tour
Fresh Starts
Frida's
Froggy's
Gilardi's
Jerome's Red Ginger
Jia's
La Bocca Verità
La Donna
La Rosetta
Las Bellas Artes
Louis' Bon Appetit/I
Lou Malnati's
LuLu's
Mangia Trattoria/W
Mantuano
Max's Deli
Mia Cucina
Miller Bakery Cafe/I
Miller's Country Hse./M
Millrose Brewing Co.
Oceanique
Oo-La-La!
Osteria del Mondo/W
Pandl's in Bayside/W
Papagus
Pappagallo's
Pegasus

Redfish
Red Rock Cafe/W
Rist. DeMarco's
Rose Angelis
Rosebud/Naperville
Rosebud/Rush
Spago
Spasso
Steven Wade's/W
Strongbow Inn/I
Tania's
Taza
Tomboy
Topo Gigio
Tratt. Dinotto
Tratt. Parma
Tratt. Pizzeria Roma
Twilight
Va Pensiero
Via Veneto
Village
Vinci
Vivaldi Trattoria
Vivo
Walter's
Wishbone
Work of Art Café
Zealous

Cigar Friendly
America's Brewpub
Bar Louie
Basil's/I
Bice Rist.
Biggs
Biloxi Grill
Bluepoint Oyster
Butcher Shop
Cafe Iberico
Cafe Luciano
Capital Grille
Carmine's
Carson's Ribs
Centro Rist.
Chicago Chop Hse.
Clubhouse
Club Lucky
Club Macanudo
Coco Pazzo
Cohiba
Courtright's
Dick's Last Resort
Eddie Martini's/W
Edelweiss Bistro
Edwardo's

Elm Grove Inn/W
Entre Nous
Erie Cafe
Fernando's
56 West
Fly Me to the Moon
Founders Hill
Francesca's on Taylor
Franconello's
Gale St. Inn
Gibsons Steakhse.
Gilardi's
Gino's Steak Hse.
Golden Ox
Goose Island
Green Dolphin St.
Hackney's
Harry Caray's
Havana Café
Hudson Club
Iron Mike's Grille
Jack Gibbons Garden
Jimmy's Steakhse.
Kerouac Jack's
La Strada
Le Colonial
Lindo Mexico
Madison's
Maggiano's
Maple Tree Inn
Mia Cucina
Mi Casa Su Casa
Michael Jordan's
Millennium Steaks
Morton's
Mrs. Park's Tavern
Myron & Phil's
Narcisse
Osteria del Mondo/W
Outback Steakhse.
Palette's
Palm
Pete Miller's
Phil Smidt's/I
P.J. Clarke's
Ranalli's
Redamak's/M
Redfish
Red Lion Pub
Rhumba
Rico's
Rock Bottom Brew.
Rosebud Cafe
Rosebud/Naperville
Rosebud/Rush

Rudy's Mexican/W
Rupert's
Saloon
Savannah's
Shark Bar
Spago
Stanley's Kitchen
Tania's
Tarantino's
Tony Spavone's
Tosi's/M
Village
Weber Grill
Zaven's

Dancing/Entertainment
(Check days, times and
performers for entertainment;
D=dancing; best of many)
Adagio (varies)
Babaluci (blues/jazz)
Barn of Barrington (piano)
Basta Pasta (D/jazz)
Bella Notte (piano)
Blackhawk Lodge (bluegrass)
Boulevard (piano)
Boulevard Inn/W (piano)
Brasserie Jo (jazz)
Bricks (D/blues)
Brother Jimmy's (varies)
Cafe Luciano (piano)
Carlos' (band)
Carmine's (band)
Catch 35 (piano)
Chicago Chop Hse. (piano)
Chip and Py's/W (jazz/piano)
Ciao Tutti (jazz)
Cielo (jazz/piano)
Cité (cabaret/piano)
Club Macanudo (jazz)
Crawdaddy Bayou (varies)
Cucina Paradiso (jazz)
D'Agostino's (blues/jazz)
Da Nicola (jazz/piano)
Dick's Last Resort (varies)
Entre Nous (piano)
Fadó Irish Pub (varies)
Fly Me to the Moon (band)
Fond de la Tour (piano)
Fondue Stube (classical)
Founders Hill (bands/blues)
Gale St. Inn (D/contemporary)
Geja's Cafe (classical/flamenco)
Giannotti Steak Hse. (D/varies)
Gibsons Steakhse. (piano)

Gilardi's (piano)
Golden Ox (varies)
Gordon (D/piano)
Granada (D/flamenco)
Green Dolphin St. (jazz)
Grenadier's/W (piano)
Hacienda Tecalitlan (mariachi)
Hackney's (piano)
Heartland Cafe (varies)
Heaven City/W (D/guitar/piano)
House of Blues (blues)
Iron Mike's Grille (piano)
Joe's Be-Bop Cafe (jazz)
Karl Ratzsch's/W (piano)
Kerouac Jack's (bands)
La Crêperie (D/bands)
La Strada (piano)
Little Bucharest
  (accordion/violin)
Madison's (jazz)
Mangia Trattoria/W (accordion)
Mia Cucina (D/jazz/pop)
Mi Casa Su Casa (D)
Miller's Country Hse./M (jazz)
Myron & Phil's (piano)
Nick's Fishmarket (D/bands)
94th Aero Squadron (D)
Oo-La-La! (jazz)
Palette's (piano)
Philander's (D/jazz)
Primavera Rist. (opera)
Redfish (blues)
Restaurant Okno (DJ)
Rhumba (D/Brazilian)
Rist. Bartolotta/W (strolling
  musicians)
Ritz-Carlton Din. Rm. (piano)
Rosebud/Rush (piano)
Rudi's Wine Bar (jazz)
Salvatore's Rist. (piano)
Schulien's (magician)
Shark Bar (bands/jazz)
Signature Room (jazz)
Smoke Daddy (blues/jazz)
Sorriso (piano)
Spavone Seven (karaoke)
Spiaggia (piano)
Sylviano's Rist. (D/varies)
Tania's (D/varies)
Tapas Barcelona (flamenco)
302 West (jazz)
Tommy Nevin's (folk/Irish)
Toulouse on the Park (piano)
Yvette (piano)
Yvette Wintergarden (piano)

Zaven's (guitar/violin)
Zum Deutschen Eck (German)

Delivers*/Takeout
(Nearly all Asians, coffee
shops, delis, diners and
pasta/pizzerias deliver or do
takeout; here are some
interesting possibilities;
D=delivery, T=takeout; *call
to check range and charges,
if any)
A La Turka (D,T)
Albert's Café (D,T)
Anna Maria (T)
Ann Sather Cafe (T)
Ann Sather Express (D,T)
Arco de Cuchilleros (T)
Army & Lou's (T)
Athenian Room (T)
Babaluci (D,T)
Bacchanalia (T)
Bacchus Nibbles (T)
Bacino's (D)
Bagel (D)
Bandera (T)
Barry's Ribs (T)
Basta Pasta (D,T)
Beans & Barley/W (T)
Bertucci's (D,T)
Betise (T)
Bice Grill (T)
Big Bowl (D,T)
Biloxi Grill (T)
Bistro 110 (T)
Bistrot Zinc (T)
Bite Cafe (T)
Blackhawk Lodge (T)
Blind Faith Cafe (T)
Blue Plate Cafe/M (T)
Boston Blackie's (T)
Bricks (T)
Brother Jimmy's (T)
Bruna's Rist. (T)
Buca di Beppo (T)
Cafe BaBaReeba! (T)
Cafe Iberico (T)
Cafe Luciano (T)
California Pizza Kit. (D,T)
Cape Cod Room (D)
Carmen's (T)
Carmine's (T)
Carson's Ribs (T)
Centro Rist. (D,T)
Charlie Beinlich's (T)

Chicago Chop Hse. (T)
Chicago Diner (D)
China Gourmet/W (D)
Claim Company (D)
Clara's Pasta (D,T)
Convito Italiano (T)
Corner Bakery (T)
Cousin's (T)
Crawdaddy Bayou (T)
Cross-Rhodes (T)
Cucina Bella (T)
Cucina Paradiso (T)
Da Nicola (D,T)
Daniello's (D)
Dave's Italian (D,T)
Davis St. Fishmkt. (T)
Deleece (T)
Dellwood Pickle (T)
Del Rio (T)
Dick's Last Resort (T)
Dish (T)
Dixie Kitchen (T)
Earth (T)
Ed Debevic's (T)
Edwardo's (D)
El Jardin (D,T)
Emilio's La Perla (T)
Erie Cafe (T)
erwin (T)
Feast (D,T)
Fireplace Inn (D,T)
Fireside Beverly (T)
Flat Top Grill (T)
Fond de la Tour (D)
foodlife (D)
Fresh Starts (D,T)
Frida's (T)
Froggy's (D)
Gale St. Inn (T)
Gaylord India (D)
Gold Coast Dogs (T)
Grande Mere Inn/M (T)
Graziano's (D)
Greek Islands (T)
Gusto Italiano (D,T)
Hackney's (T)
Half Shell (T)
Happi Sushi (D)
Hatsuhana (D)
Heartland Cafe (T)
Hickory Pit (T)
Hi Ricky (D)
Houston's (T)
Hyerdall's Cafe/M (T)
Jaipur Palace (D)

Jerome's Red Ginger (T)
Jia's (D)
Johnny Rockets (T)
John's Place (D)
Kamehachi (D)
Kerouac Jack's (T)
Klay Oven (D)
La Cantina (D)
Lan's Bistro Pacific (D)
La Rosetta (D)
Las Bellas Artes (T)
La Strada (T)
Le Colonial (D)
Leona's (T)
Leona's Neighborhood (T)
Leona's on Taylor (T)
Leona's Sons (T)
Leo's Lunchroom (T)
Lindo Mexico (D)
Little Bucharest (D)
L'Olive (D,T)
Lou Malnati's (D)
Lou Mitchell's (T)
Lou Mitchell's Exp. (T)
Lucky Platter (T)
LuLu's (D)
Lupita's (T)
Mangia Trattoria/W (T)
Manny's Coffee Shop (D)
Mantuano (D,T)
Marcello's (T)
Medici (T)
Medici on 57th (D,T)
Moti Mahal (D)
My π Pizza (D)
Nana's Cafe (D,T)
Nancy's (D)
N. N. Smokehse. (D,T)
Nonna Bartolotta's/W (T)
Nookies (T)
Nookies Too (T)
Nookies Tree (T)
Northside Cafe (T)
Old Jerusalem (T)
Orbit (T)
Original Gino's (D)
Osteria del Mondo/W (T)
Pandl's in Bayside/W (T)
Papagus (D,T)
Papa Milano (D)
Pappagallo's (D,T)
Pegasus (T)
Pizza Capri (D,T)
P.S. Bangkok (D)
Ranalli's (D)

Ravinia Bistro (D)
Redfish (T)
Reza's (D,T)
Rinc. Sudamericano (T)
Rist. Bartolotta/W (T)
Robinson's Ribs (D,T)
Rosebud Cafe (T)
Rosebud/Naperville (T)
Russell's BBQ (T)
Sai Cafe (D)
Santorini (T)
Slice of Life (T)
Soul Kitchen (T)
South Gate Cafe (T)
Standard India (D)
Stevie B's (T)
Strongbow Inn/I (D)
Suprarossa (D)
Sylviano's Rist. (D)
Szechwan East (D)
Taj Mahal (T)
Tania's (D,T)
Tapas Barcelona (T)
Taza (D,T)
Tecalitlan (T)
Thai Borrahn (T)
Thai Classic (D)
Tiffin (T)
Timbers Charhse. (D)
Tratt. Dinotto (D)
Tratt. Parma (D)
Tratt. Pizzeria Roma (D)
Il Jack's (D)
Uncle Julio's (T)
Uncle Tannous (T)
Viceroy of India (T)
Village (D)
Vinci (D)
Vivaldi Trattoria (T)
Wildfire (D,T)
Wild Onion (T)
Wishbone (T)
Zarrosta Grill (D,T)
Zia's Trattoria (T)

Dessert/Ice Cream
Ambria
Brasserie Jo
Brasserie T
Carlos'
Charlie Trotter's
Crofton on Wells
Everest
Fresh Starts
Gabriel's

Gordon
Harvest on Huron
Jilly's Cafe
Le Français
Les Nomades
Le Titi de Paris
Le Vichyssois
Lutz Continental
Mango
Mantuano
Marché
Medici
Montparnasse
Osteria del Mondo/W
Park Ave. Cafe
Provence
Rest. Okno
Rhapsody
Ritz-Carlton Din. Rm.
Sanford/W
Spruce
Tallgrass
302 West
Thyme
Tomboy
Topolobampo
Trio
Va Pensiero

Dining Alone
(Other than hotels, coffee
shops, sushi bars and places
with counter service)
Ann Sather
Arco de Cuchilleros
Army & Lou's
Athenian Room
Berghoff
Bice Grill
Big Bowl
Blind Faith Cafe
Blue Plate Cafe/M
Cafe Spiaggia
Carmen's
China Gourmet/W
Chinoiserie
Claim Company
Club Creole
Convito Italiano
Dellwood Pickle
Earth
Ed Debevic's
Elaine & Ina's
foodlife
Heartland Cafe

Heaven on Seven
Heaven on Seven/Rush
Jia's
Johnny Rockets
Kamehachi
Medici on 57th
Nookies Tree
Oak Tree

Fireplaces
Adagio
Basta Pasta
Betise
Blackhawk Lodge
Blue Mesa
Chip and Py's/W
Como Inn
Courtright's
Dionne's Cafe
Don Roth's
Eddie Martini's/W
Elm Grove Inn/W
Erie Cafe
Fireplace Inn
Gale St. Inn
Gene & Georgetti
Grande Mere Inn/M
Half Shell
Hannah's/M
Heaven City/W
Les Nomades
Le Vichyssois
Louis' Bon Appetit/I
94th Aero Squadron
Old Barn
Rosebud/Naperville
Steven Wade's/W
Strongbow Inn/I
Tanglewood
Timbers Charhse.
Trio
Va Pensiero

Game in Season
Berghoff
Betise
Cafe 36
Carlos'
Charlie Trotter's
Clayton's/I
Courtright's
Crofton on Wells
Cyrano's Bistrot
Don Juan
Elm Grove Inn/W
Fireside Beverly

Fond de la Tour
Gordon
Grenadier's/W
Heaven City/W
Karl Ratzsch's/W
Le Bouchon
Le Français
Les Nomades
Le Titi de Paris
Le Vichyssois
Louis' Bon Appetit/I
Meritage Cafe
Prairie
Printer's Row
Ritz-Carlton Din. Rm.
Riversite/W
Seasons
Spago
Spruce
Steven Wade's/W
Tallgrass
302 West
Va Pensiero
Walter's
Zinfandel

Health/Spa Menus

(Most places cook to order
to meet any dietary request;
call in advance to check;
almost all Chinese, Indian
and other ethnics have
health-conscious meals,
as do the following)
Blue Plate Cafe/M
Cafe Central
Carlos'
Charlie Trotter's
Chicago Diner
Earth
Flat Top Grill
Heartland Cafe
Ritz-Carlton Din. Rm.
Seasons
Slice of Life
Trio
Walter's

Historic Interest

(Year opened; *building)
1886 Schulien's
1890 Hannah's/M*
1897 Three Brothers/W*
1898 Berghoff*
1910 Phil Smidt's/I*

1916 Del Rio*
1920 Old Barn
1920 Philander's*
1921 Golden Ox*
1921 Green Door Tavern*
1922 Salvatore's Rist.*
1923 Lou Mitchell's
1924 Como Inn*
1930 Tufano's Vernon Park*
1932 Twin Anchors*
1933 Cape Cod Room*
1933 Hickory Pit*
1945 Ann Sather*

Hotel Dining

American Club
  Immigrant Room
Carleton Hotel
  Philander's
Chicago Hilton & Towers
  Buckingham's
Doubletree Guest Suites
  Mrs. Park's Tavern
  Park Ave. Cafe
Drake Hotel
  Cape Cod Room
  Oak Terrace
Embassy Suites Hotel
  Papagus
Fairmont Hotel
  Entre Nous
  Primavera Rist.
Four Seasons Hotel
  Seasons
  Seasons Cafe
Gordon Beach Inn
  Fanny's Famous/M
Hampton Inn & Suites
  Fog City Diner
Hilton Lisle/Naperville
  Allgauer's
Hilton Northbrook
  Allgauer's
Hotel Allegro
  312 Chicago
Hotel Inter-Continental
  Boulevard
Hyatt on Printer's Row
  Prairie
Knickerbocker Hotel
  Osteria del Mondo/W
Lenox Hotel
  Houston's
Marriott Suites
  Jaipur Palace

Oak Brook Hills Hotel
 Waterford
Omni Ambassador East
 Pump Room
Omni Chicago Hotel
 Cielo
Orrington Hotel
 Gary Barnett's
Palmer House
 Trader Vic's
Pfister Hotel
 Cafe at the Pfister
 English Room
Renaissance Hotel
 Cuisines
Ritz-Carlton Hotel
 Ritz-Carlton Cafe
 Ritz-Carlton Din. Rm.
Seneca Hotel
 Saloon
Summerfield Suites Hotel
 Benihana
Swissôtel
 Palm
Tremont Hotel
 Iron Mike's Grille
Westin River North
 Celebrity Cafe
Wyndham Milwaukee Ctr.
 Kilbourn Cafe/W

"In" Places

Ambria
Bice Rist.
Bistrot Zinc
Blackbird
Brasserie Jo
Brasserie T
Cafe Absinthe
Cafe BaBaReeba!
Campagnola
Carlos'
Centro Rist.
Charlie Trotter's
Coco Pazzo
Con Fusion
Crofton on Wells
erwin
56 West
Francesca's North
Francesca's on Taylor
Frontera Grill
Gene & Georgetti
Gibsons Steakhse.
Gordon

Grapes
Harry Caray's
Harvest on Huron
House of Blues
Hudson Club
Iron Mike's Grille
Jenny's/M
KiKi's Bistro
La Sorella
Le Bouchon
Le Colonial
Le Français
Maggiano's
Mangia Trattoria/W
Mango
Marché
Meritage Cafe
Mia Francesca
Mon Ami Gabi
Morton's
North Pond Café
one sixtyblue
Pasteur Cafe
Pizzeria Uno & Due
Printer's Row
Provence
Red Light
Restaurant Okno
Rhumba
Ritz-Carlton Din. Rm.
Rosebud Cafe
Rosebud/Naperville
Rosebud/Rush
Sanford/W
Scoozi!
Seasons
Shaw's Crab Hse.
Smith & Wollensky
Soul Kitchen
Spago
Spruce
Starfish Cafe
Tavern on Rush
Thyme
Topo Gigio
Topolobampo
Toque
Trio
Vivo

Jacket Required

Ambria
Arun's
Cafe La Cave
Cape Cod Room

Carlos'
Charlie Trotter's
Cité
Cuisines
English Room/W
Entre Nous
Everest
Fond de la Tour
Gordon
Grenadier's/W
Immigrant Room/W
Le Français
Les Nomades
Le Titi de Paris
Old Barn
Pump Room
Ritz-Carlton Din. Rm.
Sanford/W
Seasons
Spiaggia
Tallgrass
Trio

Late Late — After 12:30
(All hours are AM)
Bar Louie (2)
Belden Deli (24 hrs.)
El Presidente (24 hrs.)
Father & Son Pizza (1:15)
Half Shell (1)
Hong Min (2)
Hopcats Brewing Co. (2)
Irish Oak (2)
Iron Mike's Grille (2)
Julio's Latin Cafe (24 hrs.)
Lindo Mexico (2)
Lou Mitchell's Exp. (24 hrs.)
Miller's Pub (1:30)
Mrs. Park's Tavern (1:30)
Nancy's (1)
Narcisse (1:30)
Northside Cafe (1)
Pasha (3)
Pizzeria Uno & Due (1)
Smoke Daddy (1)
Three Happiness (3)
Wonton Club (1)

Meet for a Drink
(Most top hotels and the
following standouts)
Bandera
Bistro 110
Blackhawk Lodge
Brasserie Jo

Catch 35
Chicago Chop Hse.
Club Macanudo
Fadó Irish Pub
56 West
Frontera Grill
Gibsons Steakhse.
Gordon
Green Dolphin St.
Harry Caray's
Harvest on Huron
Havana Café
Hopcats Brewing Co.
Hubbard St. Grill
Hudson Club
Les Nomades
Lino's Rist.
Manhattan's
Mantuano
Marché
Palette's
P.J. Clarke's
Pump Room
Redfish
Scoozi!
Shark Bar
Shaw's Crab Hse.
Smith & Wollensky
Spago
Tavern on Rush
Tratt. No. 10
Tratt. Parma
Voila
Weeghman Park
Wildfire

Noteworthy Newcomers (27)
Aubriot
Blackbird
Bubba Gump Shrimp
Carmichael's
Cohiba
Crofton on Wells
Fog City Diner
Gilles
Harvest on Huron
Jack's
La Sardine
Madam B
Meritage Cafe
Mimosa
Mon Ami Gabi
North Pond Café
one sixtyblue

Provence
Rhapsody
Smith & Wollensky
Souk
Tagine
Tavern on Rush
312 Chicago
Thyme
Toque
Trocadero

Noteworthy Closings (17)

Avanzare
Brown Dog Cafe
Bub City Crabshack
Busy Bee
Churrascos
Gavroche
Grappa
Gypsy's Cove
Harry's Velvet Room
Hat Dance
House of Hunan
Petros Dianna's
Sage's Sage's
Tra Via
Tucci Milan
Un Grand Cafe
Widow Newton's Tavern

Offbeat

Addis Abeda
Bite Cafe
Brother Jimmy's
Dave & Buster's
Dish
Ethiopian Village
Johnny Rockets
Leo's Lunchroom
Mama Desta's
Manny's Coffee Shop
Narcisse
Rainforest Cafe
Restaurant Okno
Rhumba
Sarkis Grill
Soul Kitchen
Tomboy

Outdoor Dining

(G=garden; P=patio;
S=sidewalk; T=terrace;
W=waterside; best of many)
Albert's Café (S)
Athenian Room (S)
Barrington Country (P)

Bartolotta's Lake Park/W (W)
Bice Grill (S)
Bice Rist. (S)
Big Bowl (S)
Biloxi Grill (P,T,W)
Bistro Banlieue (P)
Bistro 110 (S)
Bistrot Zinc (S)
Blackbird (S)
Blackhawk Lodge (S)
Blue Mesa (P)
Blue Plate Cafe/M (G)
Bluepoint Oyster (S)
Boulevard Inn/W (T)
Brasserie Jo (S)
Brett's (S)
Brother Jimmy's (S)
Buca di Beppo (P)
Burgundy Bistro (S)
Cafe BaBaReeba! (P)
Cafe Borgia (P,S)
Cafe Central (S)
Cafe Luciano (S)
Cafe Selmarie (S)
Cafe 36 (P,S)
Campagnola (G)
Carmine's (S)
Carpaccio Rist. (S)
Centro Rist. (S)
Charlie's Ale Hse. (G)
Cheesecake Factory (P)
Chicago Flat Sammies (S)
Chip and Py's/W (P)
Ciao Tutti (S)
Clark St. Bistro (S)
Club Macanudo (S)
Coco Pazzo (S)
Coco Pazzo Cafe (P,S)
Cohiba (G)
Con Fusion (S)
Convito Italiano (P)
Corner Bakery (S)
Crawdaddy Bayou (P)
Crofton on Wells (S)
Cucina Bella (G,S)
Cyrano's Bistrot (S)
Dao (G)
Deleece (S)
Dick's Last Resort (P)
Dionne's Cafe (S)
Dish (S)
Dixie Kitchen (P)
Elaine & Ina's (S)
El Jardin (G,P)
Emilio's La Perla (P)

172

Emilio's Tapas Bar (P)
Famous Dave's (P)
Feast (G)
Fireplace Inn (G,P,S)
Fireside Beverly (T)
Flatlander's (P)
Flat Top Grill (S)
Four Farthings (S)
Frida's (S)
Frontera Grill (S)
Grande Mere Inn/M (W)
Greek Islands (S)
Green Dolphin St. (G,P)
Green Door Tavern (T)
Hackney's (P)
Heaven City/W (W)
Iron Mike's Grille (S)
Jackson Harbor Grill (P,W)
Jerome's Red Ginger (P)
Jia's (S)
Joe's Be-Bop Cafe (P)
Johnny Rockets (S)
John's Place (S)
Kamehachi (G,P)
King Crab (G)
Kinzie Chophse. (S)
La Bocca Verità (S)
La Borsa (P)
La Crêperie (G)
La Rosetta (T)
La Sorella (P)
Le Colonial (P,S,T)
Le Loup Cafe (G,P)
Louis' Bon Appetit/I (G)
Louisiana Kitchen (P)
Lou Malnati's (P)
Lutz Continental (G)
Madison's (T)
Mambo Grill (S)
Mangia Trattoria/W (P)
M Cafe (T)
Medici on 57th (P)
Meritage Cafe (G)
Merlot Joe (G)
Mesón Sabika (G,P)
Mia Cucina (P,S)
Mia Francesca (G)
Mi Casa Su Casa (P)
Millennium Steaks (P,S)
Miller's Country Hse./M (G,P)
Mill Race Inn (P)
Millrose Brewing Co. (P)
Mon Ami Gabi (P)
Mrs. Park's Tavern (S)
Nana's Cafe (S)

Nick & Tony's (S)
94th Aero Squadron (G,P)
North Pond Café (P)
Northside Cafe (G,S)
O'Neil's (S)
Oo-La-La! (G)
Original Gino's (S)
Osteria del Mondo/W (P)
Papagus (S)
Pegasus (G,P)
Pizzeria Uno & Due (S)
Provence (P)
Quincy Grille (S,T,W)
Ranalli's (P)
Red Arrow Roadhse./M (P)
Redfish (P)
Red Tomato (S)
Relish (S)
Restaurant Okno (S)
Rhapsody (P)
Rhumba (S)
Rist. Bartolotta/W (P,S)
Rivers (S,T)
Robinson's Ribs (G)
Rose Angelis (G)
Rosebud/Naperville (P,S,W)
Rosebud/Rush (S)
Rudi Fazuli's (P)
Russell's BBQ (P)
Salpicón (S)
Salvatore's Rist. (G,P)
Sarkis Grill (P)
Schulien's (G)
Shark Bar (S)
Smith & Wollensky (P)
Sorriso (P,W)
South Gate Cafe (P)
Spasso (P)
Starfish Cafe (S)
Stefani's (P)
Strega Nona (S)
Suprarossa (S)
Szechwan East (S)
Tanglewood (T)
Tapas Barcelona (P)
Tavern on Rush (S)
Thyme (P)
Tilli's (P)
Topo Gigio (G,S)
Topolobampo (S)
Toque (S)
Tratt. Parma (S)
Tratt. Pizzeria Roma (S,T)
Tre Kronor (G,S)
Tuscany (G)

173

Il Jack's (S)
Va Pensiero (T)
Via Veneto (S)
Vinci (S)
Vivaldi Trattoria (P)
Vivo (S)
Voila (P,S)
Wild Onion (P,S)
Wishbone (P)
Zarrosta Grill (S)

Parking/Valet

(L=parking lot;
V=valet parking;
*=validated parking)
Adagio (V)
Allgauer's (L)
Ambria (V)
Angelina Rist. (V)
Arco de Cuchilleros (V)
Athenian Room (V)
Aubriot (V)
Aurelio's (L)
Bandera*
Barn of Barrington (L,V)
Beans & Barley/W (L)
Bella Notte (L,V)
Bella Vista (V)
Ben Pao (V)
Berghoff*
Bertucci's (L)
Betise (L)
Bice Grill (V)
Bice Rist. (V)
Big Bowl (V)
Biggs (V)
Bistro Banlieue (L)
Bistro 110 (V)
Bistrot Zinc (V)
Blackbird (V)
Blackhawk Lodge (V)*
Blue Mesa (V)
Bluepoint Oyster (V)
Bob Chinn's (L,V)
Bohemian Crystal (L)
Bones (L)
Boston Blackie's (V)
Boulevard (L,V)*
Boulevard Inn/W (V)
Brasserie Jo (V)
Brasserie T (L)
Brother Jimmy's (V)
Buca di Beppo (L,V)*
Buca di Beppo/W (L)
Buckingham's (V)

Burgundy Bistro (L)
Butcher Shop (V)
Cafe Absinthe (V)
Cafe BaBaReeba! (V)
Cafe Bernard (V)
Cafe Borgia (L)
Cafe Iberico (V)
Cafe La Cave (L,V)
Cafe Luciano (V)
Cafe Matou (V)
Cafe Med (V)
Cafe Pyrenees (L)
California Cafe B&G (L)
Cape Cod Room (V)
Capital Grille (V)
Capriccio's (L)
Carlos' (V)
Carmen's (L)
Carmichael's (V)
Carmine's (V)
Carpaccio Rist. (L)
Carson's Ribs (L,V)
Catch 35 (V)
Ceiling Zero (L)
Celebrity Cafe (L,V)
Centro Rist. (V)
Charlie Beinlich's (L)
Charlie Trotter's (V)
Cheesecake Factory (V)
Chicago Chop Hse. (V)
Chicago Pizza (V)
China Gourmet/W*
Chip and Py's/W (L)
Cielo (V)
Cité (V)
Clark St. Bistro*
Club Creole (V)
Clubhouse (L,V)
Club Macanudo (V)
Coco Pazzo (V)
Coco Pazzo Cafe (V)
Cocoro*
Cohiba (V)
Como Inn (L,V)
Convito Italiano (L)
Costa's (L,V)
Courtright's (L)
Cousin's (V)
Crawdaddy Bayou (L,V)
Crofton on Wells (V)
Cucina Bella*
Cucina Paradiso (V)
Cucina Roma (L)
Cuisines (V)
Cyrano's Bistrot (V)

Cy's Steak (V)
D'Agostino's (V)
Dee's (V)
Deleece (V)
Del Rio (L,V)
Dick's Last Resort*
Don Juan (V)
Don Roth's (L)
Don's Fishmarket (L)
Dover Straits (L)
Earth (V)
Ed Debevic's (L,V)
Ed Debevic's/W*
Eddie Martini's/W (L)
Edelweiss Bistro (L)
EJ's Place (V)
Elaine & Ina's*
Eli's*
Elm Grove Inn/W (L)
Emilio's La Perla (L)
Emilio's Tapas Bar (V)
Emperor's Choice*
Entre Nous (V)*
Erie Cafe (L,V)
erwin (V)
Everest (V)*
Fadó Irish Pub (V)
Fanny's Famous/M (L)
Feast (V)
56 West (V)
Fireplace Inn (V)
Fog City Diner (V)
Fond de la Tour (L,V)*
foodlife*
Four Farthings (V)
Francesca's North (L)
Francesca's on Taylor (V)
Franconello's (L)
Frida's (L)
Fritzl's (L)
Frontera Grill (V)
Furama (L)
Gale St. Inn (L)
Gaylord India (V)
Geja's Cafe (V)
Gene & Georgetti (L,V)
Giannotti Steak Hse. (V)
Gibsons Steakhse. (V)
Gilardi's (V)
Gino's Steak Hse. (L,V)
Giordano's (L)
Gladys Luncheonette (L)
Golden Ox (L,V)
Gordon (V)
Grande Mere Inn/M (L)

Grapes (V)
Greek Islands (L,V)
Green Dolphin St. (L,V)
Grenadier's/W (V)*
Hacienda Tecalitlan (V)
Hackney's (L)
Hannah's/M (L)
Hard Rock Cafe (V)
Harry Caray's (V)
Harvest on Huron (V)
Havana Café (V)
Heaven City/W (L)
Historic Turner/W (L)
Hopcats Brewing Co. (V)
House of Blues (V)
Houston's (V)*
Hubbard St. Grill (V)
Hudson Club (V)
Hyerdall's Cafe/M (L)
Immigrant Room/W (L)
Iron Mike's Grille (V)
Jack's American (V)
Jackson Harbor Grill (L)
Jaipur Palace (V)*
Jenny's/M (L)
Jerome's Red Ginger*
Jia's (L)*
Joe's Crab Shack (L,V)
Kamehachi (V)
Karl Ratzsch's/W (V)
Kent's/M (L)
KiKi's Bistro (V)
Kilbourn Cafe/W (L)
Kinzie Chophse. (V)
Kyoto (L)
La Borsa (L)
La Canasta (V)
La Cantina (V)
La Donna (V)
La Gondola (V)
La Rosetta (V)
La Salle Grill/I (L)
La Sardine (V)
La Strada (V)
Lawry's (V)
Le Bouchon (L)
Le Colonial (V)
Le Français (V)
Leona's (L)
Leona's on Taylor (L)
Leona's Sons (L)
Les Nomades (V)
Le Titi de Paris (L)
Le Vichyssois (L)
Lino's Rist. (V)

Lone Star Steakhse. (L)
Louisiana Kitchen (V)
Lucky Platter*
Lupita's (L)
Lutnia (L)
Lutz Continental (L)
Madam B (V)
Mader's German/W (V)
Madison's (V)
Maggiano's (L,V)
Magnum's (L,V)
Mama Desta's*
Mandar Inn (L)
Mango (V)
Manny's Coffee Shop (L)*
Mantuano (V)
Maple Tree Inn (L)
Marché (V)
Mashed Potato Club (V)
Max's Deli (L)*
Meritage Cafe (V)
Mesón Sabika (L)
Mia Francesca (V)
Michael Jordan's (V)
Millennium Steaks (V)
Miller's Country Hse./M (L)
Miller's Pub*
Mill Race Inn (L)
Millrose Brewing Co. (L,V)
Mimma's Cafe/W (L)
Mon Ami Gabi (V)
Monastero's (L)
Montparnasse (L)
Morton's (V)*
Mrs. Park's Tavern (V)
My Favorite Inn (L)
My π Pizza (V)*
Myron & Phil's (V)
Narcisse (V)
Nick & Tony's (V)
Nick's Fishmarket (V)
94th Aero Squadron (L)
Nonna Bartolotta's/W (L)
Oak Terrace (V)
Oak Tree*
Old Barn (L,V)
O'Neil's (L)
one sixtyblue (V)
Oo-La-La! (V)
Osteria del Mondo/W (V)
Palette's (V)*
Palm (V)
Panda Panda (L)
Pandl's in Bayside/W (L)
Pane Caldo*

Papagus (L,V)
Papa Milano*
Pappadeaux (L)
Park Ave. Cafe (V)*
Parthenon (V)
Pasha (V)
Pasteur Cafe (L)
Pegasus (V)
Pete Miller's (V)
Philander's (V)
P.J. Clarke's*
Planet Hollywood (V)
Prairie (V)*
Primavera Rist. (V)*
Printer's Row (V)
Provence (L)
Public Landing (L)
Pump Room (V)
Pump's on 12/I (L)
Quincy Grille (V)
Rainforest Cafe (L,V)
Ranalli's (V)
Ravinia Bistro (L)
Redamak's/M (L)
Red Apple (L)
Red Arrow Roadhse./M (L)
Redfish (L,V)
Red Light (V)
Relish (V)
Restaurant Okno (V)
Rest. Su Casa/M (L)
Reza's (L,V)*
Rhapsody (V)*
Rhumba (V)
Rico's (V)
Ritz-Carlton Cafe*
Ritz-Carlton Din Rm.*
Riva (L,V)*
River Lane Inn/W (L)
Rivers*
Riversite/W (L)
R.J. Grunts (V)
Robinson's Ribs (L)
Rock Bottom Brew. (V)
Ron of Japan (L,V)
Rosebud Cafe (V)
Rosebud/Naperville (L,V)
Rosebud/Rush (V)
Rudi Fazuli's (V)
Rudy's Mexican/W (L)
Rupert's (L)
Russell's BBQ (L)
Ruth's Chris (V)
Sabatino's (L)
Sai Cafe (V)

Saloon (V)
Salpicón (V)
Salvatore's Rist. (V)
Sanford/W (V)
Santorini (V)
Sarkis Grill (L)
Savannah's (V)
Scoozi! (V)*
Seasons (V)*
Seasons Cafe (V)*
1776 (L)
Shark Bar (L,V)
Shaw's Crab Hse. (V)
Shaw's Seafood (L)
Shish Kabab Hse. (L)
Signature Room (L)*
Sixty-Five*
Skip's Other Place/M (L)
Smith & Wollensky (V)
Sole Mio East/M (L)
Sorriso (V)
Souk (V)
Soul Kitchen (V)
Spago (V)
Spasso (L)
Spavone Seven (L)
Spruce (V)
Starfish Cafe (V)
Stefani's (V)
Steven Wade's/W (L)
Strega Nona (V)
Strongbow Inn/I (L)
Sunset (L)
Suntory (V)
Sylviano's Rist. (L,V)
Szechwan East*
Szechwan North (L)
Szechwan Rest. (L)
Tanglewood (L)
Tania's (V)
Tarantino's (V)
Tavern in the Town (L)
Tavern on Rush (V)
Tecalitlan (L)
312 Chicago (V)
Thyme (V)
Tilli's (V)
Timbers Charhse. (L)
Tommy Nevin's (V)
Tony Spavone's (L)
Topo Gigio (V)
Topolobampo (V)
Toque (V)
Tosi's/M (L)
Toulouse on the Park (V)

Trader Vic's (V)
Tratt. Dinotto (L,V)
Tratt. Gianni (V)
Tratt. No. 10 (V)
Tratt. Parma (V)
Tratt. Pizzeria Roma (V)
Trio (V)
Trocadero (V)
Tsunami (V)
Tucci Benucch*
Tufano's Vernon Park (V)
Tuscany (V)
Uncle Julio's (L,V)
Un DiAmo Rist. (V)
Va Pensiero (V)
Via Emilia (V)
Village (V)
Vinci (V)
Vivaldi Trattoria (L)
Vivere (V)
Vivo (V)*
Voila (V)
Volare (V)
Washington Gardens (V)
Waterford (L)
Wayside Manor (L)
Weber Grill (L)
Wildfire (V)
Wishbone (V)
Wonton Club (V)
Woo Lae Oak (V)
Yoshi's Cafe (V)
Zarrosta Grill (L,V)
Zaven's*
Zealous (V)
Zia's Trattoria (V)
Zinfandel (V)*
Zofia's (L)
Zum Deutschen Eck (L)

Parties & Private Rooms
(Any nightclub or restaurant
charges less at off-times;
* indicates private rooms
available; best of many)
Abril
Adagio*
Addis Abeda
Ambria*
Angelina Rist.*
Arun's*
Babaluci*
Bacchus Nibbles*
Barn of Barrington*
Barrington Country*

Basil's/I*
Bella Vista*
Ben Pao
Betise
Bice Grill*
Big Bowl
Biggs*
Bill Knapp's/M
Bistro 110
Bistrot Zinc
Blackhawk Lodge
Blind Faith Cafe*
Bohemian Crystal*
Bones*
Boulevard*
Boulevard Inn/W*
Brasserie Jo*
Brasserie T*
Cafe BaBaReeba!*
Cafe Iberico*
Cafe La Cave*
Cafe Pyrenees*
Cafe Venezia/I*
Capital Grille*
Carlos'*
Carmen's
Carmine's
Catch 35*
Centro Rist.*
Chicago Chop Hse.*
Clubhouse*
Club Macanudo*
Coco Pazzo
Como Inn*
Con Fusion
Courtright's*
Crofton on Wells*
Cyrano's Bistrot*
D & J Bistro*
Don Juan*
Don Roth's*
Don's Fishmarket*
Earl of Loch Ness
Ed Debevic's*
Ed Debevic's/W*
Elm Grove Inn/W*
Emilio's La Perla*
Emilio's Tapas Bar*
English Room/W*
Entre Nous*
Erie Cafe*
Everest*
Fifth Ave. Bistro
56 West
Fireside Beverly

Fog City Diner*
Fond de la Tour*
Francesca's on Taylor*
Froggy's*
Frontera Grill*
Gabriel's*
Gene & Georgetti*
Gibsons Steakhse.*
Gilardi's*
Golden Ox*
Gordon*
Granada
Greek Islands*
Green Dolphin St.*
Grenadier's/W*
Hacienda Tecalitlan*
Hard Rock Cafe
Harry Caray's*
Harvest on Huron
Heaven City/W*
Historic Turner/W*
Hubbard St. Grill
Hudson Club*
Immigrant Room/W
Iron Mike's Grille*
Kamehachi
Karl Ratzsch's/W*
Kerouac Jack's*
Kilbourn Cafe/W
King and I/W
Kinzie Chophse.
La Cantina*
La Salle Grill/I*
Las Bellas Artes*
La Sorella*
La Strada*
Lawry's*
Le Colonial*
Le Français*
Le Titi de Paris*
Le Vichyssois*
Lino's Rist.*
Louis' Bon Appetit/I*
Mader's German/W
Madison's*
Maggiano's*
Mango*
Mantuano*
Maple Tree Inn*
Marché*
Meritage Cafe*
Mesón Sabika*
Mia Francesca*
Michael Jordan's*
Millennium Steaks*

Miller Bakery Cafe/I
Miller's Country Hse./M*
Mill Race Inn*
Mimma's Cafe/W*
Montparnasse*
Mrs. Park's Tavern
Narcisse*
Nick & Tony's
Nick's Fishmarket*
94th Aero Squadron*
Oceanique*
Old Barn*
O'Neil's
one sixtyblue*
Palm*
Pandl's in Bayside/W*
Papagus*
Park Ave. Cafe*
Parthenon*
Pasta Tree/W*
Philander's*
Phil Smidt's/I*
Planet Hollywood*
Prairie*
Primavera Rist.*
Provence
Public Landing*
Redfish*
Red Light*
Relish*
Restaurant Okno*
Rest. Toulouse/M*
Rhapsody*
Rhumba*
River Lane Inn/W*
Riversite/W
Rosebud Cafe*
Rosebud/Naperville*
Rosebud/Rush
Salpicón
Sanford/W
Santorini
Saz's/W
Scoozi!
Seasons*
1776*
Shark Bar*
Shaw's Crab Hse.*
Shaw's Seafood*
Signature Room*
Smith & Wollensky*
South Gate Cafe*
Spago*
Spiaggia*
Spruce*

Strongbow Inn/I*
Tallgrass*
Tanglewood*
Tania's*
Tavern in the Town*
Tavern on Rush
302 West
Thyme*
Tomboy
Tony Spavone's*
Topo Gigio*
Topolobampo*
Tosi's/M*
Toulouse on the Park
Tratt. No. 10*
Tratt. Parma*
Trio*
Tuscany*
Va Pensiero*
Vinci*
Vivaldi Trattoria*
Vivere*
Vivo*
Voila*
Walter's*
Waterford*
Wild Onion*
Woo Lae Oak*
Yvette*
Yvette Wintergarden
Zealous
Zinfandel*
Zofia's*
Zum Deutschen Eck*

People-Watching
Bice Rist.
Bite Cafe
Blackbird
Brasserie Jo
Cafe Absinthe
Carmine's
Centro Rist.
Charlie Trotter's
Club Macanudo
Con Fusion
56 West
Gene & Georgetti
Gibsons Steakhse.
Hudson Club
Le Colonial
Madam B
Marché
Mon Ami Gabi
one sixtyblue

Oo-La-La!
Red Light
Restaurant Okno
Rhumba
Scoozi!
Shark Bar
Smith & Wollensky
Soul Kitchen
Spago
Spiaggia
Tavern on Rush
Thyme
Tomboy
Toque
Vivo

Power Scenes
Ambria
Bice Rist.
Catch 35
Charlie Trotter's
Chicago Chop Hse.
Coco Pazzo
Everest
Gene & Georgetti
Gordon
KiKi's Bistro
Le Français
Les Nomades
Lino's Rist.
Morton's
one sixtyblue
Palm
Ritz-Carlton Din. Rm.
Rosebud/Rush
Seasons
Smith & Wollensky
Spago
Spiaggia

Pre-Theater/
Early Bird Menus
(Call to check prices,
days and times)
Entre Nous
Everest
Gordon
Jilly's Cafe
Relish
Russian Palace
Russian Tea Time
Schulien's

Prix Fixe Menus
(Call to check prices,
days and times)
Ambria
Boulevard
Cafe Pyrenees
Carlos'
Charlie Trotter's
Entre Nous
Everest
Grenadier's/W
Le Français
Le Titi de Paris
Le Vichyssois
Pandl's in Bayside/W
Pump Room
Ritz-Carlton Din. Rm.
Seasons
Strongbow Inn/I
Tallgrass
Zealous

Pubs/Bars/
Microbreweries
America's Brewpub
Charlie's Ale Hse.
Duke of Perth
Earl of Loch Ness
Fadó Irish Pub
Founders Hill
Four Farthings
Goose Island
Green Door Tavern
Hopcats Brewing Co.
Irish Oak
Miller's Pub
Millrose Brewing Co.
P.J. Clarke's
Red Lion Pub
Rock Bottom Brew.
Rose & Crown
Stanley's Kitchen
Taylor Brewing Co.
Tommy Nevin's
Weeghman Park

Quiet Conversation
Akai Hana
Allgauer's
Ambria
Antoinette's/I
Arun's
Aubriot
Bacchus Nibbles
Bando

Bangkok
Bangkok Star
Bank Ln. Bistro
Barn of Barrington
Barrington Country
Basil's/I
Benihana
Ben Pao
Betise
Biggs
Blackhawk Lodge
Boulevard
Boulevard Inn/W
Brett's
Buckingham's
Bukhara
Cafe Bernard
Cafe La Cave
Cafe Pyrenees
Cafe Selmarie
Cafe Spiaggia
Cafe 36
Cafe Venezia/I
Cape Cod Room
Capital Grille
Carlos'
Ceiling Zero
Charlie Trotter's
Cité
Clark St. Bistro
Clayton's/I
Coco Pazzo
Coco Pazzo Cafe
Cocoro
Courtright's
D & J Bistro
Daniel J's
Dellwood Pickle
Dionne's Cafe
Earth
Elaine & Ina's
Eli's
Elm Grove Inn/W
Elsa's on the Park/W
English Room/W
Entre Nous
Everest
56 West
Fond de la Tour
Fondue Stube
Gaylord India
Geja's Cafe
Genesee Depot
Gilardi's
Gilles

Gordon
Grande Mere Inn/M
Green Dolphin St.
Grenadier's/W
Gusto Italiano
Hatsuhana
Historic Turner/W
Immigrant Room/W
Indian Garden
Jenny's/M
Jia's
Jilly's Cafe
Julie Mai's
Kamehachi
KiKi's Bistro
Kilbourn Cafe/W
King and I/W
Kinzie Chophse.
Kuni's
Kyoto
La Bocca Verità
La Cantina
La Crêperie
La Gondola
La Salle Grill/I
Las Bellas Artes
La Strada
Le Français
Les Nomades
Le Titi de Paris
Le Vichyssois
Louis' Bon Appetit/I
Lucca's
Lutz Continental
Miller Bakery Cafe/I
Miller's Country Hse./M
Mill Race Inn
Mimosa
Mirabell
Montparnasse
New Japan
Oak Terrace
Oceanique
Old Barn
Osteria del Mondo/W
Palette's
Palm
Pandl's in Bayside/W
Pane Caldo
Park Ave. Cafe
Philander's
Prairie
Printer's Row
Pump Room
Pump's on 12/I

Ravinia Bistro
Relish
Rest. Toulouse/M
Rhapsody
Rist. Bartolotta/W
Ritz-Carlton Cafe
Ritz-Carlton Din. Rm.
River Lane Inn/W
Rivers
Ron of Japan
Rudi's Wine Bar
Russian Palace
Russian Tea Time
Salvatore's Rist.
Sanford/W
Seasons
1776
Shaw's Crab Hse.
Signature Room
Spasso
Spiaggia
Steven Wade's/W
Strongbow Inn/I
Suntory
Sylviano's Rist.
Tallgrass
Tandoor/I
Tanglewood
302 West
Toulouse on the Park
Tratt. No. 10
Tratt. Parma
Tre Kronor
Trio
Tsunami
Va Pensiero
Vinci
Vivere
Walter's
Waterford
Wayside Manor
Windows of Cuisine
Woo Lae Oak
Work of Art Café
Yvette
Yvette Wintergarden
Zaven's

Raw Bars

Bluepoint Oyster
Bob Chinn's
Catch 35
Crawdaddy Bayou
Davis St. Fishmkt.
Half Shell

King Crab
Rhapsody
Shaw's Crab Hse.
Starfish Cafe

Reservations Essential

Ambria
Arun's
Bice Rist.
Bistro Banlieue
Blackbird
Boulevard Inn/W
Cafe Absinthe
Cafe 36
Carlos'
Centro Rist.
Charlie Trotter's
Coerper's/W
Crofton on Wells
Dionne's Cafe
Elm Grove Inn/W
Everest
Fond de la Tour
Francesca's on Taylor
Geja's Cafe
Gibsons Steakhse.
Gordon
Heaven City/W
Immigrant Room/W
KiKi's Bistro
Le Bouchon
Le Colonial
Le Français
Les Nomades
Millennium Steaks
Mon Ami Gabi
Nick's Fishmarket
North Pond Café
one sixtyblue
Pasteur Cafe
Ritz-Carlton Din. Rm.
Rosebud Cafe
Rosebud/Rush
Sanford/W
Seasons
Signature Room
Smith & Wollensky
Spago
Spiaggia
Spruce
Tallgrass
Thyme
Topolobampo
Trio
Vivere

Romantic Spots

Ambria
Aubriot
Barrington Country
Basil's/I
Betise
Biggs
Bistrot Zinc
Boulevard
Boulevard Inn/W
Buckingham's
Cafe Absinthe
Cafe Bernard
Cafe La Cave
Cafe Pyrenees
Cafe 36
Cafe Venezia/I
Cape Cod Room
Capital Grille
Carlos'
Ceiling Zero
Charlie Trotter's
Cité
Clark St. Bistro
Coco Pazzo
Coco Pazzo Cafe
Courtright's
Crofton on Wells
Cyrano's Bistrot
D & J Bistro
Daniel J's
Dionne's Cafe
Eli's
Elm Grove Inn/W
Elsa's on the Park/W
English Room/W
Entre Nous
erwin
Everest
Fifth Ave. Bistro
56 West
Fond de la Tour
Froggy's
Gabriel's
Geja's Cafe
Gilardi's
Gilles
Golden Mast Inn/W
Gordon
Grande Mere Inn/M
Harvest on Huron
Immigrant Room/W
Jenny's/M
Jilly's Cafe
KiKi's Bistro

La Bocca Verità
La Crêperie
Las Bellas Artes
La Sorella
La Strada
Le Bouchon
Le Colonial
Le Français
Les Nomades
Le Titi de Paris
Le Vichyssois
Louis' Bon Appetit/I
Mangia Trattoria/W
Mango
Marché
Meritage Cafe
Miller Bakery Cafe/I
Miller's Country Hse./M
Mill Race Inn
Mimosa
Mon Ami Gabi
Montparnasse
North Pond Café
Oceanique
Osteria del Mondo/W
Palette's
Palm
Pane Caldo
Park Ave. Cafe
Philander's
Prairie
Printer's Row
Provence
Pump Room
Ravinia Bistro
Relish
Rest. Toulouse/M
Rhapsody
Rist. Bartolotta/W
Ritz-Carlton Din. Rm.
Rivers
Rudi's Wine Bar
Salvatore's Rist.
Sanford/W
Savannah's
Seasons
1776
Signature Room
South Gate Cafe
Spasso
Spiaggia
Steven Wade's/W
Strega Nona
Strongbow Inn/I
Sylviano's Rist.

Tallgrass
Tanglewood
Tavern in the Town
302 West
Topo Gigio
Topolobampo
Toulouse on the Park
Tratt. No. 10
Tratt. Parma
Trio
Va Pensiero
Via Emilia
Vinci
Vivere
Walter's
Waterford
Wayside Manor
Yvette
Yvette Wintergarden
Zaven's

Saturday – Best Bets
(B=brunch; L=lunch;
best of many)
Abril (L)
America's Brewpub (L)
Ann Sather (L)
Ann Sather Cafe (L)
Ann Sather Express (L)
Army & Lou's (L)
Athenian Room (L)
Aurelio's (L)
Bacchus Nibbles (L)
Bagel (B,L)
Bandera (L)
Barn of Barrington (L)
Barrington Country (L)
Barry's Ribs (L)
Beans & Barley/W (L)
Belden Deli (L)
Berghoff (L)
Bertucci's (L)
Best Hunan (L)
Betise (L)
Bice Grill (L)
Bice Rist. (L)
Big Bowl (L)
Bill Knapp's/M (L)
Biloxi Grill (L)
Bistro 110 (L)
Bistrot Zinc (L)
Bite Cafe (B)
Blackhawk Lodge (L)
Blind Faith Cafe (B,L)
Blue Plate Cafe/M (L)

Bones (L)
Boston Blackie's (L)
Boulevard Inn/W (L)
Brasserie T (L)
Breakfast Club (L)
Brett's (B)
Brother Jimmy's (L)
Bubba Gump Shrimp (L)
Cafe BaBaReeba! (L)
Cafe Borgia (L)
Cafe Central (L)
Cafe Iberico (L)
Cafe Luciano (L)
Cafe Spiaggia (L)
Cafe Venezia/I (L)
California Pizza Kit. (L)
Carmen's (L)
Carmine's (L)
Carson's Ribs (L)
Centro Rist. (L)
Charlie Beinlich's (L)
Charlie's Ale Hse. (L)
Cheesecake Factory (L)
Chequers/M (L)
Chicago Diner (B,L)
Chicago Pizza (L)
Chip and Py's/W (L)
Claim Company (L)
Clubhouse (L)
Coco Pazzo Cafe (B,L)
Convito Italiano (L)
Corner Bakery (L)
Cousin's (L)
Crawdaddy Bayou (L)
Cross-Rhodes (L)
Cucina Bella (L)
Cucina Roma (L)
Daily B&G (B,L)
Dao (L)
Dave & Buster's (L)
Dick's Last Resort (L)
Dish (B,L)
Duke of Perth (L)
Earth (L)
Ed Debevic's (L)
Edwardo's (L)
Elaine & Ina's (L)
El Jardin (B,L)
El Presidente (L)
El Tipico (L)
Emilio's La Perla (L)
Emilio's Tapas Bar (L)
Erie Cafe (L)
Fadó Irish Pub (L)

Feast (L)
Flat Top Grill (L)
Fluky's (L)
foodlife (L)
Founders Hill (L)
Four Farthings (L)
Fresh Starts (L)
Frontera Grill (B)
Giordano's (L)
Gladys Luncheonette (L)
Gold Coast Dogs (L)
Goose Island (L)
Granada (L)
Graziano's (L)
Greek Islands (L)
Hackney's (L)
Hannah's/M (B,L)
Hard Rock Cafe (L)
Harry Caray's (L)
Heartland Cafe (L)
Heaven on Seven (L)
Heaven on Seven/Rush (L)
Hi Ricky (L)
Historic Turner/W (L)
Houston's (L)
Hyerdall's Cafe/M (L)
Iron Mike's Grille (L)
Jane's (B)
Jerome's Red Ginger (B,L)
Joe's Be-Bop Cafe (L)
Johnny Rockets (L)
John's Place (B,L)
Karl Ratzsch's/W (L)
Kilbourn Cafe/W (L)
La Canasta (L)
La Crêperie (B)
La Donna (L)
La Rosetta (L)
Las Fuentes (L)
Las Palmas (L)
Le Colonial (L)
Leona's (L)
Leona's Neighborhood (L)
Leona's on Taylor (L)
Leona's Sons (L)
Leo's Lunchroom (B,L)
Lou Malnati's (L)
Lucky Platter (B,L)
LuLu's (L)
Maggiano's (B,L)
Mambo Grill (L)
Max's Deli (L)
M Cafe (L)
Medici (L)
Medici on 57th (B,L)

Michael Jordan's (L)
Miller Bakery Cafe/I (L)
Miller's Country Hse./M (L)
Mity Nice Grill (L)
Mrs. Park's Tavern (L)
My Favorite Inn (L)
My π Pizza (L)
Nancy's (L)
N. N. Smokehse. (L)
Nookies (L)
Nookies Too (L)
Nookies Tree (B,L)
Northside Cafe (B,L)
Oak Terrace (L)
Oodles of Noodles (L)
Orbit (L)
Original Gino's (L)
Pandl's in Bayside/W (L)
Papagus (L)
Papa Milano (L)
Parthenon (L)
Penny's Noodle Shop (L)
Pizza Capri (L)
Pizzeria Uno & Due (L)
P.J. Clarke's (L)
Planet Hollywood (L)
Prairie (B,L)
Primavera Rist. (L)
Provence (B)
Pump's on 12/I (L)
Rainforest Cafe (L)
Ranalli's (L)
Ravinia Bistro (B,L)
Redamak's/M (L)
Red Lion Pub (L)
Red Rock Cafe/W (L)
Red Tomato (L)
Rest. Su Casa/M (L)
Rhapsody (L)
Ritz-Carlton Cafe (L)
Riva (L)
R.J. Grunts (L)
Rock Bottom Brew. (L)
Roditys (L)
Rosebud/Rush (L)
Roxy Cafe (L)
Russell's BBQ (L)
Santorini (L)
Saz's/W (L)
South Gate Cafe (L)
Southport City (L)
Stanley's Kitchen (B,L)
Stir Crazy Cafe (L)
Strongbow Inn/I (L)
Su Casa (L)

Tavern on Rush (L)
Taylor Brewing Co. (L)
Taza (L)
Tecalitlan (L)
Three Happiness (L)
Tilli's (B,L)
Topo Gigio (L)
Tosi's/M (L)
Tre Kronor (B,L)
Tucci Benucch (L)
Tuscany (L)
Twilight (B)
Twin Anchors (L)
Village (L)
Volare (L)
Wild Onion (L)
Wishbone (B)
Wonton Club (L)
Zarrosta Grill (L)
Zinfandel (B,L)
Zofia's (L)
Zum Deutschen Eck (L)

Sunday Dining – Best Bets

(B=brunch; L=lunch;
D=dinner; plus all hotels
and most Asians)
Abril (L,D)
America's Brewpub (L,D)
Angelina Rist. (B,D)
Ann Sather (L,D)
Ann Sather Cafe (L,D)
Ann Sather Express (L)
Arco de Cuchilleros (B,D)
Army & Lou's (L,D)
Athenian Room (L,D)
Aubriot (B,D)
Aurelio's (L,D)
Bacchus Nibbles (B,L,D)
Barn of Barrington (B,L,D)
Barry's Ribs (L,D)
Beans & Barley/W (L,D)
Bertucci's (L,D)
Betise (B,L,D)
Bice Rist. (L,D)
Bill Knapp's/M (L,D)
Bistro 110 (B,L,D)
Bistrot Zinc (L,D)
Bite Cafe (B,D)
Blackhawk Lodge (B,D)
Blind Faith Cafe (B,D,L)
Blue Mesa (B,D)
Blue Plate Cafe/M (B,L)
Bogart's (L,D)
Bohemian Crystal (L,D)

Bones (L,D)
Boston Blackie's (L,D)
Boulevard Inn/W (B,D)
Breakfast Club (L)
Brett's (B,D)
Bricks (L,D)
Brother Jimmy's (B,L,D)
Bubba Gump Shrimp (L,D)
Bukhara (L,D)
Cafe BaBaReeba! (L,D)
Cafe Borgia (L,D)
Cafe Iberico (L,D)
Cafe Luciano (L,D)
Cafe Spiaggia (B,L,D)
California Pizza Kit. (L,D)
Carmen's (L,D)
Carmichael's (D)
Carmine's (L,D)
Carson's Ribs (L,D)
Chaplin's on Church (D)
Charlie's Ale Hse. (B,L,D)
Cheesecake Factory (B,L,D)
Chequers/M (L,D)
Chicago Diner (B,L,D)
Chicago Pizza (L,D)
Chinoiserie (D)
Cité (B,D)
Claim Company (L,D)
Clara's Pasta (L,D)
Clubhouse (L,D)
Coco Pazzo Cafe (B,L,D)
Como Inn (L,D)
Convito Italiano (L,D)
Corner Bakery (L,D)
Costa's (L,D)
Cousin's (L,D)
Crawdaddy Bayou (L,D)
Cucina Bella (B,L,D)
Cucina Roma (L,D)
Cy's Crab House (L,D)
Czech Plaza (L,D)
Daily B&G (B,L,D)
Dave & Buster's (L,D)
Davis St. Fishmkt. (L,D)
Deleece (B,D)
Dellwood Pickle (L,D)
Dick's Last Resort (B,L,D)
Dish (B,L,D)
Don Juan (L,D)
Duke of Perth (L,D)
Ed Debevic's (L,D)
Edwardo's (L,D)
El Jardin (B,L,D)
El Presidente (L,D)
El Tipico (L,D)

Emilio's La Perla (B,L,D)
Emilio's Tapas Bar (L,D)
erwin (B,D)
Fadó Irish Pub (L,D)
Father & Son Pizza (L,D)
Feast (B,L,D)
Fireplace Inn (L,D)
Fireside Beverly (L,D)
Flat Top Grill (B,L,D)
Fluky's (L,D)
Fly Me to the Moon (D)
Fog City Diner (D)
Founders Hill (L,D)
Four Farthings (B,L,D)
Frida's (L,D)
Fritzl's (B,L,D)
Gaylord India (L,D)
Genesee Depot (L,D)
Giordano's (L,D)
Gladys Luncheonette (L,D)
Gold Coast Dogs (L,D)
Goose Island (L,D)
Graziano's (L,D)
Greek Islands (L,D)
Gusto Italiano (L,D)
Hackney's (L,D)
Half Shell (L,D)
Hannah's/M (B,L,D)
Hard Rock Cafe (L,D)
Harry Caray's (L,D)
Heartland Cafe (L,D)
Heaven on Seven/Rush (L,D)
Hickory Pit (L,D)
Historic Turner/W (L,D)
Hyerdall's Cafe/M (L,D)
Indian Garden (L,D)
Jaipur Palace (L,D)
Jalapeño's Hottest/I (B,L,D)
Jane's (B,D)
Jerome's Red Ginger (B,L,D)
Jilly's Cafe (B,D)
Jimmy's Charhse. (L,D)
Joe's Be-Bop Cafe (B,L,D)
Joe's Crab Shack (L,D)
John's Place (B,L,D)
Karl Ratzsch's/W (L,D)
Kerouac Jack's (B,L,D)
King Crab (L,D)
Klay Oven (L,D)
La Canasta (L,D)
La Crêperie (B,D)
La Donna (B,L,D)
Las Fuentes (L,D)
Las Palmas (L,D)
Leona's (L,D)

Leona's Neighborhood (L,D)
Leona's on Taylor (L,D)
Leona's Sons (L,D)
Leo's Lunchroom (B,L,D)
Lindo Mexico (L,D)
Lone Star Steakhse. (L,D)
Louisa's Trattoria/W (L,D)
Louis' Bon Appetit/I (B)
Louisiana Kitchen (D)
Lou Malnati's (L,D)
Lou Mitchell's (L)
Lou Mitchell's Exp. (L,D)
Lucky Platter (B,L,D)
Lutnia (L,D)
Lutz Continental (L,D)
Mader's German/W (B,D)
Madison's (L,D)
Maggiano's (B,D,L)
Mama Desta's (L,D)
Marcello's (L,D)
Mashed Potato Club (L,D)
Max's Deli (L,D)
Medici (B,L,D)
Medici on 57th (B,L,D)
Merlot Joe (B,D)
Mesón Sabika (B,D)
Michael Jordan's (L,D)
Miller Bakery Cafe/I (L,D)
Miller's Country Hse./M (L,D)
Miller's Pub (L,D)
Mill Race Inn (L,D)
Millrose Brewing Co. (B,D)
Mimosa (D)
Mity Nice Grill (L,D)
Mon Ami Gabi (D)
Mongolian BBQ (L,D)
Moti Mahal (L,D)
My Favorite Inn (L)
My π Pizza (L,D)
Nancy's (L,D)
94th Aero Squadron (B,D)
N. N. Smokehse. (L,D)
Nookies (L,D)
Nookies Too (L,D)
Nookies Tree (B,L,D)
North Pond Café (B,D)
Northside Cafe (B,L,D)
Nuevo Leon (L,D)
Old Jerusalem (L,D)
Oo-La-La! (B,D)
Orbit (L,D)
Original Gino's (L,D)
Original Pancake Hse. (L)
Outpost (B,D)
Pandl's in Bayside/W (B,L,D)

Pane Caldo (L,D)
Papa Milano (L,D)
Pappadeaux (D)
Pappagallo's (B,L,D)
Parthenon (L,D)
Pasta Tree/W (L,D)
Pegasus (L,D)
Phoenix (L,D)
Pizza Capri (L,D)
Pizzeria Uno & Due (L,D)
P.J. Clarke's (B,L,D)
Planet Hollywood (L,D)
Prairie (B,L,D)
Provence (B)
Pump Room (B,D)
Pump's on 12/I (L,D)
Rainforest Cafe (L,D)
Ranalli's (L,D)
Ravinia Bistro (B,L,D)
Redamak's/M (L,D)
Red Apple (L,D)
Redfish (L,D)
Red Lion Pub (L,D)
Red Tomato (L,D)
Rest. Su Casa/M (L,D)
Retreat (B)
Reza's (L,D)
Rhapsody (L,D)
Rinc. Sudamericano (L,D)
Riva (L,D)
R.J. Grunts (B,L,D)
Robinson's Ribs (L,D)
Rock Bottom Brew. (L,D)
Roditys (L,D)
Rose & Crown (L,D)
Rosebud/Naperville (L,D)
Rosebud/Rush (L,D)
Roxy Cafe (B,D)
Rudy's Mexican/W (L,D)
Russell's BBQ (L,D)
Russian Palace (L,D)
Russian Tea Time (L,D)
Salpicón (B,D)
Santorini (L,D)
Sarkis Grill (L,D)
Saz's/W (B,L,D)
Shark Bar (B,D)
Signature Room (B,L,D)
Slice of Life (L,D)
Smith & Wollensky (D)
Souk (B,D)
Soul Kitchen (B,D)
South Gate Cafe (L,D)
Southport City (B,L,D)
Spiaggia (L,D)

Standard India (L,D)
Stanley's Kitchen (B,L,D)
Stefani's (L,D)
Stevie B's (L,D)
Strongbow Inn/I (B,D)
Su Casa (L,D)
Tagine (D)
Taj Mahal (L,D)
Tandoor/I (L,D)
Tanglewood (L,D)
Tavern on Rush (B,D)
Taylor Brewing Co. (L,D)
Taza (L,D)
Tecalitlan (L,D)
312 Chicago (D)
Thyme (B,D)
Tiffin (L,D)
Tommy Nevin's (L,D)
Toque (D)
Tosi's/M (L,D)
Tratt. Gianni (B,D)
Tre Kronor (B,L)
Tucci Benucch (L,D)
Tuscany (L,D)
Twilight (B,D)
Twin Anchors (L,D)
Uncle Tannous (L,D)
Viceroy of India (B,L,D)
Village (L,D)
Vinci (B,D)
Volare (L,D)
Walker Bros. (L,D)
Weber Grill (L,D)
Wild Onion (B,D)
Wishbone (B)
Zarrosta Grill (L,D)
Zofia's (L,D)

Senior Appeal

Allgauer's
Ann Sather
Ann Sather Cafe
Antoinette's/I
Athenian Room
August Moon
Bacchanalia
Bagel
Barn of Barrington
Belden Deli
Berghoff
Best Hunan
Bill Knapp's/M
Bohemian Crystal
Bones
Breakfast Club

188

Bruna's Rist.
Charlie Beinlich's
Clara's Pasta
Clayton's/I
Como Inn
Convito Italiano
Cy's Crab House
Cy's Steak
Czech Plaza
Da Nicola
Daniello's
Dave's Italian
Dellwood Pickle
Del Rio
Don Roth's
Don's Fishmarket
Dover Straits
Edelweiss Bistro
Elaine & Ina's
Emperor's Choice
Father & Son Pizza
Fondue Stube
Francesco's
Franconello's
Fritzl's
Gale St. Inn
Genesee Depot
Golden Ox
Greek Islands
Grenadier's/W
Gusto Italiano
Hannah's/M
Hi Howe
Historic Turner/W
Hong Min
Hyerdall's Cafe/M
Indian Garden
Jack Gibbons Garden
Jia's
Julie Mai's
Karl Ratzsch's/W
La Cantina
La Gondola
La Salle Grill/I
Lawry's
Little Bucharest
Lou Mitchell's
Lucky Platter
Lutnia
Lutz Continental
Mader's German/W
Mandar Inn
Manny's Coffee Shop
Marcello's
Miller's Pub

Mirabell
Myron & Phil's
Oak Terrace
Old Barn
Orbit
Panda Panda
Pandl's in Bayside/W
Papa Milano
Phil Smidt's/I
Pine Yard
Red Apple
Ritz-Carlton Cafe
River Lane Inn/W
Skip's Other Place/M
Spavone Seven
Three Brothers/W
Tony Spavone's
Tosi's/M
Tre Kronor
Zofia's
Zum Deutschen Eck

Singles Scenes
Adagio
America's Brewpub
Aurelio's
Babaluci
Bar Louie
Bistrot Zinc
Bite Cafe
Blue Agave
Bricks
Brother Jimmy's
California Pizza Kit.
Carmen's
Charlie's Ale Hse.
Chequers/M
Chicago Pizza
Claim Company
Daily B&G
Dave & Buster's
Dick's Last Resort
Dish
Duke of Perth
Ed Debevic's
Fadó Irish Pub
Four Farthings
Frontera Grill
Global B&G/M
Goose Island
Hackney's
Hard Rock Cafe
Hopcats Brewing Co.
Hudson Club
Joe's Be-Bop Cafe

189

Kerouac Jack's
Madam B
Mambo Grill
Mantuano
Northside Cafe
Original Gino's
Pizzeria Uno & Due
P.J. Clarke's
Rainforest Cafe
Ranalli's
Redamak's/M
Redfish
Red Lion Pub
Restaurant Okno
Rock Bottom Brew.
Scoozi!
Soul Kitchen
Stanley's Kitchen
Starfish Cafe
Strega Nona
Tavern on Rush
Taylor Brewing Co.
Wild Onion
Zarrosta Grill

Sleepers
(Good to excellent food,
but little known)
Arco de Cuchilleros
Bacchanalia
Boulevard
Boulevard Inn/W
Bricks
Cafe Matou
Cafe Venezia/I
China Gourmet/W
Chip and Py's/W
Clara's Pasta
Clayton's/I
Cornelia's Roosterant
Cucina Paradiso
Czech Plaza
Dionne's Cafe
Eddie Martini's/W
Fifth Ave. Bistro
Franconello's
Fresh Starts
Gladys Luncheonette
Grande Mere Inn/M
Grenadier's/W
Heaven City/W
Immigrant Room/W
King and I/W
La Salle Grill/I
Louis' Bon Appetit/I

Lutnia
Mimma's Cafe/W
Osteria del Mondo/W
Pasta Tree/W
Public Landing
Red Rock Cafe/W
Retreat
Rinc. Sudamericano
Rist. Bartolotta/W
Rist. DeMarco's
River Lane Inn/W
Sanford/W
Shiroi Hana
Spavone Seven
Steven Wade's/W
Strongbow Inn/I
Tavern in the Town
Thai Classic
Thai Little Home
Three Brothers/W
Tiffin
Tre Kronor
Udupi Palace
Volare
Walter's
Waterford
Wayside Manor
Work of Art Café
Zia's Trattoria

Teflons
(Get lots of business, despite
so-so food, i.e. they have
other attractions that prevent
criticism from sticking)
Belden Deli
Claim Company
Dave & Buster's
Dick's Last Resort
El Jardin
Father & Son Pizza
Goose Island
Hard Rock Cafe
Marcello's
Max's Deli
Michael Jordan's
Planet Hollywood
Rainforest Cafe
Ranalli's
Rock Bottom Brew.

Smoking Prohibited
(May be permissible at
bar or outdoors)
Akai Hana
Arun's

a tavola
Athenian Room
Bank Ln. Bistro
Beans & Barley/W
Benihana
Blind Faith Cafe
Blue Plate Cafe/M
Breakfast Club
Brett's
Butcher Shop
Cafe Central
Cafe Luciano
Cafe Pyrenees
Campagnola
Charlie Trotter's
Chicago Diner
Clayton's/I
Convito Italiano
Dave's Italian
Dellwood Pickle
Dionne's Cafe
Don's Fishmarket
Earth
Elaine & Ina's
Fifth Ave. Bistro
Fireplace Inn
foodlife
Francesco's
Golden Ox
Jilly's Cafe
John's Place
Kuni's
La Bocca Verità
La Crêperie
La Rosetta
Las Bellas Artes
Le Français
Le Titi de Paris
Lucky Platter
LuLu's
Lupita's
Lutz Continental
Mader's German/W
Mango
Mesón Sabika
Miller Bakery Cafe/I
Montparnasse
My π Pizza
New Japan
Next Door
Nonna Bartolotta's/W
O'Neil's
Oodles of Noodles
Original Pancake Hse.
Pasta Tree/W

Pasteur Cafe
Patrick & James
Penny's Noodle Shop
Pine Yard
Provence
Pump's on 12/I
Rainforest Cafe
Ravinia Bistro
Red Rock Cafe/W
Retreat
Rist. Bartolotta/W
Russian Tea Time
Salpicón
Sanford/W
Savoy Truffle
Slice of Life
Stir Crazy Cafe
Tandoor/I
Tiffin
Tre Kronor
Trio
Va Pensiero
Viceroy of India
Washington Gardens
Work of Art Café
Zealous

Teas
Drake Hotel
Hotel Inter-Continental
Renaissance Hotel
Ritz-Carlton
Seasons

Teenagers & Other Youthful Spirits
Arco de Cuchilleros
Aurelio's
Bacino's
Barry's Ribs
Bertucci's
Bubba Gump Shrimp
California Pizza Kit.
Carmen's
Cheesecake Factory
Chicago Pizza
Claim Company
Dave & Buster's
Ed Debevic's
Ed Debevic's/W
Edwardo's
El Jardin
El Presidente
El Tipico
Father & Son Pizza

Fernando's
Fluky's
Giordano's
Gold Coast Dogs
Graziano's
Hackney's
Hard Rock Cafe
Joe's Crab Shack
Johnny Rockets
La Canasta
Leona's
Leona's Neighborhood
Leona's on Taylor
Lindo Mexico
Lou Malnati's
Marcello's
My π Pizza
Nancy's
Original Gino's
Planet Hollywood
Rainforest Cafe
Ranalli's
Redamak's/M
Red Tomato

Visitors on Expense Accounts

Ambria
Arun's
Biggs
Boulevard
Boulevard Inn/W
Buckingham's
Butcher Shop
Cape Cod Room
Capital Grille
Carmichael's
Charlie Trotter's
Chicago Chop Hse.
Clubhouse
Coco Pazzo
Crofton on Wells
Eli's
Elm Grove Inn/W
Entre Nous
Erie Cafe
Everest
Fond de la Tour
Gene & Georgetti
Gibsons Steakhse.
Gino's Steak Hse.
Grenadier's/W
Immigrant Room/W
Iron Mike's Grille
Kilbourn Cafe/W

Le Français
Les Nomades
Le Titi de Paris
Le Vichyssois
Lino's Rist.
Magnum's
Morton's
Nick's Fishmarket
one sixtyblue
Osteria del Mondo/W
Palm
Pump Room
Ritz-Carlton Din. Rm.
Ruth's Chris
Saloon
Sanford/W
Seasons
Shaw's Crab Hse.
Signature Room
Smith & Wollensky
Spago
Spiaggia
Spruce
Suntory
Tavern on Rush
Topolobampo
Vivere
Waterford

Wheelchair Access
(Most places now have wheelchair access; call in advance to check)

Wine/Beer Only

Akai Hana
Anna Maria
Antoinette's/I
Beans & Barley/W
Blind Faith Cafe
Cafe Borgia
Cafe Venezia/I
Clayton's/I
Convito Italiano
Cross-Rhodes
Dave's Italian
Earth
Francesco's
Jilly's Cafe
Kuni's
M Cafe
Miller Bakery Cafe/I
Mrs. Levy's Deli
Pine Yard
Ravinia Bistro

Taj Mahal
Tandoor/I
Thai Little Home
Three Happiness
Tokyo Marina

Winning Wine Lists

Ambria
Cafe 36
Carlos'
Charlie Trotter's
Con Fusion
Courtright's
Everest
Geja's Cafe
Le Français
Les Nomades
Le Titi de Paris
Mimma's Cafe/W
Mon Ami Gabi
one sixtyblue
Printer's Row
Restaurant Okno
Ritz-Carlton Din. Rm.
Salpicón
Seasons
1776
Shaw's Crab Hse.
Smith & Wollensky
Spago
Spiaggia
Spruce
Steven Wade's/W
Tallgrass
302 West
Topolobampo
Trio
Vivere

Worth a Trip

Arlington Heights
  Le Titi de Paris
Crystal Lake
  1776
Des Plaines
  Cafe La Cave
Elmhurst
  Zealous
Evanston
  Jilly's Cafe
  New Japan
  Trio
  Va Pensiero

Geneva
  Granada
  Mill Race Inn
  302 West
Glenview
  Gusto Italiano
Highland Park
  Carlos'
  Gilles
  Mimosa
Highwood
  Froggy's
  Gabriel's
Hillside
  Emilio's La Perla
  Emilio's Tapas Bar
La Grange
  Cafe 36
Lakemoor
  Le Vichyssois
Lake Zurich
  D & J Bistro
Libertyville
  Tavern in the Town
Lockport
  Tallgrass
Lombard
  Bistro Banlieue
Momence
  Dionne's Cafe
Naperville
  Fifth Ave. Bistro
  La Sorella
  Mesón Sabika
  Montparnasse
Northfield
  Brasserie T
Oak Brook
  Fond de la Tour
Oak Park
  Philander's
Park Ridge
  Walter's
Vernon Hills
  Cafe Pyrenees
Wauconda
  Spasso
Westmont
  Waterford
Wheeling
  Le Français
Willow Springs
  Courtright's
Wilmette
  Akai Hana

Woodridge
  Clara's Pasta
INDIANA
Hammond
  Phil Smidt's
WISCONSIN
Elm Grove
  Elm Grove In
Kenosha
  Mangia Trattoria

Young Children
(Besides the normal fast-food places; * indicates children's menu available)
Abril
Ann Sather
Ann Sather Cafe
Arco de Cuchilleros
Athenian Room
Aurelio's
Bagel*
Bandera*
Barry's Ribs
Belden Deli
Bertucci's*
Big Bowl
Bistro 110*
Blackhawk Lodge*
Blue Mesa*
Blue Plate Cafe/M*
Bob Chinn's*
Brett's*
Bricks
Brother Jimmy's*
Bubba Gump Shrimp*
Butcher Shop*
California Pizza Kit.*
Carmen's
Cheesecake Factory
Chicago Diner*
Chicago Flat Sammies
Chicago Pizza
Claim Company*
Crawdaddy Bayou*
Daily B&G*
Dave & Buster's
Davis St. Fishmkt.*
Dixie Kitchen*
Ed Debevic's
Ed Debevic's/W
Edwardo's
El Jardin
El Presidente

El Tipico
Father & Son Pizza
Fernando's
Flat Top Grill*
Fluky's
Four Farthings*
Giordano's
Gold Coast Dogs
Graziano's*
Hackney's*
Hard Rock Cafe
Hyerdall's Cafe/M*
Joe's Be-Bop Cafe*
Johnny Rockets
John's Place*
Karl Ratzsch's/W*
La Canasta
Las Palmas*
Leona's
Leona's Neighborhood
Leona's on Taylor
Lindo Mexico
Lou Malnati's*
Lou Mitchell's*
Lupita's*
Mader's German/W*
Mantuano*
Marcello's
Max's Deli
Mia Cucina*
Michael Jordan's*
Miller's Country Hse./M*
My π Pizza
Nancy's
N. N. Smokehse.*
Nonna Bartolotta's/W*
Original Gino's
Original Pancake Hse.*
Pandl's in Bayside/W*
Pappadeaux*
Phil Smidt's/I*
Planet Hollywood*
Rainforest Cafe
Ranalli's
Redamak's/M
Redfish*
Red Rock Cafe/W*
Red Tomato
Rest. Su Casa/M
R.J. Grunts
Seasons Cafe*
Strongbow Inn/I*
Walker Bros.

Rating Sheets

To aid in your participation in our next *Survey*

F | D | S | C

⌐⌐⌐⌐

Restaurant Name _____
Phone _____
Comments _____
_____
_____

⌐⌐⌐⌐

Restaurant Name _____
Phone _____
Comments _____
_____
_____

⌐⌐⌐⌐

Restaurant Name _____
Phone _____
Comments _____
_____
_____

⌐⌐⌐⌐

Restaurant Name _____
Phone _____
Comments _____
_____
_____

⌐⌐⌐⌐

Restaurant Name _____
Phone _____
Comments _____
_____
_____

⌐⌐⌐⌐

Restaurant Name _____
Phone _____
Comments _____
_____
_____

	F	**D**	**S**	**C**

Restaurant Name _____
Phone _____
Comments _____
_____
_____

Restaurant Name _____
Phone _____
Comments _____
_____
_____

Restaurant Name _____
Phone _____
Comments _____
_____
_____

Restaurant Name _____
Phone _____
Comments _____
_____
_____

Restaurant Name _____
Phone _____
Comments _____
_____
_____

Restaurant Name _____
Phone _____
Comments _____
_____
_____

F	D	S	C

⎣⎦⎣⎦⎣⎦⎣⎦

Restaurant Name _____
Phone _____
Comments _____
_____
_____

⎣⎦⎣⎦⎣⎦⎣⎦

Restaurant Name _____
Phone _____
Comments _____
_____
_____

⎣⎦⎣⎦⎣⎦⎣⎦

Restaurant Name _____
Phone _____
Comments _____
_____
_____

⎣⎦⎣⎦⎣⎦⎣⎦

Restaurant Name _____
Phone _____
Comments _____
_____
_____

⎣⎦⎣⎦⎣⎦⎣⎦

Restaurant Name _____
Phone _____
Comments _____
_____
_____

⎣⎦⎣⎦⎣⎦⎣⎦

Restaurant Name _____
Phone _____
Comments _____
_____
_____

F | D | S | C

⅃⅃⅃⅃

Restaurant Name _____
Phone _____
Comments _____
_____
_____

⅃⅃⅃⅃

Restaurant Name _____
Phone _____
Comments _____
_____
_____

⅃⅃⅃⅃

Restaurant Name _____
Phone _____
Comments _____
_____
_____

⅃⅃⅃⅃

Restaurant Name _____
Phone _____
Comments _____
_____
_____

⅃⅃⅃⅃

Restaurant Name _____
Phone _____
Comments _____
_____
_____

⅃⅃⅃⅃

Restaurant Name _____
Phone _____
Comments _____
_____
_____

Restaurant Name _____
Phone _____
Comments _____
_____
_____

Restaurant Name _____
Phone _____
Comments _____
_____
_____

Restaurant Name _____
Phone _____
Comments _____
_____
_____

Restaurant Name _____
Phone _____
Comments _____
_____
_____

Restaurant Name _____
Phone _____
Comments _____
_____
_____

Restaurant Name _____
Phone _____
Comments _____
_____
_____

F | D | S | C

⌐ ⌐ ⌐ ⌐

Restaurant Name _____
Phone _____
Comments _____
_____
_____

⌐ ⌐ ⌐ ⌐

Restaurant Name _____
Phone _____
Comments _____
_____
_____

⌐ ⌐ ⌐ ⌐

Restaurant Name _____
Phone _____
Comments _____
_____
_____

⌐ ⌐ ⌐ ⌐

Restaurant Name _____
Phone _____
Comments _____
_____
_____

⌐ ⌐ ⌐ ⌐

Restaurant Name _____
Phone _____
Comments _____
_____
_____

⌐ ⌐ ⌐ ⌐

Restaurant Name _____
Phone _____
Comments _____
_____
_____

F	**D**	**S**	**C**

⌐⌐⌐⌐

Restaurant Name _____
Phone _____
Comments _____
_____
_____

⌐⌐⌐⌐

Restaurant Name _____
Phone _____
Comments _____
_____
_____

⌐⌐⌐⌐

Restaurant Name _____
Phone _____
Comments _____
_____
_____

⌐⌐⌐⌐

Restaurant Name _____
Phone _____
Comments _____
_____
_____

⌐⌐⌐⌐

Restaurant Name _____
Phone _____
Comments _____
_____
_____

⌐⌐⌐⌐

Restaurant Name _____
Phone _____
Comments _____
_____
_____

	F	D	S	C

⌐⌐⌐⌐

Restaurant Name _____
Phone _____
Comments _____
_____
_____

⌐⌐⌐⌐

Restaurant Name _____
Phone _____
Comments _____
_____
_____

⌐⌐⌐⌐

Restaurant Name _____
Phone _____
Comments _____
_____
_____

⌐⌐⌐⌐

Restaurant Name _____
Phone _____
Comments _____
_____
_____

⌐⌐⌐⌐

Restaurant Name _____
Phone _____
Comments _____
_____
_____

⌐⌐⌐⌐

Restaurant Name _____
Phone _____
Comments _____
_____
_____

Wine Vintage Chart 1985-1997

This chart is designed to help you select wine to go with your meal. It is based on the same 0 to 30 scale used throughout this *Survey*. The ratings (prepared by our friend **Howard Stravitz**, a law professor at the University of South Carolina) reflect both the quality of the vintage and the wine's readiness for present consumption. Thus, if a wine is not fully mature or is over the hill, its rating has been reduced. We do not include 1987 or 1991 vintages because, with the exception of cabernets and '91 Northern Rhônes, those vintages are not especially recommended.

	'85	'86	'88	'89	'90	'92	'93	'94	'95	'96	'97
WHITES											
French:											
Burgundy	24	25	20	29	24	24	–	23	28	27	26
Loire Valley	–	–	–	26	25	19	22	23	24	25	23
Champagne	28	25	24	26	28	–	24	–	25	26	–
Sauternes	22	28	29	25	26	–	–	18	22	24	23
California:											
Chardonnay	–	–	–	–	–	25	24	23	26	23	22
REDS											
French:											
Bordeaux	26	27	25	28	29	19	22	24	25	24	22
Burgundy	25	–	24	27	29	23	25	22	24	25	24
Rhône	26	20	26	28	27	16	23*	23	24	22	–
Beaujolais	–	–	–	–	–	–	20	21	24	22	23
California:											
Cab./Merlot	26	26	–	21	28	26	25	27	23	24	22
Zinfandel	–	–	–	–	–	21	21	23	20	21	23
Italian:											
Tuscany	27	16	24	–	26	–	21	20	25	19	–
Piedmont	26	–	25	27	27	–	19	–	24	25	–

*Rating is only for Southern Rhône wine.

Bargain sippers take note: Some wines are reliable year in, year out, and are reasonably priced as well. These wines are best bought in the most recent vintages. They include: Alsatian Pinot Blancs, Côtes du Rhône, Muscadet, Bardolino, Valpolicella and inexpensive Spanish Rioja and California Zinfandel.